CW01083031

Riding
Some Kind
of
Unusual
Skull Sleigh

Riding Some Kind of Unusual Skull Sleigh

On the Arts
of Don Van Vliet

W.C. Bamberger

ALAP EDITIONS

ISBN 0-917453-35-2

Alap Editions is now an imprint of
Bamberger Books
P.O. Box 350
Whitmore Lake, Michigan 48189

First printing: October, 1999
Second printing: August, 2000

for Aja

"I think people have had too much to think and ought to flex their magic muscles."

"A widely held misconception about me is that I'm a mystic. I'm not. I believe in black and white, I believe organically."

"The only leader is in your backbone and moves your feet. I don't want to lead people to a goal."

"When it comes to art I have a real streak of fascism. I want it to be exactly the way I conceive it, and if one line is changed it's like hey, the hell with it. . ."

"When I was three years old I was very disappointed to open a dictionary and read: the Great Auk—extinct. Now that didn't leave me with much faith in humanity."

"All tongues are connected, you know—we all drink from the same pond."

"The stars are matter. We're matter. It doesn't matter."

"I want to try and hold my brush like an ass swinging its tail. Donkeys swing their tail without thinking about it . . . . Like them, I want to swing my tail in the air—to me: the air, that's the painting."

"It's nice when people appreciate what you do, but I'm an artist, so thanks for the hand, but don't touch me. . . . "

—Don Van Vliet

Introduction

"Genius" is a word we all use, but few of us bother to define. Don Van Vliet has been nominated for the title of "possibly rock and roll's only true genius" for the music he created and recorded during his seventeen-year career as Captain Beefheart. And if we sharpen the word "genius" until it means something specific, applies only to someone who creates music of great power, the likes of which no one has heard before, music which we can imagine no one else imagining, then Van Vliet is a genius.

From 1964 to 1982, when Van Vliet was performing and recording as Captain Beefheart ("the shingle that gave me shingles," as he later referred to his musical alias), his chosen medium for musical expression was the standard rock and roll or blues band—the Magic Band, as the varying roster was always known : a pair of electric guitars, bass and drums, an occasional keyboard or marimba, fronted by Van Vliet's own accomplished blues harmonica, untutored reed-playing, and powerful voice— so powerful that it once destroyed a recording studio microphone.

For many years Van Vliet maintained that he personally created every note of the music, taught the musicians to play from scratch, wrote whole albums in single sittings, and rarely found anyone who could keep up with his creative genius. But the reality behind these claims has begun to emerge in recent years. The new picture is that of a man driven to create a music indeed formed from his own rhythms and abilities, but also from his shortcomings, a music which he was only able to realize by gathering together young, impressionable musicians, and driving them through 12 to 18-hour days of practice for months to learn difficult music—music they helped to create, yet received no credit for. In particular, the musicians who worked with him from 1968 through early 1974 might be said to have been as much "Captain Beefheart" as was Van Vliet himself in this period. It is surely no coincidence that when this core of musicians—the most magic of the Magic Bands—abandoned him in frustration and anger, and he could not find others willing to be so subsumed by his will, his music dried up. The image of Van Vliet as a solitary, self-sufficient genius has been wiped away permanently. It has been replaced by the picture of a man who, along with unique talents, is shot through with insecurities, human frailties (including greed and ego of epic proportions), and fanatic determination. And yet, even as the Captain Beefheart image has cracked and fallen, the air of genius about the music remains.

The music made by Captain Beefheart and the Magic Band (originally called "*his* Magic Band," the band was given nominal autonomy not long before they walked away from their leader) falls into the category of rock and roll because it is electric and loud, and because there is no other musical category capacious enough to accommodate its angular, elbows-out sound. But, at its best, on such albums as *Trout Mask Replica, The Spotlight Kid, Doc At the Radar Station* and a handful more, the music is like none which had ever been heard before in the world of rock and roll, or anywhere else. The best of the compositions on these albums offer a layering of melodies and fragments, riffs and dead stops, often with the instruments playing in several different time and/or key signatures simultaneously. And once the listener has had almost enough time to sort out the complex braid of rhythms and melodies, all will change, so that many of the compositions are long chains of non-repeating links. Lyrics too tend to be loose chains, of puns, non-sequiturs, jokes and word play; a definite meaning can rarely be put to them. Van Vliet never chose to pin them down in that way, earnestly offering completely different interpretations to different interviewers.

2

Despite, or more likely because of, the originality and power of this music and the reputation he gained among the more progressive factions in rock and roll, Van Vliet was never able to make a living from playing music. The two albums on which he attempted to consciously create commercial pop music sold even fewer copies than had his most difficult music. After this failed attempt at selling-out, Van Vliet instead bottomed out: contractually unable to record, he was nearly destitute.

A few years later, he returned to recording, with music which consciously echoed his classic (meaning "uncompromising") style. And in fact these were more than echoes, they were in large part rerecordings of leftover music from 1967 - 72. Leftovers, retro, recreations, whatever, his fans were ecstatic. But Van Vliet only made three of these comeback albums before he grew disillusioned with music—or ran out of music to record. After *Ice Cream for Crow* in 1982, he abruptly left the music business behind, and returned to his first love: art.

Van Vliet had been sculpting, drawing and painting since the age of three. He finally gained entry into the art world in 1984. Taken on and advised by a major gallery based in Germany, Van Vliet quickly became an internationally recognized and collected painter, and he has never looked back. Van Vliet once said that "Talking about different art-forms is like counting raindrops: there are rivers and streams and oceans, but it's all the same substance."[1] But he also has compared music and painting, and declared a preference for the latter:

> One you can physically drown in, being paint. The other you can mentally drown in. I prefer swimming in paint.[2]

Yet, the ending to this story of artistic struggle and unexpected recognition is not a completely happy one. Van Vliet has withdrawn from public life in recent years, and unconfirmed reports have him wheelchair-bound and ill with MS.

Even while it has become clear that Van Vliet, either by choice or physical disability, will never return to music, long-time fans, and new ones who come to Van Vliet's music either on their own or by way of comments from more recent rock and roll phenomena, continue to find the Captain Beefheart persona fascinating. Any famous person's fame characterizes those who bestow it as much as those who receive it. A famous person's fans are a flock, a tribe, not quite a cult; and without their object an important part of their identity is put in jeopardy. This tribe refuses to sign off the Captain Beefheart wavelength in part because there is no one else they can turn to as a substitute.

Rock and roll has had its share of eccentrics, and Van Vliet certainly qualifies. Fans gather together anecdotes of eccentricity, and debate their truthfulness. There is much Van Vliet lore which may be apocrypha, and some which could be nothing else. Not a little of this originated with Van Vliet himself. He has told of being called to Igor Stravinsky's house, while working on the *Trout Mask Replica* album, and refusing to go. He claims to have sold a vacuum cleaner to Aldous Huxley (then living in Lano, in the California high desert) by pitching the machine with "Well, I assure you sir, this thing sucks." This story is barely plausible, in an unsettling way. But then there is the story that he and guitarist Alex Snouffer changed their names because they were wanted by police for smuggling sponges into California from Nevada. (It is difficult to credit, but one writer took this at face value.) The motives for such outrageous yarn-spinning? One is to give those who encounter his music a total character experience. Another is to conceal whoever is behind the yarn. There is some of each of these in Van Vliet's presentation of himself, as Captain Beefheart and as a painter.

Other rock and roll eccentrics may match or even better Van Vliet, but few of them survived long enough in the music business to create as varied a catalog of music, and none have created music as singular and unique, as far outside the boundaries of conventional music, as resolutely uncommercial (with the lapses noted above), as did Captain Beefheart and the various Magic Bands. A certain kind of music fan, one with an interest in—even an insistence on—unconventional music, in a total experience of an "other," *needs* Captain Beefheart.

4

This tribe of Captain Beefheart fans refuse to give up their identity just because Van Vliet has given up his. Fans continue to seek out and soak up minutiae such as dates and personnel of recording sessions, and variant labels on *Trout Mask Replica.* They collect bootleg tapes of performances of songs which the various bands all endeavored to play identically to one another, and exactly the same every time, prizing them for such snippets of dialogue as when Van Vliet mentions that he is wearing "a hot hat," or when he jokes about "that orange juice chick" (Anita Bryant, briefly well-known for her anti-feminist and anti-gay pronouncements). There are a number of internet sites devoted to Van Vliet, CDs are appearing, books are in the making.

A look ahead to the post-Magic Band career of one of its last recruits, guitarist Gary Lucas, may help clarify this need which many fans have for sustaining the example of Captain Beefheart. Lucas himself began as a fan, became (with his first wife) Van Vliet's manager and chief handholder-by-phone, made guest solo guitar appearances at concerts, and became a full member of the Magic Band for the last album. Lucas has since become the premier solo guitar virtuoso on the NYC and European alternative music circuits. (Only in 2000, twenty years after his Magic Band period, did Lucas release recordings of him playing any of Van Vliet's music.) Lucas' solo career as the One True Innovative Solo Guitar Monster means that he has come to share at least one thing with Van Vliet, something not narrowly musical. Lucas has given us a revealing nod in its direction by recording the theme to *Cool Hand Luke* on his CD *Evangeline.* In the film, Paul Newman's Luke is a man at the point of a flying wedge of collective wishes. Behind him stand any number of eggers-on, of Cool-Hand-wanna-bes, whose pressure leads Luke to extend his stunts to greater and greater degrees of difficulty. What Luke feels about his stunts remains opaque, even as they wear him down and finally destroy him. What is clear is that he is a vehicle for the needs of the penned-in populace: he manifests all the reckless defying they wish they had in them. Don Van Vliet as Captain Beefheart does this for all the latent verbal/musical outsiders among us, all of us who need to feel that our sensibilities can continue to thrive on a different level than that of the vast majority of music fans. A cold way of saying this would be to admit that being a fan of Captain Beefheart music has a decided snob appeal. A more generous way would be to point out that any such sensibility can use all the reinforcement it can get in a music world which is growing more commercially committed each day.

This need for Captain Beefheart as a survival tool is part of the reason so many fans stoned Van Vliet with disdain whenever he chose not to sacrifice all for their listening pleasure. Van Vliet was, in effect, allowed only to stay poor, to stay arrhythmic, to stay verbally opaque, to stay off the radio, to remain the classic starving artist, so that fans might have his uncompromising example to identify with. (Van Vliet, however, wasn't willing to accept his end of this deal. He had always hoped for, and believed he could have, commercial success, no matter how difficult his music.)

Van Vliet is no longer a starving artist in any economic sense. He is now an internationally known and widely collected painter. Die-hard fans of Van Vliet as Captain Beefheart often clip off his post-recording life with a cursory "he quit music for a career as a successful painter." Many fans of the music ignore the art almost completely, except that which appears on album covers and inner sleeves. This is certainly understandable. Music travels wonderfully through our daily lives, endlessly adapting itself to our moods like an aura we can tune, never making us feel it is slumming. But the world of modern art, the world where Van Vliet's expressionist swirls and melting bio-boundaries are understood and accepted, is a place apart, in many ways, from the daily lives most of us live; a place few fans of his music find interesting or even comfortable.

Taking the short ride in the very small elevator up to the Michael Werner Gallery in New York City, walking into the well-lighted area with its "hushed" aura, the soberly polite and eminently helpful staff, the careful way the drawings are laid on the viewing table and held until the viewer gives the nod—all make for a very different experience than that of going to a large hall or theater and seeing Captain Beefheart and the Magic Band in concert in the company of scores of fellow enthusiasts.

And there are differences, hard to explain but easy to feel, in the differing natures of the two art forms, as well. As idiosyncratic and difficult as is the music made by Captain Beefheart and the Magic Bands, most listeners are able to make up their minds about it based on listening and personal taste, without feeling there is some esoteric key they are missing. In contrast to this, many who look at his paintings—the earlier ones done in a style which hovers somewhere between whimsical cartooning and De Kooning-like expressionist intensity, the later work much more disconnected and unformed-looking are at a loss as to how to begin to judge or even look at the work. There is an air of "conniseurship required," as well as a suspicion that it all means nothing, that discourages casual acquaintance with the work. For many, Van Vliet has passed into a very different, incomprehensible world. (Unfortunately, this same feeling keeps many people away from not just Van Vliet's work, but much of modern art.) Enthusiasts of modern art, however, enjoy knowing about Van Vliet's history as Big Bad Wolf of the rock and roll world. It is only the gallery owners, for reasons of their own, who act as if this part of Van Vliet's past is something to be disdained— even as they utilize it for its publicity value.

This book will be a look at, and a critical meditation on both of Van Vliet's arts, and the almost opposite worlds he has found himself living in as he has gone about the business of creating his works in these different mediums. This book will attempt to place them in contexts which may point the way toward answers to some questions these arts and Van Vliet himself have raised.

Central to the answering of any number of questions about Van Vliet, as I hope to show, is the fact that he is and has been an "ecological" man and artist. By this I don't mean simply that he wants to help save the earth, but that he is aware of the fact that we are all—man, animal, plant, air, light—interconnected.

And not only does he understand and believe this, but to be ecologically or systemically connected to other musicians or mediums or life forms is one of *his* needs. Van Vliet's experiences serve to highlight both sides of a truly ecological philosophy: the well-known light side of humanistic creativity, and the almost overlooked dark side of totalitarian domination.

Like most of us, Van Vliet can seem more than one man. In his case, however, the extremes of his personality seem much further apart than is the case for most of us. On the one hand, Van Vliet can be funny, warm, concerned with the environment and all sentient beings, even while, on the other hand, he has been tyrannical and bullying—even physically abusive—to his band members. He has been a glory-hound who has taken credit and monetary rewards for the musical ideas of Magic Band, even while fuming about the greed of others around him.

In looking at some of the questions raised by Van Vliet's relationship to his arts and to those who have helped him to realize them, I will refer to the new conception of "mind" which was being formulated contemporaneous with Van Vliet's emergence as Captain Beefheart. I do not claim that Van Vliet was influenced by, or even aware of, the conception of mind held by anthropologist Gregory Bateson, or the "Gaia" theory formulated by James Lovelock. Still, I believe that looking at Van Vliet's approach to musical composition by way of these theories can throw new light on what he has accomplished, as well as why it became so difficult for him to create new music in the last half of his musical career.

My look at Van Vliet's art, too, will suggest alternative ways of looking at the art and the career. The title *Riding Some Kind of Unusual Skull Sleigh* is taken from a 1986 - 87 painting by Van Vliet, one which marks a crucial point in the progress of his art, and perhaps of his life. It is one of Van Vliet's larger paintings, four foot by just under five, but it is not his largest; it is painted in his most favored colors—dark red, ocher, black, tan, pearly white. But there is something singular about the painting: among those which have been reproduced it is the last which includes a human figure. Before 1987 quite a few Van Vliet paintings include people, some are even portraits; even more include animals. But after 1987, no people appear. There are a few animals, but the paintings grow increasingly abstract and fragmented; with the disappearance of the human subject, nearly all the warmth, humor and intimacy, the connectedness which are so common in the early works as to seem to be the reason they were created also disappear.

In my view, Van Vliet's long time philosophy, his ecological view of the interconnectedness of all things, was clearly reflected in his art from his earliest known works to approximately 1987. From that point on, signs of such a philosophy disappear. An artist is likely to change his or her style any number of times in a life-time, for reasons known and unknown, as an aspect of true artistic growth. But the change evident in Van Vliet's work— from the interconnected and humorous, to the fragmented and hermetic isolated from the human community—does more than signal a change in painting style. I will attempt to throw some light on why this might be so by looking at some of the business realities of the art world. The world of art as business is now Van Vliet's world, and one which, much as was the music world, has been a mixed blessing for him.

So in the pages which follow, the answer to the question of who it is who is riding the unusual kind of skull sleigh is a double one. I believe, and will show, that Van Vliet has been doing just that, letting his body (his skull is only the central radar station, not a control tower) be his vehicle in nearly all of what he has created. Secondly, as I have no privileged access to Van Vliet's innermost thoughts or psychology, I will be riding on the surface of his works, trying to see everything there is to see along the route, and making of it what I can. When I hear Van Vliet sing his composition "Sue Egypt," and he asks "Who are these people who ride on my bones?" I suffer a cold shot of self-recognition.

Yet I feel this ride needs to be risked, because the approach I will take here has not yet been taken. Essays and articles about Van Vliet's arts have rarely gone beyond the simplest descriptive approach. Little attempt has been made at taking a wider or deeper view. And Van Vliet's career and arts deserve deeper looks, deserve explication and contextualization. Artists who draw have a number of different varieties of paper they can choose from, depending upon the medium with which they choose to work. One of these variables is "tooth." This is a measure of how much drag an pastel crayon, for instance, will encounter as it moves across a sheet of paper. The more "tooth" the more medium will be left behind on the paper. Don Van Vliet's work presents a great deal of tooth to someone wanting to take an approach different from the skimming passage of the usual "Rock's only genius . . . He talks to gila monsters," personality-centered approach which well-meaning or awe-stricken critics have most often taken. If Van Vliet's arts are going to be appreciated beyond the Captain Beefheart cult and wealthy art collector circles, new approaches need to be opened up. This is the intent of the following ride on Van Vliet's unusual skull sleigh.

Don Van Vliet now declines to be interviewed. What follows has been assembled primarily from secondary sources. Important details would not have been included without the resources assembled by three internet sites devoted to Van Vliet and his work: *Homepage Replica, Electricity,* and *The Radar Station.* Their addresses are listed with the other sources at the back of this book. Also, the lively interchanges of those on the Radar Station's "Fire Party" discussion group also suggested important areas of speculation. Some of what has been posted on these sites include incomplete original source references. I have included as much source information as I have been able to gather. In at least one case (the "choker-setter" story) what is included comes from memory, and no source can be located.

Particularly important to me were published interviews with and the writings of John French and Bill Harkleroad. Gary Lucas patiently answered my many questions about the role he played in helping Van Vliet enter the New York art world. (The reader is urged to seek out the recordings these men made after leaving the Magic Band, all of which are excellent. Several of these are included in the discography here.) Two interviewees who provided some important general information have requested not to be credited. Ron Ledford read parts of the *Light the Fire Piano* chapter and made important suggestions about the presentation of musical ideas. Becci Downing lent her ear to the measurement of Van Vliet's vocal range.

Any factual or musical errors are, of course, solely my responsibility.

As regards the discussion of the paintings, I have chosen to refer only to those which have been reproduced in catalogues or magazines which a reader might reasonably expect to be able to locate. Works seen during my two vists to the Michael Werner Gallery in New York City gave me no reason to believe the unreproduced body of Van Vliet's work may be fundamentally different from that which I am using for my commentary. That this is an artifically small selection, much of it made by his gallery, is part of what I will have to say about Van Vliet's experience of the world of art, its galleries and its dealers. Sources where each of the paintings may be seen in reproduction are listed by the title of the work at the back of this book, and "untitled" works have source and page number noted in the body of the text.

Born in the Desert

Don Glen Vliet was born January 15, 1941 in Glendale, California. He was reluctant to join us: his mother, Willie Susan Vliet, was in labor for more than fourteen hours before Don was coaxed into the world with a pair of forceps. Don was to be Glen and Sue Vliet's only child. The Glendale home glimpsed in the BBC documentary *The Artist Formerly Known as Captain Beefheart*[1] is a pleasant looking two-story, complete with an appropriately green suburban yard. Photos exist of a very young Donny in a cowboy outfit, looking quite pleased with himself. So, if stories of his from-the-cradle antics are true, the budding young eccentric managed to co-exist with the movie-loving boy.

Van Vliet reports that he had set out on his own path by the time he was three. At that age he began sculpting in the bathtub— "[Like] everyone does: my genitals, then a bar of soap, and on out from there."[2] He used the vacuum to collect hairs lost by the family cat so he could include them in his sculptures. Also when he was three, he tried to jump into the tar pits outside Los Angeles, enticed by the musical sound of the bubbling tar. His mother pulled him back at the last minute. It was also at age three, Van Vliet tells us, that he told his mother that if she would stay on her side of the room he would stay on his and they could remain friends.

Almost forty years later he would sing that we should all send our mothers home our navels. There are other references to

"Mother," even "Mommy" in Van Vliet's work, some quite dismissive, but knee-jerk Freudians should beware of making too much of Van Vliet's use of one of the most common and most loaded of words in any language.

Perhaps the best way to view his relationship to his mother is the simple one offered by Anton Corbijn's short film *Some Yo-yo Stuff*, which aired with the BBC documentary. This opens with Sue Vliet, a pleasant if here somewhat tired-looking woman, walking onto a desert path carrying a small cut-out of Van Vliet from the *Ice Cream for Crow* album cover. She proceeds to secure this in the sand. "This is my son, Don," she says, then turns and leaves the rest of the film to him. This is a bow by the archetypal "widow woman," put-upon but strong, doing what she can for her son.

Van Vliet's claim that he was already finding his personal and artistic identity at three may raise eyebrows for a moment, but this is known to be the age at which children suddenly realize that marks they can make can represent elements in the world around them. And such an early calling is by no means unheard of. Yehudi Menhuin knew he wanted to be a concert violinist at age four, and stormed off in tears when his uncomprehending parents presented him with a toy violin. Van Vliet also brings to mind the poet/engraver William Blake. Blake was identifiably the Blake of legend by the time he was four: God's face came through his nursery window and set him screaming.

In *The Soul's Code* psychologist James Hillman discusses the fact that the influence of genetically inherited factors in our make-up waxes and wanes at different times in our lives. At times, genetic influence is dominant, and at other times it withdraws to allow other, less easily defined parts of our character to take the lead. Hillman identifies the years from age three to approximately thirteen as being one common cycle.[3] Van Vliet has identified just these years as being his first artistic period. He blames his parents' move to the desert for his desertion of art, but this is an age which in itself inflicts much greater displacements than simple geographical ones. He was not to take up art again until he was 24, the same period in which he began concentrating more on his music.

According to Van Vliet, he appeared on a television program broadcast from the Griffith Park Zoo (the forerunner of the present Los Angeles Zoo) at seven years of age, sculpting animals while a Brazilian sculptor named Augustino Rodriquez looked on and made comments. At eleven, again according to his own account, he was lecturing in sculpture at the Barzell Art Institute of UCLA, and, again at age 13, won a scholarship from Knudeson's Creamery to "go to Europe to study for six years." He was to have gone when he was sixteen. But this was not to be.[4]

When Don was 13, the Vliets moved to Lancaster, in the Mojave Desert. Van Vliet's story is that they moved in reaction to his winning the scholarship, because they thought all artists were crazy or gay. The idea of a 16-year-old going off on his own to Europe would have been an unsettling one in and of itself, but neither reason would have been enough to cause the elder Vliets to up stakes and move to the desert. They certainly would not have had visions of a powerful scholarship board showing up at their door and dragging away their son. More likely it was something more pedestrian, perhaps relocating to find work. A promotional map of the Antelope Valley area, which includes Lancaster, issued at this time carries the legend "New Empire of Urban and Industrial Progress in the Southland."[5] Whatever young Don's promise as an artist, this map's very American promise is much more likely to have been the impetus behind the family's move.

Don's parents were originally from the American heartland, Glen from rural Kansas and Sue from Arkansas. They brought Don into the world in an America which was just coming out of the Great Depression. Those unhappy days would have been the background for their adolescence and courtship. This may even have been what led to their coming to California, where so many migrated in search of better opportunities. (And it seems that they found them: when Don was born his father was part owner of a gas station, and the Vliets owned their home.) Glen Vliet was 31 when his son was born, Sue was 27. Like so many who grew to adulthood in this period, it is likely that the effects of the time would have played an important part in how they saw their lives to come, including their responsibilities as parents.

When Don was eleven months old, America entered World War II. California, and Southern California in particular, would perhaps have felt the disruptions of the war to a greater degree than any other area in the country outside Washington, D.C. On the West Coast an attack or invasion by the Japanese was felt to be a very real possibility. Japanese-Americans in the area were sent away to internment camps (some in the Mojave itself) for the duration, the film industry was affected, as were the nearby agricultural areas. The Vliets certainly would have felt the uncertainty which shadowed all American lives for four years. To have their son, early-on or not, display signs of wanting to be an artist or musician, must have dismayed them.

Besides being financially insecure, the life of an artist would have seemed unthinkably distant from the work ethic which continued to mean financial survival for the Vliets. Don had to drop out of high school his senior year because his father had a heart attack. "Vliet" (as he was known in high school) had to drive his father's *Helms Bread* truck, to maintain an income for the household, which was a large one. According to Frank Zappa, living in the Vliet home were Don, his parents, Don's girlfriend Laurie, and Don's Aunt Ione and Uncle Alan. His grandmother lived across the street. Zappa's recollection is that Don would sit in his room and scream at his mother, "Sue! Get me a Pepsi!" This was the Vliet family's reality, a working class reality: when a choice had to be made between education and income, income had to win out.

When Van Vliet gave up art from age of 13 to 24, he became interested instead in cars and clothes and girls, normal teenage and young adult concerns. (His car did prompt one exception to his abandonment of art: he sculpted a werewolf's head to add to the steering wheel of his light-blue Olds.) Little time, according to Van Vliet, was taken up with that other primary concern of children, school. He claims to have had only a few scattered days of formal schooling in his entire childhood, to have rejected school upon first experiencing it, and so stayed away. This at a time when that now almost extinct bogeyman, the Truant Officer, still stalked the land.

Whatever the concrete truth of Van Vliet's claims, however many hours he may or may not have spent at a desk in a public school, there can be little argument that his intelligence is of a kind that has little to do with formal schooling. He claims to be largely self-taught; to be deliberately a-literate. Even while suggesting acquaintance with Aldous Huxley's work, Van Vliet has always claimed never to have read a book. ("My wife reads to me sometimes, though," he told an interviewer. "And that's nice.") One rationalization he gives for this is to avoid any possible influence. Reading someone else's work, he worried, might give him "a restriction on tuning." Not only did Vliet not finish high school, he dropped out of the local junior college soon after enrolling. This otherwise unremarkable school was the scene for the first collaborations between Van Vliet and Frank Zappa.

The day may come when Van Vliet's work can be discussed without delving into his on-and-off friendship and numerous collaborations with Zappa, but that time has not yet arrived. For the thirty-plus years they knew each other, the pair took turns in the lead: Zappa availing himself of Van Vliet's record collection and Van Vliet of Zappa's tape recorder; Zappa of Van Vliet's voice and Van Vliet of the former's recording expertise; Zappa of Van Vliet's stream-of-consciousness verbal brilliance, Van Vliet of Zappa's business sense. They were, classically for high school friends, opposites in most ways: Van Vliet was physical, instinctive where Zappa was almost totally cerebral. They did have some things in common: both were zealots of black rhythm and blues, neither was interested in working toward a conventional middle class life, and both had a taste for shocking those they felt were less hip than they. But what is most significant in the short list of what they shared is that both went on to create music which deliberately broke from the tradition of the well-made song, both favoring segmented music with unexpected shifts in tempo and key. Zappa and Van Vliet both found cult followings, but Zappa

16

was able to capitalize on this base, and work his way into wider commercial success. When Van Vliet tried to do the same, he failed so completely he had to ask Zappa for work.

Was there something in the desert air that produced these two amazing musicians, with their very different geniuses, something which also produced the musicians which made up the early and mid-period Magic Bands—Doug Moon, Jeff Cotton, Alex St. Clair, Bill Harkleroad, John French, and Mark Boston? If so, it also exacted a price. Zappa died of prostate cancer in December of 1993, and it seems undeniable that Van Vliet is very ill. Evidence suggests that those who were early Mothers of Invention and Magic Band members have paid an enormous psychic toll for their experiences. Van Vliet, as we shall see, must bear a large share of the responsibility for the psychological fallout suffered by the members of his bands, particularly the players who holed up in a small house in a California canyon and collectively created the masterpieces *Trout Mask Replica* and *Lick My Decals Off, Baby*. But the seeds of what was to come must have been in them from the beginning.

What may be the first capture of Van Vliet on tape is "Lost in a Whirlpool," issued on the posthumous Zappa release *The Lost Episodes*. This dates from 1958 or '59, when Van Vliet would have been 17 or 18. This anthropological curiosity is a field recording of sorts, recorded at Antelope Valley Jr. College. Van Vliet and Zappa, along with another guitar player, chanced upon an unguarded reel-to-reel tape recorder in an empty classroom. Zappa played blues leads over the other guitarist's 9th chords while Van Vliet improvised lyrics. The words were likely inspired by the adolescent boys' room baptism known as "giving a swirly." They tell the surrealistic tale of a rejected lover being flushed down a toilet, and of the things seen there, such as a "big brown fish"—which is obviously not a fish at all. He begs his woman to come with a toilet plunger and save him. What is most striking about this recording is Van Vliet's voice. For more than a verse he sings falsetto, not a thin Beach Boy's falsetto, but a powerful and controlled high blues voice that could easily have been a female blues singer from the 1920s or

30s. In the second verse he drops down to what is recognizable as the Beefheart baritone-to-come. Van Vliet's voice is already powerful enough to cause noticeable distortion in the recording. It is easy to see why Zappa, who at this time had only recently begun playing guitar, would keep coming back to Van Vliet. Only a few years after the cracks of puberty had healed over, the future Captain Beefheart's voice was already a magnificent instrument.

Van Vliet used to perform spontaneous monologues which fell somewhere between comedy routines and poetry. Zappa was an obsessive recorder of friends and acquaintances then and in later years, and he recorded some of these monologues. From these tapes Zappa extracted a number of catch phrases which were to become associated with his group the Mothers of Invention. These include "Suzy Creamcheese, what's got into you?", "Brown Shoes Don't Make It," "Hot Rats" and "Lumpy Gravy"—by which Van Vliet meant the ups and downs of life. These appropriations (although Van Vliet was so inventive it is likely that without Zappa these would have been left behind by their originator, lost to history if not for the tapings) helped fuel the later animosities between the two.

In 1963, Zappa took advantage of Van Vliet's voice to try to break into the commercial recording business. Van Vliet sang a "Howling Wolf-style" version of "Slippin' and Slidin'" for Zappa, and this was among a trio of recordings Zappa tried to sell to Dot Records as being by a group called "The Soots" (pronounced "suits"). Zappa at this time was spending most of his time in his "Studio Z" in Cucamonga, honing his compositional and record producing skills. "The Soots," which has been described in some articles as being a working band, was never more than a studio assemblage, put together by Zappa with the sole intent of selling demos to record companies. Dot rejected these. The conditions they were recorded under were primitive to say the least. For "Slippin' and Slidin'" and others done at the same time the band played in the studio, and Van Vliet was miked out in the hallway, listening to the band through the door, reading an *X-Men* comic he had pinned to the wall while he sang.

"Metal Man Has Won His Wings," which shows up on several bootleg recordings, was recorded at this same time. The lyrics are so far down in the mix that they are indecipherable, but on a 1975 radio show taped on Long Island Zappa and Van Vliet explained that the words were graffiti scratchings on the walls Van Vliet faced as he sang. "Metal Man," and "Tiger Roach," another track on *The Lost Episodes* show Van Vliet well on the way to finding the Captain Beefheart within him. He introduces "Tiger Roach," with the statement, "This album is not available to the public. Even if it were, you wouldn't want to listen to it." The lyrics are a "rant" (Zappa's word) by Van Vliet, a series of obdurate images much like the poems and lyrics which would begin to emerge with *Strictly Personal* a half-dozen years later. The track also features Van Vliet's astoundingly well-done imitation of a squealing pig.

Van Vliet's adoption of the name "Captain Beefheart" dates from this period. His response years later to a question about the origin of the name reveals more about the angles at which his thoughts join one another than it does about the name:

> I have a beef in my heart against the world. . . . The way they treat humanity and animals. It's the shingle that's given me shingles. . . . My friends don't call me Captain. I don't even have a boat. It's funny how a name like that can stick to you like mashed potatoes. Some of these new kind they have stick to you forever. Poor colon.[6]

Some less poetic details: Van Vliet and Zappa had plans to make a film, *Captain Beefheart and the Grunt People.* A fragment of the script shows that it was to have been a science-fictionalization of Van Vliet's own life: Captain Beefheart watches happenings on the moon on a monitor screen, while his parents yell at him for leaving dirty socks on the floor and for not clipping his toe nails. The film was never made, but the name stuck. The adoption of this "shingle that gave [him] shingles," appears to predate the addition of "Van" to his given name.

Several stories have been told about how the name Captain Beefheart came about—one involving a relative of Van Vliet exposing himself—but it was almost certainly coined by Zappa, whatever the circumstances. When Zappa left Cucamonga to go to Los Angeles and eventually form the Mothers of Invention, Van Vliet's homing instinct kicked in; he returned to Lancaster and was drafted into a band being formed by an old friend, Alex Snouffer.

Many of the bands in the Lancaster area were playing blues. Van Vliet has always claimed to have had no musical influences whatever (the larger question of his total rejection of influence will be taken up later), but it is undeniable that much of his music has roots in the blues, much more so than Zappa, who favored the more pop "rhythm and blues" styles and modern orchestral music. Van Vliet shows affinities with both country bluesmen and the first generation of electric blues players. Country blues were for the most part sung by men to their own guitar accompaniment, often slide guitar, where the strings are fretted with a knife or a bottle or a metal tube, to achieve a sound at once more vocal and harder ringing. This style had had its heyday in the 1930s. But the form, and a number of the rediscovered players, had recently been taken up by the folk music crowd. An elderly Son House, who had taught or played with such legends as Robert Johnson and Charlie Patton, had returned to the stage in 1964, and an excellent comeback album had been released by Columbia. Columbia also had issued the first of its compilation LPs of Robert Johnson's 78s. Both albums were widely available, and Van Vliet's music from 1965 through '68 shows their influence, especially that of House's album. "Ah Feel Like Ahcid" on the *Strictly Personal* album is very much in the style of Son House. Electric players such as Muddy Waters, whose version of "Rollin' and Tumblin'" inspired dozens of songs, including Van Vliet's "Sure 'Nuff and Yes I Do," and fellow Chicago bluesmen Howlin' Wolf and Elmore James were also entering the consciousness of young white musicians.

A number of British Invasion bands, the Animals and the Rolling Stones most successfully, had popularized electric blues for young white audiences. By the time the first Paul Butterfield Blues Band album was released in 1965, homegrown white blues bands were already common all over the country, including the Mojave Desert. Captain Beefheart and the first Magic Band were playing music influenced by blues and R&B records when they came together in early 1964. A classmate of some of the Magic Band members remembers there being "this whole high desert blues subculture and each of our bands had these cliques."[7] As John French has said, "If you wanted to get gigs in the desert you had to have a four piece band with a stand-up singer," and you had to play blues.[8] Van Vliet eventually became the reigning king of this scene. His ability to sing blues was to become so well-known in the Los Angeles area that at one Muddy Waters performance in L.A., Waters came to Van Vliet's table and explained that his singing was below par that night because of a bad cold.[9] When not playing, Van Vliet frequented clubs in Lancaster and nearby Palmdale, sitting at a back table with his sketch pads, poetry journals and his pipe.

In those periods when Zappa was out of favor with Van Vliet, his party line of his musical history would begin when he joined Alex Snouffer's band. Snouffer (soon to be known as Alex St. Clair) called and told Van Vliet he was going to sing with the band. ("He's a real Prussian," Van Vliet once said.) Van Vliet had never sung with a band before, and, apart from a knack for vocally imitating some of the best blues singers' styles, his singing at local parties had seemed nothing exceptional. But there were no other candidates among the musicians Snouffer knew, and Van Vliet became the vocalist. The band was called Captain Beefheart and His Magic Band (Snouffer had heard about the planned movie), but Captain Beefheart was a free-floating name, not yet attached to anyone in particular.

Van Vliet claims to have been so nervous at the band's first performance that he took along some "art things"—a Hoover Superchief vacuum cleaner and some Mexican jumping beans. During the intermission he put a spotlight on a tiny curtain, then unveiled the jumping beans. "I was doing an artistic show," he later said. "That's what got me on the wrong track, because I went on into that." Despite such antics, Van Vliet soon took control of the group from Snouffer.

At an event called "The Teenage Fair" at the Hollywood Palladium in 1965, Captain Beefheart and His Magic Band "Made such an impact on the audience that numerous fan clubs sprouted up before they even had a recording contract."[10] The band played blues covers and Rolling Stones songs—Van Vliet even danced in an imitation of Mick Jagger's style. The bands all played in "booths," small areas like stalls. In the next booth, playing their first job, was a group called The Rising Sons, which included Taj Mahal on guitar and harmonica, Gary Marker on bass, and teenaged Ry Cooder on slide guitar. The band was playing a repertoire which included Robert Johnson material, and Van Vliet was awed by Cooder's abilities. He berated Magic Band guitarist Doug Moon for not being able to play as well as Cooder.[11]

By mid-1965 Captain Beefheart and His Magic Band had a recording contract for two singles to be issued by A&M records. The band, which included Moon and St. Clair on guitars, Jerry Handley on bass and Paul Blakely on drums, went into the studio with producer David Gates (later the lead singer of Bread) and recorded five songs.

The group's lead-off single was a version of Bo Diddley's "Diddy Wah Diddy," and it became a local hit. The arrangement, dictated by Gates, revolves around a fuzz-tone guitar riff and a heavily thumping bass. Van Vliet reaches deep and sings the nonsense words with a straight face, pushing them through the got-every-base-covered arrangement. A film clip exists of the band lip- and hand-syncing to the record as they stand in the middle of a beach party. Guys and girls (in notably chaste two-piece swim suits) dance around the band, and occasionally run into the water. This clip, credited as "Courtesy of Dick Clark Productions," was likely filmed for Clark's *Where the Action Is*, a lip-sync music show featuring the once and future unknown Steve Alaimo (who would pretend to sing while swimming in a pool, etc,), and Paul Revere and the Raiders. It is doubtful that the clip ever aired, as the record had no national impact.

The Bo Diddley song was backed by a Van Vliet original, "Who Do You Think You're Foolin'," a good vehicle for Van Vliet's voice, but an unremarkable "my girlfriend can't fool me" song (though he would later claim this was a song about the government, and that the girl was the Statue of Liberty). The second single had a tune by the producer, "Moonchild," for its A-side. This forgettable ballad was backed by "Frying Pan," another Van Vliet original based on the "Rollin' and Tumblin'" riff. This is a blues about getting out of the title location and into the fire. The vocal shows Van Vliet just beginning to work on the received conventions of blues playing. He is clearly, if gently, mocking the southern black accent and diction most other white blues players of the time adopted with a fidelity bordering on hagiography. The harmonica playing here, as on all the tracks recorded at this time, is at the top of the instrument—in the Jimmy Reed rather than the Little Walter range—to allow the sound to come through the jangling, early-60s-primitive, mix.

The fifth title the band recorded was not released until 1984. Seen from our end of the career of Captain Beefheart, "Here I Am, Always Am" is a fascinating composition, the first suggestion of the structures of the music which was to follow. The verses are backed by a slightly-jazzy three chord progression in 3/4 time, but midway through the chorus the backing changes to a strong 4/4, almost a march rhythm. This structure was quite different from nearly everything else being played in rock and roll at that time. (The Beatles song "We Can Work it Out" alternated between 4/4 and 3/4 but did so in a much smoother manner.)

The band also recorded demos of other compositions at this time, recordings which remained unreleased until 1999's five CD rarities set *Grow Fins*. "Obeah Man" is a delight, a driving, oddly accented hoodoo song, while "I Just Got Back from the City," is based on a "Who Do You Love?" style one-chord riff. A third compostion, "Triple Combination," is another one-chord piece, but is murky and uninspired. Doug Moon, guitarist with this first incarnation of the Magic Band, remembers that many of these early songs (through the first album and beyond) were group compositions. But the best of these exhibit the rhythmic variety that was to mark all of Van Vliet's best work. The composer credits (as always) go to Van Vliet alone. John French remembers other compositions—"Frisco's So Free," "Garden of Nowhere," and others which were never recorded.[12]

In 1966, with only a local hit under their belts, Captain Beefheart and His Magic Band could still be found playing such venues as the Exposition Hall at the Antelope Valley Fairgrounds. But they had also begun playing bigger halls. Recordings of the band playing at the Avalon Ballroom in San Francisco have been preserved.[13] All the songs are blues tunes, including a cover of Howling Wolf's "Evil."

Van Vliet's voice has often been compared to that of Howling Wolf. Wolf (whose real name was Chester Burnett) sang in a rough and powerful voice, occasionally giving out near-falsetto howls in imitation of his namesake. He would stalk up and down the stage as he sang, though more slowly than Van Vliet's quick stalking style during the early-1970s tours. Wolf also played harmonica in a wheezy, rhythmic style, a style Van Vliet used only when deliberately nodding toward the country blues tradition. Van Vliet's voice can be said to be somewhat similar to Wolf's in that both are powerful and rough, but Wolf had a much more limited range. He sometimes seemed as if he were singing only one note, but bending it so powerfully that it formed an entire melody. Van Vliet, on the other hand, has always swooped from part of his range to another, very suddenly and dramatically. Wolf's howls are really not much like the vocal jumps Van Vliet employs at the end of many of his phrases, which are sudden pops like bottle caps being blown off by some fizzing pressure. Little Richard's vocal mannerisms are actually much closer to Van Vliet's than are Wolf's—listen to how Little Richard ends the vocal lines in "Lucille," for instance, and compare it with Van Vliet's "don't wanna kill" in "China Pig." That Little Richard, campy rock and roll entertainer, does not carry the cachet of the bluesman may be why his name is rarely invoked in this connection. (Van Vliet once told Magic Band guitarist Bill Harkleroad that he took this effect from singer Teresa Brewer.) Most likely, Van Vliet's voice was formed out of its own materials—he found out he could do things that few others could do, and stayed with his unique strengths.

But Howling Wolf's music, with his voice considered as only one element, can still be compared with the music of Captain Beefheart and the Magic Band. Here is one (to those of us lucky enough to have seen Burnett perform, very accurate) description of Howling Wolf and his music:

> . . . Wolf brings out of his band an ensemble counterpoint unlike anything else in the blues. His voice seems to hang in the air, and makes the room rumble with echo. . . . Notes blend together and merge into melody lines that are not being "played" by any one instrument. Wolf is not bound by the three-chord blues pattern, and often seems to erase the bar lines of western music. He is a Primitive-Modernist. . . .[14]

As time passed, the music made by Captain Beefheart and the Magic Band would grow more and more to prompt the kind of amazed and spooked reaction Howling Wolf provoked.

But first the band had to be rebuilt. And here Van Vliet began assembling the body electric which would create and play music like no one had ever made before. And he was fortunate enough to find the man who would be the backbone not just of the band, but of the creation of the startling music to come; be Richards to his Jagger, Strayhorn to his Ellington, an unassuming local drummer named John French.

Safe As Milk

For a time, Alex St. Clair played drums and Doug Moon handled all the guitar chores. Then, in October of 1966, Van Vliet asked John French to join as the group's drummer. Doug Moon worked at an aircraft factory with French's father, and had taken him to jams. French had also attended the Magic Band's rehearsal for the Teenage Fair and loaned the band some of his drum equipment. French was primarily a drummer, but for a time fronted his own blues band, singing and playing harmonica, once opening for the Magic Band. French's band, Blues in a Bottle, had also included Mark Boston on bass and Jeff Cotton on guitar, both of whom were later to join the Magic Band.

French accepted Van Vliet's offer, thinking he was joining the best blues band around. But Van Vliet immediately set about "hipping him up," by playing records by John Coltrane, Ornette Coleman, Roland Kirk and other progressive jazz players, musicians Van Vliet had been led to by Gary Marker. Van Vliet, who was using LSD and other recreational drugs, also persuaded French to smoke enormous amounts of marijuana out in the desert with him

French, Moon and others who played with Van Vliet in the earliest Magic Bands joined for much the same reason. Van Vliet had become a brilliant blues singer and harmonica player, they all felt, and by joining with him they were joining the best blues band around. But Van Vliet was too restless to stay with the blues form for long. By the year after "Frying Pan" he had written—with much uncredited help from the band members—the songs which were to give the band's first album, *Safe As Milk*, its experimental, surrealistic feel.

Life as part of the Magic Band could be surrealistic in itself. French recalls one evening when Van Vliet was very restless, and asked French to go for a drive. They drove aimlessly through L.A. for a while, then Van Vliet pulled up to a delicatessen. Inside were Bob Krasnow, a record producer, and his associate, Richard Perry. "Are you Captain Beefheart?" they asked Van Vliet. "We've been looking for you."[1] Whether this was staged or an example of Van Vliet's supposed "psychic powers" French was unable to tell.

So it came to be that *Safe As Milk* was recorded with Richard Perry, who had no experience as a producer. Krasnow now acted as the band's manager. As the band began to compose and rehearse *Safe As Milk*, Van Vliet made a number of behind-the-scenes deals designed to get Ry Cooder into the band, and to force Doug Moon out. Gary Marker wanted to produce the album, thinking Van Vliet could create hit records, and Van Vliet suggested he could do so if he delivered Ry Cooder. Krasnow called Cooder in, ostensibly as a studio musician to help the band prepare. Moon was not told that he was to be ousted. Relations between Van Vliet and Moon were tense. Van Vliet felt that Moon was a second-rate guitarist, and Moon felt that Van Vliet's constant tinkering with the songs was destroying the music he had sweated to help write.

While it would not be until 1970 that Van Vliet's claim to have composed and taught every player every note would become Beefheart Gospel, Cooder recalls this being Van Vliet's claim even in 1967. (He also made it clear to Cooder that he felt music which kept to a single groove for very long was "bourgeois,"[2] and so his music would attempt to subvert that tendency, to, as he would later describe it, do away with the "Mama heartbeat" of popular music.) John French, too, recalls the composition of the music as always being more of a cooperative experience:

> . . . Don is an incredibly complex person, but he's also a very lazy person. So when he wrote complex music for the first Magic Band he depended heavily on the band to arrange it—to teach it to him. . . .[3]

Van Vliet may be able to read music, as he once claimed, but if so not well enough to write out his own compositions. He has stated that he considers written music "a useless obstacle. Those written notes look like black ants crawling over white paper, on lines. . . . There are no lines in nature. Einstein has proven that.[4]"

The matter of credit for composition and conflict over Van Vliet changing parts written by others were part of a greater struggle Van Vliet felt he was having with the other members of the band. Gary Marker, who observed the band at work, has said that Van Vliet had a "flip/flop superiority/inferiority complex."[5] He felt he was not given enough respect for his ideas because he didn't play any instrument other then the harmonica, and he had had no musical training. At the same time that he felt slightly inferior for this lack of knowledge, he also had enormous faith in his own creativity. In may have been in part to help insure that his ideas would prevail despite his lack of musical knowledge that Van Vliet became increasingly abusive and domineering with the band in this period.[6]

On Cooder's first day of rehearsals with the band, Moon suddenly appeared with a loaded cross-bow and threatened Van Vliet. Cooder ducked behind a guitar amp, but Van Vliet only raised his voice and ordered Moon back to his room. Moon went.[7] He was present for the recording of some demos, but on the day the band was scheduled for the album cover photo shoot Krasnow fired him. The *Safe As Milk* album as released included no musician credits, but Ry Cooder and Alex St. Clair were the guitarists. (Several studio musicians were brought in, and another guitarist may have played on some of the material.)

In much this same way, Marker was bumped out of the producer's chair by Krasnow while Van Vliet sat silent.

The album, or a selection of similar demos, had earlier been rejected by A&M. In an exchange which has become legendary in fan circles, A&M's Jerry Moss declared the songs written for *Safe As Milk* "too negative," and added that *"Electricity* wouldn't be good for [his] daughter." "Negativity" is not quite the right word for the music on the album, but it doesn't take much listening to understand what Moss was responding to; it is even present in the title. The phrase *Safe as Milk* refers to an environmental hazard that had recently been in the news. Both the insecticide DDT and Strontium 90 (this latter a fission by-product with a half-life of nearly 30 years) were found to have saturated some environments to the point where it was present in mothers' milk. (Van Vliet's first ecological realization was tied to something similar: "When I drank my first cola," he has explained, "I realized with a shock that the bottle had the form of a woman . . . the shape is very sexy, but the content is poison."[8])

The song "Safe as Milk" does not appear on the album, rather on its follow-up, and it is a catalogue of dangers lurking everywhere in our homes, with an accent on spoiled food: cheese with a mile-long beard, blue bacon; domestic life as toxic event. When the phrase appeared as the title of the first album it unavoidably became a declaration of the nature of music inside. The words "Safe as Milk" seem to declare that while this music may seem wholesome at first, in reality it holds hidden dangers. That Moss, presented with this at times aggressive music with its often secretive-sounding lyrics, should have "read the title" (that is, heard the music) as he did is understandable. No one likes signing a dotted line when they suspect they are being duped, perhaps ridiculed.

With Krasnow's help Van Vliet began trying to make *Safe As Milk* a bridge between his drive toward experimentation and an awareness of commercial realities. One consequence of this is that co-writer's credit for most songs goes to one Ed Bermann. Little is known about Bermann, though French and others did meet him, and French remembers him as a poet and lyricist. Van Vliet's comment was:

> He was a fellow that I met up in the desert; he was a
> writer and I sort of collaborated with him on some of
> the songs on the album. I got together with him
> because at that time the group that I was with wouldn't
> listen to one thing that I said—you see, my stuff
> seemed too far out for them—and I thought that if I
> was with what they thought was a professional writer
> that they would listen to me.[9]

This exhibits some of the inferiority/superiority split Marker saw, but also sounds like Van Vliet talking his way around the fact that a song doctor of some sort was brought in. The Captain Beefheart legend, like that of Picasso who insisted he was born a brilliant draftsman, requires that no creative help was ever actually *needed.* It has been proven not to be true of Picasso— or of anyone else in the history of the arts, for that matter—so it would be no slur to conclude that help was indeed needed. Bermann's name appears on eight of the album's twelve tracks, including the first "classic" Captain Beefheart song, "Electricity." (His name will appear again, as co-writer of "Owed T'Alex" on 1978's *Shiny Beast (Bat Chain Puller)* album—a sign that Van Vliet had begun recycling old, unrecorded material.) It is interesting to note that the "straightest" or most conventional of the songs—"I'm Glad" for example, which even features male falsetto background voices—are credited to Van Vliet alone, while the most innovative compositions—"Autumn's Child," "Electricity"—are credited as collaborations.

John French also played an important part in the assembling of the lyrics. Van Vliet used to carry his lyric ideas around in a paper shopping bag, his "bag o' tricks," as the band called it. When the time for the recording session drew near, French discovered that all Van Vliet had of his lyrics were these scraps. French sorted these out and created lyric sheets. During the sessions , producer Perry made a number of suggestions about where Van Vliet should sing, and French stood at Van Vliet's side to hand him lyrics, drinks, and deal with his growing hypochondria as the vocal tracks were recorded.[10]

Perry, who would go on to become a very well respected producer, had no experience with the state-of-the-art eight-track recording process, and after recording a few songs moved the band to a more old-fashioned four-track studio, with a resulting loss of sound quality.

The album opens with "Sure 'Nuff 'N Yes I Do." After a quick guitar quote from Son House, Cooder plays the "Rolling and Tumbling" riff while Van Vliet sings "I was born in the desert." The lyrics are solidly within the blues braggart tradition, but the music (arranged by Cooder) moves away from its strict blues roots. When the full band enters for a second verse, playing a chugging rhythm, the opening riff moves to the background and finally disappears. During the third verse everyone but Van Vliet drops out at the fourth beat, and crashes back in on an off-beat, a rhythmic variation that keeps the listener from going on auto-pilot. "Zig-Zag Wanderer," which follows, is an unremarkable quest song, with some simplistic if razor-toned guitar work.

"Call On Me" is a smooth ballad with pop-soul guitar changes. But there is rhythmic variation here, too. Between two of the verses the band relaxes and a solo guitar plays a free-time riff, and the last section of the song is an entirely new riff. "Dropout Boogie" is a song made up of some of the "Generation Gap" rhetoric of the time: Dad wants son to stay in school, get a job, get married and "bring home the butter," while the son wants to drop out. Van Vliet sets this dialogue against the heavily-fuzzed rise and fall of a simple guitar riff, while he sings the lyrics in a low gargling voice. There are again breaks for rhythm changes, in this case shifts to a tinkling carousel waltz, which provides mocking relief to the relentless nagging argument. The music comes to a full-stop more than once, an unusual technique in a time when radio feared even seconds of dead air.

The only other composer in rock and roll of the time who was making effective use of such stops was Brian Wilson, just a few miles down the coast from Van Vliet. There are a number of similarities between these two men: both created rock and roll music which was "incorrect" by existing standards (session musicians would sometimes ridicule Wilson behind his back), both changed textures and time signatures frequently within two-and-a-half-minute tunes, and both reached unprecedented creative peaks which were followed (in Wilson's case almost immediately, while Van Vliet suffered a slow drying-up) by an inability to finish new music. A detailed look at the parallels between these two men would be fascinating.[11]

"I'm Glad" is a slow ballad with falsetto background vocals and syrupy brass. Like "Call On Me," this tries for a smooth sheen, but falls just short.

"I'm Glad" is followed by "Electricity." This song was still being put together scant minutes before the tape was set rolling. With everyone set to go, Van Vliet told French he wanted the drum part changed, from a straight 4/4 to a shifting pattern of syncopations, and French—as he would continue to do—rose to the occasion. "Electricity" sets off with a chugging guitar, then stops dead and a slow intro section comes in. The music then gallops off, but not without a number of stops and starts, all with a thermin's scribbled contrail flying above.

The thermin is an electronic instrument, which had until recently most often been played for film soundtracks—the spooky "ooh-eee!!" effects. But Brian Wilson had recently used it on the Beach Boys hit "Good Vibrations." This was released in October 1966, after Wilson had been at work on the song for six months. The sessions for *Safe as Milk* began in the late summer or early fall of that year, and released in April of 1967. It would have been quite reasonable for Van Vliet to decide to integrate the novel "new" sound of the thermin then so prominent on the radio into one of the songs for the album, to increase its chances for success. Van Vliet and the thermin player got along very well, with the former writing his ideas in graphic form , and the latter getting the part right on the first take.

This recording of this song occasioned one of the most famous moments of Van Vliet's music career: the power of his voice destroyed a $1,200 microphone (in 1966 dollars) with the explosive force of a bellowed *"Eeeeeee. . . "* The engineer on the session verifies that this indeed happened. This anecdote captures

32

the characteristic shape of Van Vliet's interactions with the world, both with inanimate objects and with people. He has never made much in the way of concessions to equipment, economics, other people's abilities, limitations or taste, et al. He always has exerted the full force of the ideas he has at a given time, and again and again something in his path has been crushed. These have ranged from the microphone, to friendships, to the entire Magic Band in 1974, to his music career itself.

In contrast to the whirling dynamo power of "Electricity," the second side opens with whimsy. "Yellow Brick Road" has a ricky-ticky rhythm and thinned-out guitar sounds. This song is meant, much like the Jefferson Airplane's "White Rabbit," to capture the power of a tale for children and place it within the frame of adult pleasures. The flower power lyrics mention smiling children and sunshine and candy sticks. But Van Vliet doesn't quite muster the friendly vocal tone needed to make this work; only the sudden vocal bursts warning us not to look back are convincing.

For "Abba Zabba" Van Vliet asked French if he could play an "African" rhythm. What French plays here he later dismissed as probably coming from a King Kong movie, but the dancing tom-centered rhythm is compelling, whatever its source. The dips and swings of the melody fit nicely over this. There are more starts and stops here, and even a bass solo. Van Vliet's voice is double tracked and he briefly sings in counterpoint with himself. "Abba Zabba" received a good deal of underground radio play, at least in California.

"Plastic Factory" is a less successful take on some of the same concerns Van Vliet sings about in "Dropout Boogie." Still, the lyrics employ an effective device: the verses concentrating on the joys of being outdoors, while the chorus simply says that a factory is no place to be, and leaves the listener to make the obvious connection. There are, again, shifts to 3/4 here, but this time they add nothing. The high points of this track come with Van Vliet's straight-forward and nimble harmonica playing.

"Where There's Woman" is another ballad, a woman-as-refuge song, and Van Vliet sings this in a wonderfully yearning voice. The percussion arrangement is unusual—dominated by hi-hat and bongos for the verses, with full drum kit coming in for the choruses. There is some tricky syncopation here, which keeps the track interesting.

Ry Cooder arranged the Robert Pete Williams song "Grown So Ugly," a blues, though not in 12-bar form. An insistent rhythmic figure (played in open D tuning, with most of the fretting being done at the third fret) alternates with the vocal for the verses, the melody sung where the guitar rests or holds a chord. The starts and stops of the verses give way to a second, descending rhythmic figure, which drives the chorus: "I've grown so ugly I don't even know myself."

Williams was a country blues player who had been discovered during field recording sessions at Angola prison in Louisiana, where he had been imprisoned. "Grown So Ugly" is the story of a man getting out of prison and finding that he has changed so radically that no one he knows recognizes him. Williams, a short stocky man who favored a huge black hat, sang in a high voice that could actually achieve that which is so often promised and so rarely delivered: he could give his listeners chills. Van Vliet's baritone is much more aggressive, investing the song with anger rather than Williams' jittery desperation. Williams wrote a number of songs which are as brilliant as "Grown So Ugly." His lyrics and music stand apart from most blues compositions as being more structurally singular, rhythmically inventive and deeply thoughtful. Either by chance or by way of brilliant musical insight, Cooder brought Van Vliet a song from the man closest to being his counterpart among living blues players. (Van Vliet would later declare that he had too much respect for the classic bluesmen to cover their songs. He also dismissed Ry Cooder's solo albums with the comment, "I don't like using the past. . . . It's very warlike to do things out of the past. Why does he need that shield?")[12]

Van Vliet's recording of "Grown So Ugly" serves to point out an overlooked aspect of his own music: that it is country music. It is not simply that Van Vliet has chosen to live away from cities so much of his adult life. Country blues can be very irregular, especially west of Mississippi. (Delta players were dismissive of the great Blind Lemon Jefferson because the Texan "broke time.") Bar lengths might change, the players speed up or slow down, verse lengths change. Country blues are a record of the motions and breath of a particular body. When the blues went to the city it had to conform, to become the steady pulse of a collective body electric. All of the players had to know what the music would do next. Van Vliet's music is country because it records the vital forces of a particular body, and does not give way to the composite body that produces music from and for crowd-think. Listening to "Well," "The Dust Blows Forward and the Dust Blows Back" and "Orange Claw Hammer," the *a capella* Beefheartian field hollers on *Trout Mask Replica*, a listener can feel the rhythms expanding and relaxing, with lungs, rib cage, and consciousness itself as it processes the words. This body-rhythm base is at the heart of even the most "difficult" of Beefheart music. Some kinds of African music seem polyrhythmic beyond even Beefheart, and yet dancers dance to it. This is because everyone listening knows what core rhythm they need to supply to unify the music; their minds and bodies complete the music and make it flow. Such a core rhythm can be found for Beefheart music; listeners should try letting their bodies lead them in, without using the bridle of "understanding"—who among us, after all, "understands" how another's body moves? This appreciation of the idiosyncratic body of the composer is the opposite of the conformity of city music, which erases the individual body as surely as the city itself does. Participation and sympathy are the country virtues needed for country music, including that of Captain Beefheart and the Magic Band.

The album's last track, "Autumn's Child," begins with the guitars whispering back and forth, interweaving short lines with Asian-sounding harmonies. This gives way to a series of guitar arpeggios, and some heavily-echoed background vocals. There follows a broken series of chords and thermin wriggles, and a return to the first theme. These sections continue to alternate, relieving and boosting one another, throughout the song. A series of broken chords and a new rhythm pattern lead to the end, an unexpectedly corny last melody line and ending chord. Cooder has singled this out as being the composition which most impressed him.

The band began performing the new compositions at concerts; performing them before they were ready, in Cooder's opinion. Krasnow kept telling them they were going to be "underground heroes," and as big as the Rolling Stones. Van Vliet was feeling and showing the strain. He would suffer anxiety attacks while riding in a car with the band, and the driver would have to pull over while Van Vliet regained his breath and his composure. At times he would swear he was having a heart attack and demand to be driven to the hospital. This became almost a daily occurrence.

The collapse of the band came, fittingly, on stage. They were performing at the Mount Tamalpais Music Festival ("and, believe me," Cooder told the BBC interviewer, "it wasn't going very well") when, in the middle of "Electricity," Van Vliet fell silent, turned, walked straight off the back of the stage and fell on top of Krasnow. Cooder packed up his guitar, and told the band he was through. John French followed him across the grounds trying to talk him into giving Van Vliet another chance, but Cooder was soon on a plane to somewhere far away.

This was shortly before the group was scheduled to appear at the Monterey Pop Festival, and their appearance had to be cancelled because another guitar player could not have learned the complex material in time. Would Captain Beefheart and His Magic Band have become "underground heroes" or something even bigger if they had played Monterey? Jimi Hendrix's star rose from there, as did one or two others. But just as many who played there sank. To say that Cooder ruined Van Vliet's shot at the big time may be to engage in wishful thinking. Or denial: it was, after all, Van Vliet who quit the stage first.

This would not be the last time Van Vliet's behavior would prompt a Magic Band member to gather himself together and flee.

Strictly Personal

The tracks for the band's second album were recorded between October 1967 and May 1968. One reason for giving the album the title *Strictly Personal* was that Van Vliet (again making extensive use of the band's abilities) wrote all the songs, with no outside song doctor looking over his shoulder. The results were for the most part variations on the blues and more basic rock forms of the time. Where many of the tracks on the first album included both straight and slide guitar, Van Vliet here begins assembling his music around the rasping, whining sound two slide guitars make, a sound he would continue to favor. The album is much more monochrome, the songs more sound-alike than those on the first album. *Strictly Personal* has an overall tone as unflashy as its manila cover art. Without Bermann's input, the lyrics become less structured, more impressionistic, and at the same time sparser; some barely developing beyond their titles.

The music on *Strictly Personal* doesn't immediately impress the way *Safe As Milk* does. The compositions are simpler, more a beginner's, even a naif's music—there is nothing here with the complex structure of a "Dropout Boogie" or the harmonic richness of "Autumn's Child." But neither are there any songs which seem to be aimed toward Top 10 radio play, as there were on the first album. What Van Vliet is doing with the music here is almost literally levelling his musical landscape, stripping everything down to its bare bones so that he can begin to build something new. While *Safe As Milk* is certainly the first album by Captain Beefheart and His Magic Band, *Strictly Personal*, true to its title, is the first album shaped solely by Van Vliet's sensibility. There is an immediacy and a physicality to the music which is missing from most of the previous album, which for all its originality comes from a more commercially calculated approach. Both compositionally and in its occasional feel of trying too hard to please, *Safe As Milk* (one or two tracks excepted) has more in common with the reviled Mercury albums of 1974 than it does with what came immediately before or after it. The second album's cubist blues forms are in a direct line from the A&M "Diddy Wah Diddy."

The album opens with "Ah Feel Like Ahcid," a reworking of Son House's "Death Letter Blues." Van Vliet imitates something of House's urgent singing style, but is overall more relaxed. The words at once pay homage to and parody the themes of traditional blues—Van Vliet sings about a woman with big "chicken legs" and that "the postman's groovy," while a slide guitar plays Mississippi delta-style blues behind him. The song fades, and chords like a puffed-out-chest announce the next song, "Safe As Milk." The lyrics may have been inspired by bachelor pad living—the refrigerator has a blown-out bulb and holds spoiled food, but Van Vliet still sees its chrome shelves as "looking like a harp." The slide guitars work through the verses in call and response patterns, rising treble lines answering heavily rhythmic chord passages. French's friend Jeff Cotton had joined the band after Cooder's departure. Cotton and St. Clair's guitars cross one another like a knife and sharpener. French plays in an all-out pounding style, and Handley is buried beneath French's toms. The end of the song is a blurry coda of feedback and slide-wiggling, set over French's drums as they turn and slow and finally settle into slow rolls wandering through some phasing effects which push the drums from one speaker to another.

"Trust Us" begins like movie music suggesting an exotic island religion, with "ah-ahs" and a profoundly serious-sounding spoken intro. The lyrics—"Trust us; to find us you gotta look

38

within," and an insistence that we all have to see before we see, be before we be, suggest the "us" in the title signifies our instincts, our inner feelings. One of the guitars plays a repetitive lick through most of the song. There are no solos as such, only variations on the repeated patterns. Again, as on "Safe As Milk," there is a meandering section where the guitars slowly investigate the notes they have been playing, and Van Vliet stretches out the syllables of a couple of lines. This was the era of "raga rock," and early attempts at a Western-style electric trance music, and Van Vliet uses the repetitions in the music to great effect. The chant which ends the songs—Van Vliet repeating eight words again and again, intercutting them with ever more rapturous leaps into the falsetto, and French's drums being lowered by the production into the sound of a huge chamber—is indeed compelling, almost hypnotic.

The songs fades out and another fragment of "Ah Feel Like Ahcid" fades in. The first three songs, then, are a suite. Some considered it a set of drug songs, and a case can be made for that. But what's most interesting is that the suite form suggests that the most basic delta blues riffs and the most current electronically altered experimental effects all flowed together for Van Vliet. Listening to "Moody Liz," an unfinished recording from the same time, we hear Van Vliet and other voices singing long note chants over a busy rhythm track.[1] One of the things the voices chant is "Trust Us," suggesting that Van Vliet may have pnce envisioned a suite structure for the entire album.

The fourth and final track on the first side is "Son of Mirror Man—Mere Man," an older song with music largely shaped by Doug Moon during the pre-*Safe As Milk* period.[2] The guitars again sound like anvils playing the blues. Van Vliet's voice comes up in the mix like a bullfrog singing opera: *"Mirr...orrrrrrrr."* The music is insistent, the lyrics a sing-song of opposites, "me / you," "Nearer than / farther than," that Van Vliet's voice turn to poetry. Halfway through the track the rhythm changes, cuts in half and the band plays freely until Van Vliet's harmonica enters and the other instruments all step aside while he plays, sings and scats, first fiercely and then more and more quietly until only a whispering harmonica reed remains. The album's phasing effects are at their most insistent here.

The second side opens with "On Tomorrow." The opening riff has much the same rhythm as Zappa's composition "King Kong," but stubbornly holds its place on the scale, rather than slowly swinging down as Zappa's piece does. French's tom-toms provide the steady pulse that guides the busy traffic of changes through the first minute of the track. There are a number of changes in rhythm and sound, including a sequence which employs total silence for full beats as a tension-builder. Again, there are free passages, where the guitars and drums abandon even the varying beats that have structured the piece, and play with no definite rhythm, and utilizing the slide guitar player's freedom to play any interval between the set notes of a guitar fretboard, they also play with no set pitch.

Some reverse guitar leads into "Beatle Bones N' Smokin Stones." A second, untreated guitar enters, apparently an electric guitar being played without an amplifier, from the dead sound of it. The lyrics have a simple springboard: if there are Strawberry Fields, then there must be strawberry mice, strawberry butterflies, strawberry caterpillars, etc.

John Lennon was reportedly not pleased by Van Vliet's reuse of his phrase, but if so Van Vliet bore him no ill feelings. Van Vliet had a clairvoyant episode the day before Lennon was killed, telling a journalist, "Something big is happening tonight— something horrible. You'll read about it in your papers tomorrow." The day after Lennon's assassination Van Vliet played a concert in New York City which began with him playing a soprano sax solo. He told the audience that the music was "from John, through Don, for Sean."[3]

"Gimme Dat Harp Boy" is a simple riff-driven blues. One fan described it as Willie Dixon's "Spoonful" played backward. Van Vliet's harmonica, naturally enough, dominates. "Kandy Korn," an ode to the little yellow and orange sweets is one of Van Vliet's most minor songs, both lyrically and musically. But he clearly had a soft spot for it, continuing to perform it in concert more than a decade later.

The phasing effects on *Strictly Personal* figure in one of the first of the many feuds Van Vliet would have with record producers. According to Van Vliet, Krasnow put "psychedelic Bromo-Seltzer"—by which he meant phasing—on the record without his consent. "Phasing" is a technique whereby the sounds of two or more tracks go in and out of synchronization, the result being a *whooshing* effect, as if the sound were being carried and spun by a swift current. Phasing had been used to add excitement to records at least since Toni Fischer's 1960 hit "The Big Hurt." And just a month before recording began with Krasnow, in September of 1967, the English band the Small Faces had released "Itchycoo Park," a heavily phased song which became a chart hit.

If Krasnow (who has since died) made any public statement about this, no record of it is to be found in Van Vliet literature. But rumors persist that Van Vliet in some way authorized Krasnow to alter his tapes, and an attempt at emulating the Small Faces' success could have been at the root of it, or an appeal to the growing popularity of the drug culture. Some have said that Van Vliet authorized Krasnow to do this, and only after negative comments by others did he condemn the mix. (The band members were divided on the effects.) But, despite the cries of the purists and of Van Vliet himself, the phasing doesn't really mar the music, and some aspects—some of French's drum solo work, for instance—even seem to have been arranged with the idea of leaving enough space in the music to accommodate such effects. Bill Harkleroad was present when Van Vliet first saw a copy of the album, but his account leaves open the possibility that Van Vliet's anger was directed at the fact that Krasnow misled him about the possibility of the album coming out at all more than objections to the phasing effects Krasnow added to the album. And Van Vliet remained not just a business associate of but friends with Krasnow after the album was issued. One of Van Vliet's statements about the album's mix reflect their mixed relationship:

> I told Krasner, I said I hope you had fun, but I think
> you should start playing yourself so you don't have to
> do that to mine. It didn't make me that mad at
> Krasnow, because he wanted to play. He wanted me
> to make it—he didn't do it vindictively or maliciously,
> he just wanted me to make it. . . .[4]

Phasing began as a physical manipulation of the tape, with the producer or engineer dragging his thumb along a copy of the master tape to produce the sound. It is not known whether Krasnow used physical manipulation or if he by then had the ability to produce the effect electronically, but when Krasnow asked Van Vliet to name his new label, Van Vliet chose "Blue Thumb." (*Strictly Personal* is BTS 1.) Along with the name, Van Vliet gave the ultimate endorsement of his own thumbprint: it was Van Vliet's print that became the label logo, spinning round and round as the albums played. Was this some private reference to an agreement about phasing?

Strictly Personal is a short album, totalling just over thirty-five minutes. But it had originally been planned as half of a double-album set, with the working title of *It Comes to You In a Plain Brown Wrapper*. The second disc was to be longer performances. These were actually recorded before the tracks which became *Strictly Personal*. These long tracks, an additional fifty-plus minutes of music, were recorded in November of 1967 but not released until 1971, as *Mirror Man*. These songs are even simpler than those on *Strictly Personal,* for the most part consisting of simple riffs repeated for up to nineteen minutes. "Tarotplane," is a two-chord groove, with occasionally slippery slide leads. The lyrics are Van Vliet's revision and knitting together of several songs: the old hymn "You're Going to Need Somebody On Your Bond," Son House's recording of "Grinnin' In Your Face," and (at an even further remove) Howling Wolf's "Wang Dang Doodle," as well as a couple more. The title is a pun on Robert Johnson's "Terraplane Blues," but Van Vliet makes no use of that song's lyrics or music. Van Vliet plays "first-time musette" (supposedly given to him by Ornette Coleman) as well as harmonica here. The musette is a double-reed instrument, which had made it into pop music consciousness via Brian Jones' interest in the Master Musicians of Jajouka. Van Vliet tightens his voice to form a sound close to that of the musette, does some of his formidable scat-singing, and even turns his mike on and off in places to add some John Cage-style indeterminacy to his vocal. The end of the track deliberately unravels, much the same as on "Safe As Milk," and "On Tomorrow" on *Strictly Personal*. These variations mean that, for all its basic musical simplicity, the track passes the test of time: it runs nineteen minutes and doesn't become boring. An eight minute alternate version of the logy "Kandy Korn" fails this test.

"25th Century Quaker" is based on a squarish two-bar ascending riff which is very close to the melody. The musette sounds out of place here (particularly at the end, where it sounds like a loon being strangled), and Van Vliet uses it sparingly. Here again he works his voice hard, using repetitions of words and fragments of phrases much the way Van Morrison uses them. Under this chanting the guitars slowly change the shape of the basic riff, while keeping everything available in small rhythmic boxes. The effect is again hypnotic, though the track as a whole is less successful than "Tarotplane." French here again provides the rhythmic binding that keeps the fragments together.

"Mirror Man" appears here in a much looser-limbed arrangement than on *Strictly Personal*. Where the earlier track had a hammering insistence, the longer version has an attractively swinging swagger. Its quarter-hour playing time passes pleasantly, but it doesn't leave the impression the more forceful short version does. Despite moments of excellence by the players, in the end this album is only a set of musical vocabulary and grammar exercises for Van Vliet as he searched for a new form.

In January 1968, while Krasnow was mixing the completed *Strictly Personal*, Van Vliet, French, Handley, St. Clair and

Cotton travelled to Europe. They first played a festival in Belgium, then landed in London, where they were refused entry into England. The official report of the incident includes such comments as,

> Mr. Vliet is the leader of an American "pop group" known as Captain Beefheart's Magic Band, which specializes in so-called psychedelic music and is currently very popular with a certain section of the population of the West Coast of the United States. The group arrived together and presented a very strange appearance, being attired in clothes ranging from "jeans" to purple trousers, with shirts of various hues, and wearing headgear varying from conical witches' hats to a brilliant yellow safety helmet of the type worn by engineers. . . . [It] proved somewhat difficult to interview them as they appeared to think on a completely different mental plane. . . .[5]

They told the immigration officials that they had no concerts scheduled in England, but when the officials leafed through the *New Musical Express* they found announcements for two concerts. The band had no work permits to play in the country, and they had very little money; Van Vliet had only about five dollars. They protested that they were to play for publicity purposes only and would not be paid, but the officials were suspicious.

At this point Peter Meaden, the English rep for Kama Sutra/ Buddha, arrived. But Meaden—"a gentleman dressed in the American style, with long unkempt hair and with a cigarette dangling from his lower lip," according to the report—had no proof that he was affiliated with any record company and was known by the police at the airport to have had convictions for drunk driving and illegal possession of a firearm. On the question of the illegal concerts Meaden, "pleaded for clemency on the grounds of his own stupidity." This was rejected, and the group were searched and detained in "approved detention quarters" from just after noon until five o'clock. The immigration officials decided that the group was the victim of Meaden's shenanigans, and the Chief Immigration Officer spent four hours making phone calls trying to arrange permits. But, in the end, the record company was unable to secure these. Meaden was fired on the spot, and the band was sent back to Hanover.

The band subsequently was allowed in the country. British D.J. John Peel, already a fan of the band, arranged for them to record several songs for radio broadcast. Reports of these sessions recount how Van Vliet spent time "playing with light switches" and lying on the floor to sing. English audiences, once they were able to hear and see the band perform, would champion the music to a far greater degree than would ever be the case in their home country.

Back home, after more deal-finagling by Krasnow, Van Vliet began to doubt that *Strictly Personal* would ever appear. So in early summer of 1968 he decided to record the album all over again. The most important fact about the one recording session which did take place before Krasnow abruptly delivered the finished album was that this was the first recording Van Vliet did with Bill Harkleroad, who would become "Zoot Horn Rollo" in 1969. Harkleroad, a decade or so younger than Van Vliet, spent his adolescence in Lancaster, playing in bands and at jam sessions. A photograph from 1964 shows the teenaged Harkleroad with a double necked Mosrite guitar, dressed for success in a Ventures-dominated musical world.[6] At the same time, he began seeing both Van Vliet and Frank Zappa playing in local bands. By the time Harkleroad was 14 he was jamming with Van Vliet, as were the other members of what was to become the "classic" Magic Band line-up. Van Vliet's band soon became the unit in which Harkleroad, who had begun to concentrate on playing blues, aspired to play. According to Harkleroad, the interest ran both ways; Van Vliet waited for him and the others to get old enough that they could join him, and he could eliminate the "old school" players who were resisting his musical ideas. "He knew how to get young guys [who had] good ears, and the talent, but not a lot of previous knowledge to do this, because the older guys [would say] 'fuck you, I'm not going to work that hard.'"[7] "That hard" would eventually include the nine-month period when he and the band spent up to 16 hours a day rehearsing and assembling the music for the album *Trout Mask Replica.*

The other members of the band at this belated *Strictly Personal* session included Gary Marker on bass, Jeff Cotton and John French, with Zappa doing the production. At the time Harkleroad went into the studio with Van Vliet he was playing a 1963 Fender Telecaster through a Fender Dual Showman amp. Zappa walked into the studio and turned the amp's tone and volume controls both up to ten. "I had to stand to the side of it," Harkleroad has said. "It could have cut paper for sure."[8]

The songs recorded at the session were "Kandy Korn," which appeared on *Strictly Personal* as released, and "Moonlight On Vermont" and "Veteran's Day Poppy," neither of which were recorded for Krasnow's version of the album, but would appear on *Trout Mask Replica.* On the latter album, these two are among the more conservative pieces. (On "Moonlight" Harkleroad's guitar has the "shredding" tone he complained that Zappa had adjusted his amplifier to have.) But had they been included on *Strictly Personal*, they would have ranked as the furthest extension of what Van Vliet was doing at the time. Harkleroad refers to this material as "the transition group of tunes . . . [with] open-tuning, slide, and more traditionally played stuff, but the way the parts went together wasn't so traditional."[9]

If Van Vliet was thriving artistically, well on his way to finding a unique and personal musical style and beginning to attract the calibre of musicians needed to play his new music, he was less successful on the business front. He was already falling into a pattern which would repeat itself over the years: he broke with Krasnow in indignation over the "psychedelic Bromo-Seltzer" on *Strictly Personal,* and was once again without a manager or record contract.

And so, reenter Frank Zappa.

Light the Fire Piano

The late 1960s saw the rise of artist-owned record labels. Van Vliet has said that Paul McCartney approached him about joining the roster of the Beatles new label, Apple, but Van Vliet replied, "I don't think there *is* a label for this bottle!" Instead, the next Beefheart album appeared on "Straight Records," one of two labels begun by Frank Zappa. Zappa's motives in offering Van Vliet a contract were mixed: he certainly valued his old friend's voice[1], and recognized Van Vliet's genius, so different from his own. Having participated in the abortive second round of *Strictly Personal* recordings, he knew something of the direction Van Vliet was taking. But Zappa also was staking out a territory within the record business, showing that he was willing to take the chances the more established labels would no longer take. Van Vliet would later complain of being treated as a "hood ornament" —of his name being used to gain prestige among the musically adventurous, and the aggressively "hip"— by the likes of Virgin Records, and Zappa's invitation certainly contained an element of this as well. While Van Vliet would later revile Zappa for his motives and his marketing strategies, the offer did include a promise of complete artistic freedom.

With this carrot (as good as a diamond to him at this point) in front of him, Van Vliet eagerly accepted the offer, and over the next nine months he and the Magic Band proceeded to forge an almost entirely new electric American music. In the working life of any artist deserving the title there come times when he or she decides to leave the known behind and follow their own impulses and abilities as far out on a limb as they might lead. For Van Vliet, this was one of those times.

The Magic Band that had recorded *Strictly Personal* had by this time broken up. Alex St. Clair and Jerry Handley both were gone. In an interview for the BBC documentary, Doug Moon explains that he had left the first Magic Band because Van Vliet's compositional ideas had grown more and more untraditional. (It is both a measure of the stature Van Vliet had gone on to attain as Captain Beefheart, and an illustration of how the idea of what makes a musician an artist has since the 1960s become intertwined with the idea of exploration that Moon is obviously uncomfortable saying that he didn't care to follow the experimental path.) It may be that St. Clair and Handley left in part for the same reason. But we shouldn't rule out Bill Harkleroad's suggestion that Van Vliet had been waiting for younger musicians to come of age, so that he could rid himself of the older players who not only didn't care for the new direction, but who wouldn't put up with Van Vliet's domineering side, and even (or so he felt) looked down on him as a musician.

Jeff Cotton (rechristened "Antennae Jimmy Semens") remained from the previous Magic Band, as did John French ("Drumbo"). Added were Harkleroad ("Zoot Horn Rollo") on slide guitar, and Mark Boston ("Rockette Morton") on bass. Boston was a real find. In an era when many bass players were those too uncoordinated for guitar, Boston had a technique on his instrument which equalled those of the other members. This group of musicians is considered the classic Magic Band line-up.

First Harkleroad then Boston moved into the rundown two-story house in Woodland Hills, just outside Los Angeles, where Van Vliet was already living with French and Cotton. The house had a large yard including tropical plants, eucalyptus trees, a small bridge and a laundry shed. Band members all living in the same house was not unusual at this time. Many other bands, including the English group Traffic and several San Francisco groups, as well as jazz giant Sun Ra and his Arkestra did the same. Some previous Magic Band members had lived with or close to Van Vliet since 1966, but the intensity of the arrangement would reach an unprecedented peak over the next year.

Zappa first envisioned recording the album at the Woodland Hills house—that is, in the band's native habitat; the idea being to create an album with the spirit of an anthropological field recording. Some tracks were recorded on a cassette recorder and some on a professional-quality portable reel-to-reel tape recorder. An almost complete set of recordings of the compositions intended for the album was done in this way, some of which were included on the album.[2] And these tracks do indeed capture unplanned "anthropological" moments. During the recording of "Hair Pie: Bake 1," for example, Van Vliet and "The Mascara Snake" (Van Vliet's cousin) walked around the grounds playing horns which were miked into the recorder, while the rest of the band played inside the house. As they finished, a couple, new to the area, wandered by and engaged Van Vliet in a conversation which was included on the album.

But Van Vliet almost immediately decided that Zappa was simply being "cheap," avoiding paying for studio time. He demanded the album be rerecorded in a "real" studio. Van Vliet insisted the band would play better there, as well: "Look at them, Frank," he told Zappa. "They're trapped. They can't transcend their environment!"[3] Economic considerations may well have figured into Zappa's initial scheme, but it should be pointed out that in suggesting the "field recording" technique Zappa was treating Van Vliet's music much the same as he was treating his own at this time. *Uncle Meat*, a Mothers of Invention album which Zappa released in this same period, was a collage of studio tracks, live recordings spanning several years, and tapes of band members and others commenting on (and complaining about) Zappa's music and their personal circumstances.

Considering how integral to the creation of this music was the band's forced intimacy in the ramshackle Woodland Hills house, the field recording scheme would have been a valid way of approaching the phenomena of the music created there. It would certainly have heightened the sense of the album as music from a previously undiscovered culture. But it would not have conveyed one of the messages that Van Vliet wanted the album to convey: "This is art." For that message, a more formal sound was required. Zappa relented and booked time in a Glendale studio and most of the album was rerecorded. These sessions were themselves a bit unusual. The band recorded 21 tracks in four hours—an astonishingly short time. When Van Vliet came to add his vocals to the prerecorded tracks, he chose to sing without headphones, listening to whatever sound leaked through the glass from the control room monitors.[4]

The double album which resulted was *Trout Mask Replica*. On the album cover, as on *Strictly Personal*, there are no clear images of the men behind the music. On the front, Van Vliet sports a moth-eaten-looking green coat, a high hat with a badminton birdie attached, and his face is masked by a large (and reportedly quite smelly) carp's head. On the rear cover, the band can be made out clearly, though their outlandish costumes are distracting, and Van Vliet's face is almost obliterated in a reflection caught by the camera lens. The images of the band inside the gatefold have been reversed, solarized, and otherwise obscured.

A listener putting needle to groove found what at first seemed like musical anarchy. The only tracks which sounded anything like music as it was known to blues and rock and roll players and fans in 1969 were those few which resembled *a capella* field-hollers, sung by Van Vliet in a voice which at times exhibited the *basso* resonance of a Paul Robeson. These were almost the blues, except that the lyrics sprung from Van Vliet's distinctly American word-surrealism, one which bridged Kenneth Patchen and Groucho Marx. The full-band tracks combine the givens of electric music in ways which rock had never done before, though such ideas had been implied in part in most fields of music in the same period. Similar ideas appear, for example, in Terry Riley's process music masterpiece "In C" from 1964, wherein discrete musical phrases of different lengths approach one another, lock together, then part again; in the off-kilter syncopation of the dual-guitar breaks in the Rolling Stones' "19th Nervous Breakdown;" and in some of the "harmolodic" ideas of Ornette Coleman, theories about alternate ordering of melody and harmony.

Zappa, in his capacity as head of the record company issuing the album, once described the music as a cross between delta blues and avant-garde jazz. While it is undeniable that the first of these was one of the roots from which the music grew, the second is relevant only because it had served to create a space in which this music could be taken seriously by listeners rather than dismissed as indulgent non-music. And it helped, it seems certain, to create the space within Van Vliet where he could work without the hobble of self-doubt about his own ideas. Zappa's characterization quickly became the default description for critics writing about the album—even while Zappa's comment totally misses the reality of the process Van Vliet used to form the music; a process which, as I hope to show, excluded any possibility of conscious influence.

As Van Vliet surely must have hoped, characterizing the music in any such simple way was impossible. There were two slide guitars, but this certainly wasn't blues. And there were no distinct lead and rhythm guitar parts—all the guitar parts, and each note in those parts, were equally assertive. In fact, the guitars were played with identical tone and volume, so it was at times impossible to tell where one player left off and the other began. They played lines and chords—angular, giant-step riffs alternating with chords like metal boxes being stomped—which seemed to have only the remotest relation to one another. The bass played ideas all its own, and the drums were no more locked into straight time-keeping than were the other instruments. French played as if the drums were some kind of muffled acoustic keyboard. Over the churning of these instruments Van Vliet bellowed, chanted, recited and sang lyrics full of surrealistic winking, and honked loudly through various reed instruments, at times two horns at once, *a la* Rahsaan Roland Kirk. There were no guitar or bass solos, and the harmonica was left at home this time around (an important, largely overlooked point).

"Frownland," the album's opener, is one of its most musically difficult, the guitars beginning in 7/8, an exotic time signature for rock and roll of the time. Like the *alap* section of an Indian *raga*, where the themes which will be the basis for the entire performance are presented in miniature, this short composition draws the outline of what is to come: difficult music and statements (verbal and otherwise) of personal independence: "My smile is stuck / I cannot go back to your frownland." But the music's opening howl is worse than its bite on side one. "Frownland" is the only unrelentingly difficult track on the side. The others all offer easier ways in, even if these may not be apparent on first listening. The *a capella* song-poem "The Dust Blows Forward and the Dust Blows Back" offers immediate respite, with a jaunty melody and humorous lyrics. This song-poem was improvised by Van Vliet as he clicked a small cassette player on and off. The resulting pops sound like the flaws on an old 78 rpm. Van Vliet here sings some of his most whimsically engaging lines: "I took off my pants and felt free / The wind blowing up me / And up the canyon." The last word Van Vliet sings is the wholly unexpected "Spam."

"Dachau Blues" is lyrically one of the least successful of Van Vliet's works. Rhyming "Dachau Blues" with "poor jews" is embarrassingly inadequate to the subject. The song is redeemed somewhat by an image of three little children with doves on their shoulders crying for the misery to end. The dour simplicity of the melody, however, does serve to smooth the listeners' ride around the sharp turns of the accompaniment. (That a taped monologue about trapping rats in a barn in order to kill them is placed directly after "Dachau Blues" seems a tasteless joke. As Zappa did the editing of the album, it may have been his doing.)

Jeff Cotton is credited in the album notes with "steel-appendage guitar" (a reference to his slide of choice; Harkleroad prefered the "glass-finger" approach) and "flesh horn." This latter is a reference to the hysterically tight, high voice in which he sings "Ella Guru." Van Vliet sings a more normal part and double tracks some mutterings in the background. Van Vliet's cousin Victor, here renamed "the Mascara Snake," contributes a few remarks as well. The chorus of "Ella Guru" features some of the clearest, most conventional music on the album. Cotton unleashes his helium-high voice again on side three for a recitation of the poem "Pena." On this track, Van Vliet contributes some fierce, gargled scat-singing behind Cotton.

The instrumental "Hair Pie: Bake 1" is one of the "field recordings." It begins with Van Vliet and the Mascara Snake playing free-form reeds while walking around the grounds of the house where Van Vliet and the Magic Band were living. The rest of the band, miked while playing inside the house, are faded in playing a series of riffs which tend toward (but don't quite arrive at) march time. The riffs rub each other the wrong way at times, but they are for the most part simple and symmetrical. The manner in which chords are used for emphasis here reminds us that Van Vliet was born in the 1940s. There is an underlying affinity in much of this music to the syncopated, Latin-tinged punching style of late Swing and the Big Bands, a tradition still alive in the 1960s in the form of television and film score orchestras.[5] The Big Bands' organization into riffing sections also is much closer to what Van Vliet does in his mature music than are the strummed chords of folk and country, two of rock and roll's musical roots. The studio version of this composition, "Hair Pie: Bake 2," on side 3, is nearly identical, except that it is smoother sounding. Having both included on the album shows what was gained by using a studio—clarity of tone—as well as how completely the musicians' environment was excluded from the music.

The first side concludes with "Moonlight on Vermont," one of the simplest band tracks, and one of the fiercest. Van Vliet sings a variation on "Old Time Religion" as part of the lyrics, and the guitars bite deeply into the bluesy riff that supports the gospel melody. We are caught and rushed along by the power of what the band is doing here. This is deist gospel music cranked up to eleven on a dial of ten.

The second side begins with "Pachuco Cadaver." No cadaver is mentioned, rather the song is about a beehived, tattooed woman who steers a "cartoon around" and drives all the pachucos wild. The music shifts rhythms as relentlessly here as elsewhere, but each section is atypically symmetrical, producing a succession of rhythms which are nearly danceable(!). Van Vliet's honking saxophone is present here, but used sparely. If the album was to have a single, this could have been it. ("When Big Joan Sits Up" would also have been a strong contender.) The next composition, "Bill's Corpse" was reportedly named for Harkleroad, though the lyrics offer no discernable connection to the title. The song includes some opaque coinages by Van Vliet ("formaheap"), but overall still manages to clearly convey his wish that people might come together in harmony rather than in anger or grief. "Sweet Sweet Bulbs" is a love song—such bulbs grow in his lady's garden. Again, French's drums hold together a very fragmented accompaniment which threatens to succumb to great centrifugal force. "Neon Meat Dream of a Octafish" is a poem recited against musical background, an updating of the beatnik poetry scene which Van Vliet would have known about.

"China Pig," a blues about a piggy bank, is played in the chunking style of John Lee Hooker or any number of country bluesmen. The guitar is played by the just-dropped-by Doug Moon. Van Vliet asked Moon to play this riff, then Jeff Cotton handed him one of his poems, and Van Vliet improvised from there. (The unedited tape, released on the 1999 set *Grow Fins*, includes Van Vliet trying to find a key in which to sing "Candy Man," a song by Reverend Gary Davis, then very popular with the folk-blues crowd, before going into "China Pig.") "My Human Gets Me Blues" is a very different kind of "blues," one closer to the "outside" musical style of the bulk of the album. But this is a very ordered example of the new style, one which barely disguises the fact that there is a definite "Mama heartbeat" under nearly the entire song.

The instrumental "Dali's Car" was inspired by a car in an exhibit of the campy surrealist's work at the L.A. County Museum. John French's recollection is that this was the first piece Van Vliet wrote on the piano. This was on a night when the electricity had been knocked out, and the piece was composed and written down entirely by candlelight—a fittingly ceremonial circumstance for the beginning of a new order of music. The composition, here played as a guitar duet, is stately, almost processional. Its harmonies are astringent in a way not unfamiliar to listeners of modern chamber music. If this were arranged for a string quartet it would not be out of place on a Kronos Quartet album.

For "Well" Van Vliet returns to his *a capella* Robeson voice and his Americana word collages. This track, too, is very late-40s/early-50s; a time which found the first field recordings and reissues of older black music being released for white audiences, and Jackson Pollock playing "exquisite corpses" word games with expatriate European surrealists. This track presents Van Vliet's unaccompanied voice at its most resonant and powerful.

"When Big Joan Sets Up" is an unrelenting guitar rush, highly rhythmic, with hilarious lyrics—"She ain't built for going naked/ So she can't wear any new clothes." This is Van Vliet's blues-conga rhythm style at its most insistent. "Fallin' Ditch" is a phrase that children used to use for "pretend" swearing. Here, Van Vliet literalizes it; the ditch is a hoodoo pit which the singer is trying to avoid falling into ("Ain't gonna get my bones!"). The lyrics are concerned with the dangers of letting yourself become depressed: loneliness and even frowning put the singer at risk of tripping into the fallin' ditch. A dark-sounding song that warns us we had better brighten up.

"Sugar and Spikes" is another of the songs dating from the end of the *Strictly Personal* period. Both the melody and guitar lines have an unmistakably vocal basis. The contour of the melody and the rolling drum parts make it very much one with the earlier album. The slide guitars ping and bounce the wiry-sounding notes around, especially behind the lyric beginning "Going to see the navy-blue vicar." The dynamics are the most compelling and successful of all the band tracks here.

"Ant Man Bee" is an ecology song with anti-war trimmings. Van Vliet here asserts that only man and the ants among all creatures in nature attack one another, and that we should be like the bees, who take honey and "set the flowers free." None of this is strictly true, of course, but it suits Van Vliet's non-programmatic approach to ecological thinking. Van Vliet's voice is very elastic here, swooping from a near-falsetto "Hoodoo," down to a guttural "Ant Man Bee." This is the album's best sing-along track. The harmonies here sound much more conventional and bluesy than on most of the newer material. Harkleroad compares the feel of this to Coltrane's classic *Africa Brass* (during this period Harkleroad often went to sleep with Coltrane playing in his headphones), and the comparison is not so far fetched. As Harkleroad also points out, French's drum part here is a standout.

The final side begins with "Orange Claw Hammer," another neo-field holler. The title refers to the tail of an oriole. Van Vliet improvised this on the portable cassette player he had at the house. The lyrics begin with a series of striking but isolated images, but the song soon becomes a story, almost a "tall tale." A shanghaied ex-sailor has finally come back home after thirty years to find his daughter. He takes her by the hand and leads her down to the docks to show her the beautiful ships that tempted him away to a life at sea. Lester Bangs commented on this song in a 1980 article, saying that it stood out among *Trout Mask's* material because it concerns itself with something that occurred between people, rather than the "Neon Meate Dream of a Octafish."[6] While it is true that "Orange Claw Hammer" has the most sustained emotional narrative on the album, Bangs was wrong to imply that this was the only song to include up-front emotions. There are smaller gems of emotion in the songs "Frownland," "The Dust Blows Forward...," "Dachau Blues," "Bill's Corpse," "Sweet Sweet Bulbs," "My Human Gets Me Blues," and more—in short, roughly half of the album's songs offer emotional segments. The *a capella* openness of "Orange Claw Hammer," without clashing guitars to complicate the emotional mix, allows the listener easier access. Other instances are often fragmentary, moments rather than narratives, and the accompaniment is anything but the kind of sentimental wallpaper that conventionally emotional songs are built on. This doesn't necessarily mean the more impressionistic lyrics are more shallow, only that the emotions can be harder to hear, intertwined as they are (as in life) with other images and ideas. Van Vliet doesn't spoon-feed listeners emotional content anymore than he does melody or rhythm. We have to stay awake and feel things for ourselves.

The eco-refugee song "Wild Life" offers some of Van Vliet's most upfront emotion. The lyrics tell of a man and his wife who are planning to escape to the mountains and live with the bears because their environment and their kin have been destroyed. The guitar parts in the accompaniment are among the most disjoint here, but the song retains a very clear mid-tempo rhythmic pulse throughout. Van Vliet's soprano sax playing here is among the best he put on record.

Only John French's lively, long-phrase drumming keeps the short-line guitar parts on "She Too Much for My Mirror" from chopping the music into unrelated segments. The accompaniment tracks ends before Van Vliet can get all his words in: "Shit, I don't know how I'm going to get all that in there," he complains. And he doesn't. "Hobo Chang Ba" is one of the strangest tracks on the album. The guitars whir around each other (again sounding at times like conga-line music) while sleigh bells clank. The nonsense words are sung by in a flat nasal voice by an uncredited vocalist.

Not long after the release of *Trout Mask Replica*, Van Vliet and the band members began dismissing Zappa's credit as the producer of the album, claiming that he slept through the recording session. But Van Vliet also takes a personal shot at Zappa on the album itself, on the track titled "The Blimp." Van Vliet wrote the words at home, then called Zappa at his studio and had Jeff Cotton recite them through the phone to a backing track Zappa played. (This most likely occurred after the recording of rest of the album had been finished.) Writing credits for words and music for the entire album go to Van Vliet, but the music behind "The Blimp" is Zappa's, part of a live recording of the Mothers of Invention playing a composition titled "Didja Get Any Onya?" (The complete track can be heard on the CD pressing of Zappa's *Weasels Ripped My Flesh*.) Zappa had the tape of the concert in his studio with the intent of mixing it, and pulled it out for use in this musical experiment. The rubbery bounce of the bass and drums, the woodwind squeak that is heard intermittently, provide a flexible frame which Van Vliet via Cotton fills with Zappa-mocking lyrics. Van Vliet would later agree with interviewers who suggested "The Blimp" was inspired by the Hindenburg disaster. But the lyrics—"Frank, it's the big hit! It's the blimp!"—are clearly an attack on Zappa, characterizing him as being a hit-chaser who expects Captain Beefheart and the Magic Band to make money for him, and further predicting that Zappa will soon be found floating down the gutter in need of a bottle of wine. Zappa takes all of this with good humor, laughing when the phone recitation is finished. (Though, it may be that including his own reaction on the album was Zappa's way of saving face, of saying he didn't miss what Van Vliet was putting down.)

"Steal Softly Through Snow" was one of the first of the piano pieces, and has some of the most noticeably segmental music on the album. But each of the sections has a more unified feel than most of the other compositions. French coaxes a high clacking sound from one of his drums and does more hi-hat and cymbal work here than is usual for the album. The lyrics wander from image to image, all of which suggest a desire to join with the "natural world" rather than be apart from it. The words and music here add up to one of the album's friendliest tracks.

"Old Fart at Play" is a comic poem of old-time Americana. A farmyard, with a background of fiddle-and-saw music, is the setting for a story of the title character sneaking up on a farm wife as she is "flattening lard" and dust and dough balls are collecting in her rolled-down stockings. The old fart wears an intricate wooden rainbow trout replica mask. The mask has a special dilating breathing apparatus the old fart uses to capture and seal in the smells of this high-cholesterol kitchen bliss—the aromas of baloney, wax paper and "special jellies" among others—the flip side of the toxic kitchen meltdown in "Safe as Milk." A direct descendent of this poem, "Floppy Boot Stomp" on 1976's *Shiny Beast (Bat Chain Puller)*, will set its farmyard antics to music much more conventionally organized, with dynamics clearly designed to compliment and propel the storyline. Here, the rhythms behind the recitation jump like water drops in Mama's hot skillet—and yet they do complement the tale. This is because rhythms, even irregular rhythms are unavoidably narrative. (The sight of someone "talking with their hands," conducting themselves with incomplete gestures, twists and shrugs, personal twitches which nonetheless do make their words come through more clearly, would be a good visual aid for the point I'm trying to make.) The rhythms here echo the poem's quirkiness, its "assortment of observations" transitions and even the Old Fart's eccentric inventiveness.

In general, Van Vliet's rhythms are best compared with literary models—intertwined, suspenseful of resolution, each developing line referring to the one before without repeating it—while his lyrics favor a musical model: theme and variations. And the likely source for many of the lyrics and poems, however surrealistic or esoteric they may seem, is neither a linguistic nor a musical one, nor is it esoteric. Rather, it is visual, and quite pedestrian.

In an essay on *Trout Mask Replica*, Langdon Winner approaches words and music in way most unusual in Beefheart criticism: he takes a level-headed view. After quoting lyrics from "The Dust Blows Forward and the Dust Blows Back" he observes that, "The images in the song are those of a pleasant, unromanticized American landscape described in the motley vernacular of old time rural culture. . . . He begins with elements that are ridiculously familiar to everyone and plays with them until he's produced extraordinary, unsettling effects."[7] This is all true, but Winner (one of the most perceptive critics of Beefheart music) does not go on to identify the most likely source for Van Vliet's Americana. The most likely candidate, clearly, is that shared by all of us city and suburban kids: films and television. (Did it ever occur to Van Vliet that the quaint, rural America he was sampling from for his lyrics was the America both his parents had left behind to come to urban California?)

During the *Trout Mask* cloistering, Van Vliet watched endless hours of television. Van Vliet was a child of the desert, yes, but of the desert-as-suburb. Where in the Glendale neighborhood where he grew up, or in Lancaster where he suffered through adolescence as a car, girl and clothes crazy kid with few friends, or as a member of a scuffling blues band would he have had experience of trains with cowcatchers, of hobos, of pirates or riverboats or bears in caves? At the movie theater, or on television. The narrative which takes up half of "The Dust Blows Forward," the sentimental tale of a shanghaied sailor who sires ebony children in another part of the world, and who cries when he is reunited with a long lost daughter, could easily have been a Wallace Beery film. In a clip in the BBC documentary Van Vliet declares himself a fan of black and white television, but disdains color. Black and white is the color of old B movies and cowboy serials, of early cheap TV series.

"Veteran's Day Poppy" is another of the older tunes, recorded for the planned revision of *Strictly Personal*, and its lyrics too are sentimental in the way of old films. The brief verses tell of a woman who refuses to buy a poppy from a veteran because it will only remind her of her son, killed in action. The slide guitar part is downright pretty as it answers the squarish blues-riff of the fretted guitar. Harkleroad notes that Zappa contributed some harmonic ideas, and his recollection is that the last section of the three that make up the music was Zappa's contribution. But it is the middle section that sounds distinctly like a left-over from Zappa's *Freak Out* album. The last section has a long chord-chain structure. John French's drums shine under this long coda; they sound as if French is telling an intricate tale on his drum set, the patterns and accents sound so much like a storyteller's voice. And with this long out chorus, a musical moment around a potbellied stove, the album glides almost gently to a close.

Many listeners' reactions upon first hearing *Trout Mask Replica* were much like those which cartoonist/animator Matt Groening reports as having been his own:

> The first time I heard *Trout Mask* . . . I thought it was the worst thing I'd ever heard. I said to myself, they're not even trying!

That this was Groenig's reaction is understandable. The music captured on *Trout Mask Replica* was totally unprecedented. Even those who had admired the first two albums couldn't have been prepared for this shift. Pablo Picasso has been called a "vertical invader," meaning that he appeared on the painting stage as though through a trap door from Spain's past. *Trout Mask Replica,* too, appeared on the contemporary music stage as a vertical invader, one from a contemporary but inner world all Van Vliet's own. And there are, of course, those who favor vertical invaders, who in fact seek them out. Such seekers among those who listened to the album quickly went through the second phase of Groening's listening experience:

> I listened a couple more times. . . . About the third time, I realized they were doing it on purpose; they meant it to sound exactly this way. About the sixth or seventh time, it clicked in, and I thought it was the greatest album I'd ever heard. . . . and it remains the best rock album I've ever heard.[8]

Why has this deliberately raucous, obstinately segmental, egotistical, altogether all-too-human music not simply sunk into obscurity, but rather achieved masterpiece status? Some simply chalk it up to snobbery, some to gullibility. A more thought-provoking answer to the question of why so many of us (even if not nearly as many as find it unlistenable) find this raucous, disjoint music so gripping may be found in the words of Gregory Bateson, the anthropologist and communication theorist. (A fact which Van Vliet the pan-species communicator would appreciate is that Bateson also did extensive work in dolphin communication. Van Vliet likened his untutored reed playing to the sound of a whale or a dolphin.) Bateson believed that beauty had to do with "the superposition of multiple transforms," that is, the progressive movement of energies through different levels or forms. The opposite of beauty is, in Bateson's scheme, that which disrupts this transformational process: he gave the example of a lesion which blocks flow of energy through back muscles along the spine—requiring a spinal readjustment. Beauty lies in a segmental series of transformations. After all, as Bateson pointed out, "we are segmental animals."[9] (Ant, Man, Bee—all segmental.) We can conclude that muscular composition, to be beautiful in the way a supple body is beautiful, should be segmental.

A more prosaic answer would be to point out that a major factor in what makes the songs work is Van Vliet's voice. Its power is, of course, its most noticeable characteristic, but there is also the attitude the voice conveys. While he sings with real conviction such comic lines such as those in "Big Joan Sets Up," where he says that she cannot wear any new clothes because she "ain't built for going naked," there is always a tincture (one of Van Vliet's favorite words) of self-recognition in his voice, a quality which flags that part of his presentation which winks at his own artfulness. This tone may be heard at its clearest in the dialogue snippets (he laughs at some of his own lines), but it is present in nearly all the singing. The exceptions—"Dachau Blues" and parts of "Wild Life" for instance—where his lyrics demand that his seriousness come across undiluted are his least-successful vocals; he sounds uncomfortable with his own propagandistic impulse, and they are less than convincing. In the majority of the vocal performances, even those of the most complex and oblique lyrics, there is the tone of a man saying, "Yes, I am making the art sign here; this is a little hokey, maybe, but make no mistake, it is nonetheless real." (Van Vliet can be seen acting out this attitude quite clearly in the 1982 video for "Ice Cream for Crow.") This slight undercutting of his own seriousness insures that no pretentious skin will completely congeal over the songs. This quick wink behind the bellow is enough to relax the listener, to keep the human lines open, if at times only slightly. Those of us who could hear that open line were quickly hooked, and frustration gave way to fascination.

This fascination arises, in part, from the contradictory nature of the experience of listening to the music. It is immediately strange, almost ungraspable, and yet listening with a sympathetic ear will find the music somehow familiar, unexpectedly human.

This arises from Van Vliet's decision to concentrate not, as he had done before, on his voice or his whistling as the basis of his compositions, but rather on his hands, on his personal, unintellectualized body rhythms. A few years after this, in 1972, Van Vliet talked about rhythm:

> [Everybody] has his own rhythm. Percussion is very important for the actual level of speech. Everybody walks in a different rhythm; for me it is a special way to express myself. . . . [I seek] a more natural rhythm, more healthy, less bombastic one.[10]

John French has said that Van Vliet's music changed drastically when he got a piano, on which he wrote some eighty percent of the material for the album. We can feel the difference the use of the piano made by comparing the compositions on the album with those which were composed in the interregnum between *Trout Mask Replica* and the album which preceded it. The two tracks which Van Vliet decided not to include in the *Strictly Personal* set have a different feel, noticeably less fluid than the slide-guitar-riff based music of that album. The same transitional feel is to be found in the music collected on *I May Be Hungry (But I Sure Ain't Weird)* CD. This music is stretched out, repetitive, with in some instances vocal drones which serve as harmonic arches stretching over the more jarring bodies of the interlocked guitars. This is much more relaxed music than that which followed it; and it is much more rooted in the voice, rather than the hands as on *Trout Mask*.

Van Vliet had not played a piano before acquiring one at the house, and while he acquired the instrument he did not acquire a piano teacher. The group had almost no money, but there were larger reasons why Van Vliet chose to go it alone, reasons rooted in his most basic way of being in the world. Obviously, the best way to perfect a new physical skill (including piano playing) is to find an expert to teach you its fine points. Some more subtle points are packed inside this bit of common sense. "A Computational Theory of Physical Skill," a study of juggling and computer science conducted at MIT, analyzes a few of these hidden-in-plain-sight points in a way which helps shine a little more light on what Van Vliet was after on the keys. The decision to find or not to find a teacher is, according to Howard Austin, the juggling thinker who conducted the study, actually part of an *ability*: "The ability to find or give yourself good advice." This ability is found along that uncertain line (the existence of which, as years pass and attempts are made to map it, becomes less and less certain) where we so often find Van Vliet at work, that between intellectual and physical activities. Here "advice, techniques, skill models and various other HIGH-LEVEL EDITOR features play the dominant role. . . . These activities are inherently intellectual in nature and hence lead to the claim that so-called physical skill is largely mental activity."[11]

By choosing not to seek out a piano teacher, by refusing this kind of "influence," Van Vliet kept himself cruising at his preferred depth, which is the opposite of that the MIT study explored: where supposedly mental activities—the creation of music, poetry and paintings—are largely physical. Which is to say that Van Vliet chose to "think" with his hands and ears. In this, Van Vliet participates in the historical moment of theories about cognition, agrees with those (scientists, musicians, philosophers, many others) who share a "dissatisfaction with the *cephalocentric* view of intelligence."[12] He aligns himself with those who feel "Cognition is an accomplishment of the *whole animal*. . . ."[13] It helps to clarify Van Vliet's technique to recall how all the while he was creating music, he most often characterized himself as a "sculptor" rather than a musician. What Van Vliet was telling us has to do with sculpture's special place among the arts. As art critic Peter Fuller pointed out, sculpture "in its material processes . . . is much, much more intimately linked to the biological and physical levels of existence than are, say, literature or philosophy,[14]" or painting or musical composition. Saying, "I'm more sculptor than musician," was Van Vliet's way of pointing out how he worked primarily with his body rhythms rather than restricting himself to his intellect or the vocal skills he had worked to perfect (skills which bring along their own musical habits) as bases for composing. He says as much in an explanation of the "magic muscle" he advises a "Space Age Couple" to stretch on *Lick My Decals Off, Baby:* "[It's] something like intuition or instinct, something we all have but which we ignore in favor of just thinking. There's too much rationality in this world."[15]

Langdon Winner writes of the music here, "Beneath the apparent chaos of its surfaces are structures of remarkable intricacy."[16] The fact that Van Vliet would at times just dash off a quick run of notes when the band needed another part is not incompatible with Winner's observation. Those who suspect a contradiction lurks here are forgetting that human idiosyncracies shape every discovery, even the most "objective." Scientific theories retain, as a kind of fossil poetry, the personalities of the scientists who propose them. Musical structures—those which rely least on received musical forms—have this same basis. Van Vliet's music is both intricately structured *and* spontaneous, even unthinking, in how it was assembled because this is what human beings have at their most basic operating level.

Kids, you can try this at home; get a rough feeling for how this music works as well as it does. Each of us is capable of producing any number of rhythms, more or less accurately, when we wish to do so. And every one of us, for that matter, has any number of rhythms going on inside us at any given time; some of which we can become aware of and try to copy, some of which we cannot. One thing about these body rhythms—both the on-going involuntary sort and the kind we pound out on the table top or our knees—is that the body is not set up to keep them metronome-steady. (Even that "Mama heartbeat" is not as steady as we like to think.) A rhythm by its nature "wants" to change. Only mechanical sources (or inhumanly excellent musicians) keep perfect time and, while keeping steady time is many a player and listener's ideal, it is not everyone's. Duke Ellington pointed out that "You can't swing with a metronome," and much excellent music is rhythmically elastic. One of Harkleroad's most telling comments about the music on *Trout Mask* is that, "everything was built from a rhythmic sense. . . . My feeling was that the actual notes themselves were interchangeable—it really wouldn't have mattered a whole lot as long as they created the same effect."[17] The notes do matter, of course, though this is not a contradiction of Harkleroad's thought. Any musician knows that playing, for instance, a fast triplet using the same note played three times, and the same rhythm played using three rising notes feels very different. Pitch colors rhythm. (Jazz saxophonist Roscoe Mitchell titled one of his compositions after this effect: "Off Five Dark Six.")

With all this said, try sitting, relaxed, in a chair or on a couch, in a car seat, anywhere comfortable which gives you freedom of movement. (You might want to keep in mind Van Vliet's dislike of keeping any rhythm for too extended a period of time.) Begin tapping out a rhythm on your leg with the palm of your hand. It can be done, but there is no interest here, only control. Try tapping out a second part with your other hand. Soon you will begin to feel a wish for variety in your nerves, your hands will "ask" to tap out more complex variations; let them. But then, and here is the part where you (like Van Vliet) have to exercise self-trust (think, if you need to rationalize this process, of the lyrics to "Trust Us"—to find "us," you have to look "within"—and ask yourself, who or what is this "us"?), trust that what is actually happening is not that your body is failing to do what you are asking it to do (become a machine), but that your consciousness is resisting following what your body is asking to do. Follow it, and you will find your "inability" to keep steady time will lead you through a series of varied rhythms lasting for short periods of time, unsteady or conflicting if viewed against a machine ideal, but (trust yourself) each feeling right on its own terms. When your hands feel you have done enough of what they have asked you to do, they will tell you to stop.

This exercise in listening to your body will, if done with the right kind of self-trust, produce constantly changing patterns, patterns which are oddly satisfying to follow, and which are, finally, fascinating in how they tell us something about the personal rhythms we live by.

This composition by listening to one's body, applied to the

piano (and with his use of the Magic Band to extend his body, and layer the lines his body dictated), is the basis of much of the music Van Vliet wrote at this time. This new compositional philosophy was an attempt, as Van Vliet would later put it, to "turn himself inside out." What is surprising, and hard to hear on *Trout Mask*, is the simplicity and beauty of the individual parts. Close listening will reveal that each guitar bass or drum part consists of a series of relatively simple riffs, one following another. The complexity comes in the combination of the parts, with each part (as Van Vliet intended) cutting across any lulling simplicity in the other. One guitar might be playing in 3/4, for example, and another in 4/4 so that they would share a downbeat (or "line up") only once every several measures. Some of the compositions nonetheless retain a flow and beauty even in their completed form—"Hair Pie Bake 2" is one; the repeated chord riff which closes "Veteran's Day Poppy" (a composition dating from the *Strictly Personal* period) is another. These are at one end of a spectrum that ranges across to "She's Too Much for My Mirror," where the waves of the lines cross and cut one another and produce a very choppy sea indeed.

(Others were working the same seam at this same time, if in search of a smoother result. The Grateful Dead, for one, flowered musically when Mickey Hart returned from studying with African Master Drummer Olatunji and taught the band how they might play in layers of different time signatures. This was almost exactly contemporary with *Trout Mask*.)

A look at transcriptions of two instrumental compositions from *Lick My Decals Off, Baby,* the follow-up to *Trout Mask Replica* which shares much with it musically, will further illuminate how this music works as well as it does.[18] "One Red Rose That I Mean," and "Peon" are both in the key of "C." ("A Carrot Is As Close As a Rabbit Gets To a Diamond," released on *Shiny Beast (Bat Chain Puller)* in 1978, but written years earlier, is very similar to these as well.) In looking over the transcriptions, it is striking that there are no accidentals, no notes outside the C major scale. Most blues, rock and jazz music, and many pop and classical pieces, have notes which fall outside the major scale of their key—the flatted notes of the blues scale, for instance, being essential to the music. But there are none here. Van Vliet has dismissed any worry about scales with an obvious pun: "Fish take care of the scales; as soon as I saw a fish, I realized that they had the scale department sewn up completely."[19] It appears that Van Vliet, even while not thinking of his note selections as belonging to any formal scale, composed these pieces using only the white keys on the piano, keys which comprise the C Major scale. Van Vliet, that is, never ventured onto the black keys. This restriction insures an overall consonance, or harmonic agreement of one note after or against another. Not all of Van Vliet's piano music was composed using such a restricted scale—some of his chords are dense clusters indeed—but some others were. Only the black keys, for example, were used to create fragments or musical raw material in E-flat minor. At least two pieces from *Lick My Decals Off, Baby* were constructed from these simple, individually consonant fragments.

But Van Vliet's primitive-modernist piano style has elements which keep it from falling into children's song simplicity. While each section used all white keys, it may begin on any note of the scale; and the melodies have a tendency to end on the note where they began. If this is strictly adhered to it is termed playing in a "mode"; the "Aeolian mode," the "Mixolydian," etc. This is much more common in jazz circles than in rock and roll. While an explanation involving modes could more accurately describe what happens, we might more simply say that Van Vliet takes different tones on the C scale to be the "root" of his melody. (Rarely does he play a "second" relative to the note he chooses to be his root. It is interesting to note that this "second"—for instance, "d" if the melody starts on "c"—is the note which would fall between the thumb and finger of the right hand, for the beginning pianist one of the hardest notes to hit.) Some of these choices, played against an overall C background, creates music with a shifting, unresolved feel. The feeling of dissonance (which might be said to be an "illusion," considering the limited six-note scale) is produced in part by proximity—"e" and "f" clash when adjacent, but not when played in a Fmaj7th chord:

"f-a-c-e." Some of the perceived dissonance is also due to the misalignment of rhythms produced by the arrangement process described above. The transcription of "Flavor Bud Living," recorded on *Doc At the Radar Station* in 1980, but composed at an earlier date, shows these same characteristics. The music feels as if it is being forced into too small a space.

A word which has been applied again and again to the music of this period is "atonal." This means music that has no tonal center, that mixes keys and wanders through sequences of notes which have no harmonic relation. Harkleroad even agrees with this, saying that Van Vliet could find no tonal center to anchor his singing. But this is not true of Van Vliet's music on *Trout Mask Replica* nor anywhere else. The music is jarring, tightly jammed, and certainly is not harmonic in the sense in which this word is usually used. But the tunes have tonal centers, chord progressions can be heard, and at times the compositions even modulate from one tonal center to another. Anyone trying to duplicate the chords played by the individual guitarists or the two playing in tandem had better have an extremely sharp ear, because these are not simple progressions of major and relative minor chords. But what can be identified without too much struggle are pedal notes, the most basic single notes which sketch the harmonic framework of the compositions, notes which can be played as an ostinato beneath the complexity of the music as a whole. We might play, most simply, the I and V: in the key of "C" this would be "C" and "G." The effect is something like that of the tambura which provides the drone notes behind Indian classical music, or the playing of the rhythm section in modal jazz. (Think of the 4-note bass part in the most well-known section of Coltrane's "A Love Supreme," and everything that transpires over it.)

Such a tonal center can be located (some to a less certain degree) beneath all the music on *Trout Mask*. "Pachuco Cadaver" and "Bill's Corpse," for example are both recognizably rooted on an "A." "Sweet Sweet Bulbs" suggests E-flat, and "Neon Meat Dream of a Octafish" suggests "E." "China Pig" is of course a blues, so it has a conventional key—G-sharp on the record, though the guitar sounds like it is tuned to an open G chord. "My Human Gets Me Blues" is more complex than any of these. This begins with alternating chords which are based on G and C, but it then modulates up a half step (where the lyrics are "Well, the way you been..."), and then thins out to a guitar riff much like one from "Moonlight On Vermont" and moves up again for a last section where French's drums dominate. "Dali's Car" is rooted on "C."

One thing this makes clear is that Van Vliet's decision not to play harmonica was a deliberate one, not one imposed by the structure of the music. Of those looked at above, "Pachuco Cadaver" and to a lesser degree "My Human Gets Me Blues" offer good possibilities for blues harmonica parts. But the exclusion of the harmonica helps prevent any easy vocal quality from entering the music, prevents any simple entrance into the compositions. Van Vliet's singing to music barely heard through the control booth window, and his insistence on avoiding slipping into any easy melody, have roots in the artists' unending search for ways to escape what he or she has already done. David Bowie, for instance, has recorded music where he deliberately sings in a different key from that of his accompanying musicians, and has had his band switch instruments to see what music unfamiliarity may produce. This tradition reaches back at least as far as the Symbolists and early Modernists of the late nineteenth century. Writers and musicians in particular, from Poe and Rimbaud up to William Burroughs with his cut-up writing techniques and any number of psychedelic-dropping rock and roll musicians, have searched for ways of preventing any fall into easy repetition. Unfamiliarity and dislocation, in this equation, create freshness. Van Vliet's decision to leave his harmonica at home was in this tradition. He wanted, it seems, to have to struggle with his part, to be forced (if only by his own choices) to keep away from habitual patterns, to stay as awake as he was forcing the band members to stay.

The band members, particularly the guitars, would have a great deal of work to do before there would be any danger of their sleepwalking through their parts. Ideas which might be easily played on a piano, can be virtually impossible to recreate on the guitar and bass. Gary Lucas, who played guitar with Van Vliet in the last incarnation of the Magic Band, has said that learning to play "Flavor Bud Living," a 56-second piece, involved three months of practice, with muscles pain shooting through his forearm, and the "virtual cauterization" of his fingertips to get the right fingerpicking attack. At times, the guitarists created new tunings for the guitar (a long and venerable tradition in blues guitar circles), or developed new techniques, some physically demanding. Harkleroad, for instance, had to develop a technique of moving his left hand around to the front of the guitar so as to use his thumb to help with the fretting. So far removed from standard guitar music were these compositions when they were composed, that we must take Van Vliet's frequent comment in 1969-1973 interviews that he taught the Magic Band to play from scratch as a metaphor rather than as a simple lie. The truth is that this music could never have been realized had the Magic Band members not been exceptionally gifted and dedicated (or, less charitably, subservient) musicians.

One notable characteristic of the guitar playing on the "most Beefheartesque" of Van Vliet's albums—*Trout Mask Replica; Lick My Decals Off, Baby; Doc at the Radar Station* and *Ice Cream for Crow*—is the uniformly aggressive attack given to all of the notes. Van Vliet demanded this steady hard tone from all the guitar players who played this music; he would tell them what kind of guitars and strings to use, what kind of picks, to insure that they sounded the way he wanted them to sound. The most important consequence of this aggressive attack is that it eliminates grace notes, passing tones, any trace of subordinate musical elements. The angularity and unusual phrasing of the compositions, the characteristics which give them their undeniable beauty, would, if Van Vliet had allowed any of his notes to be played softer than the rest, allow the listener to hear (or, more accurately, construct) simpler melodies amidst the hard-won complexities. If the notes were not all clearly given equal weight the unusual notes, the individual personality of the compositions, would appear to be awkward adornments. So the guitar players—as well as the drummer and the bass player—*had* to play *hard*.

(We can see a correlative insistence in Van Vliet's painting. There is a technique known as "haliation," which involves small, almost invisible points of primary complementary colors being placed around the contours of objects to make them appear as if they glow with an inner light. This puts a halo around the "important" elements in a painting. Van Vliet's technique is the opposite of haliation: he lavishes as much attention on the white spaces of his paintings as he does on the figures. There are no "grace images" in Van Vliet's art.)

As physically demanding as mastering the all-over attack undeniably was for the bands who played this music, the abruptly changing rhythms were just as difficult. A player barely had time to lock into a part, feel the rhythm of it before it would change. Rhythms might change as many as a dozen times or more in a single composition. Some shifts are relatively smooth, some jarring.

Van Vliet would respond to requests for him to characterize his music with such descriptions as "music without a lullaby," and "music to de-materialize the catatonia." But his most frequent comment was that he wanted to break music away from its attachment to the "Mama heartbeat." This comment has been repeated many times, yet it is often passed over too quickly. It is understood that this means Van Vliet dislikes a regular rhythm, considering it hypnotic, even narcotic. But the negative effects of such a rhythm may need spelling out. Why the words "Mama heartbeat" instead of something along the line of "narcotic" or "hypnotic?" Van Vliet's ability to keep all the butterfly-fixing pins out of his language makes it impossible to say for sure, but the word "Mama" implies a comfort and feeling of security the other words lack. What is wrong with a regular rhythm is that it is comfortable, and Van Vliet dislikes "comfortable" to the point of chastising band members he feels have gotten too comfortable with the music. Any time any of the bands began to relate to the music on any but a playful, physical or "feeling" level, including playing parts too well, with too much facility, Van Vliet would

72

do something to break up the automatism of the pattern which had developed. He might rewrite parts of the music, or (as he did to a later guitarist) make them listen over and over again to country blues; any strategy to keep the music fresh in the players' hands, to keep them from getting too comfortable. Comfort makes us stay happily at home, Mama's heartbeat makes children cuddle and snooze. Again, this shows how Van Vliet wants everyone to stay awake, wants everyone to explore their world and find ways of joining with it that are not to be found in any complacent state. The undancable rhythms and jumping bean riffs are a deliberate wake-up call.

This demand for unflagging musical attention certainly has an element (consciously or unconsciously) of personal identification to it: if the music was almost wholly written from his own internal rhythms any tendency to treat them thoughtlessly would have been like shrugging off Van Vliet himself, of declaring the rhythms inside him uninteresting. And no artist (nor anyone else taking the risk of expressing themselves fully) is going to expose himself to such a depth and then calmly let this exposure be absent-mindedly shrugged off. Van Vliet's ego is too large to allow this.

That this music was composed by his body not his intellect, and that he abhors the idea of anyone hearing (or playing) his music without really *listening* to it, without giving their attention to every note and word go a long way toward explaining Van Vliet's total rejection of the question of "influence" from this point on. The question has worried many who have attempted to write about Van Vliet's music from *Trout Mask* forward. (And those writing about his art, as well.) Van Vliet knows that "influences" are distractions, in more than one sense. They are, for musicians, mother-style comforts that allow less effort to be made in writing and playing music. To be influenced is to ride, at least in part, on the skull sleigh of another. But influence can be an even bigger distraction for the listener. In listening to the music on *Trout Mask* and other of the more difficult albums, a listener, no matter how enthusiastic, at some level tries to explain, at least to himself, what he is hearing. The more unusual or original a work of art—be it music, painting, dance—the harder it is to fit it into the aesthetic world each of us have assembled within ourselves. Appreciating works of art isn't a passive activity—it is an active hunting and gathering. We seek out the aesthetic experiences we enjoy, and work to make them a part of us. With works as original as the music of Captain Beefheart and the Magic Band, we lack the vocabulary (and not just the words; there is also a "vocabulary" of forms and concepts we understand and accept, think with just as we understand and speak with words) to enable ourselves to "understand" them. Influences, for the individual as well as for the critic, become an easy way of correlating the startlingly unfamiliar with forms we already understand to a comfortable degree. Such phrases as "looks like," "sounds like," "is reminiscent of" are all useful—almost unavoidable if we are trying to share our reactions to and thoughts about the music—but they are also, undeniably, defaults which tend to constrict the attention and openness of our listening.

The combination of the music of Captain Beefheart and the Magic Band on this album, and Van Vliet's stubborn insistence on keeping our attention focused on both what is in the tracks and the persona he created to be its creator, are meant to force us to stay awake. And reward us greatly for doing so.

Everything's Wrong at the Same Time It's Right

Painter Trevor Winkfield has pointed out that artists fall into two categories, those who recreate the world we all know, and those who create a world of their own. With *Trout Mask Replica* Van Vliet proved himself an artist of the second sort. Thirty years along, many of us still feel this album is a masterpiece; at the very least a monumental achievement. But like many another monument, its meaning has changed over time. The primary reason for this is that a new picture of Van Vliet as Captain Beefheart has begun to emerge, one which drastically alters the "how" of the album's creation at almost all levels.

Even as *Trout Mask Replica* was first making its way into the world, there were indications that Van Vliet was not an easy man to deal with. While the release of the album didn't make Captain Beefheart and the Magic Band household names, it did attract the attention of some of the best of the newly emerging serious rock critics. As did the man behind the trout mask. Van Vliet had by this time a clear sense of who he wanted his "Captain Beefheart" persona to be, of the image he wanted to project. This was in direct descent from the vacuum cleaner ringmaster he had been with Alex St. Clair's band.

Those who have been close to Van Vliet speak of how he can be a "normal" person, and then suddenly take on the Captain Beefheart style. In reading interviews Van Vliet gave, it is clear that he used this punning, digressive, outrageous persona—

which was certainly a part of him, not a total fabrication, despite the adoption of some mannerisms from identifiable sources—to keep interviewers at a distance. But he would stay "in character" even when it made things more difficult for the musicians. While trying to teach the bands exactly how he wanted his music played, for example, Van Vliet would only rarely resort to simple musical explanations. His instructions could be as elliptical as his lyrics: "play your drums like BBs rolling in a pan." The most likely explanation for Van Vliet having caused himself such self-difficulty is that it came about from a combination of superstition and integrity: the music had been composed out of inspirations and techniques which arose within the Captain Beefheart persona, and stepping out of it at any time in the process would have shown a lack of integrity, and put him at a remove from his inspiration. It began to be this persona who took on all comers.

Rock music criticism had only recently moved beyond the *Tiger Beat* level—"What's your favorite color?"—and these new writers, Langdon Winner, Lester Bangs, Jann Wenner among the best of them, found Van Vliet's music and persona ideally suited to the new critical tone. Winner's "The Odyssey of Captain Beefheart" was printed in *Rolling Stone* in May of 1970. Winner's article help disseminate—and shape—the legend of Van Vliet as unearthly genius. The article opens with Van Vliet knowing the phone will ring before it does (an ability others have attested to), and goes on to suggest that his genius has kept him from appearing in front of the public except for a very limited number of times—twenty-five times over six years. Winner goes on to relate how the first Magic Band wore all black leather and had hair to their waists in 1964, repeats the stories of his artistic youth and refusal to attend school, the tale of *Safe As Milk* being "too negative" for A&M, how Ry Cooder (here unnamed) quit and spoiled the band's chance to play the Monterey Pop Festival, and repeats Van Vliet's fanciful assertion that he composed *Trout Mask Replica* in a single eight-and-a-half-hour sitting.

Winner also tells the (true) story of how Van Vliet called in tree surgeons to check the eucalyptus trees on the grounds of the

Woodland Hills house to make sure the band's music hadn't hurt them in some way—and sent the bill to Straight Records. Another true story which Winner helped spread was how Van Vliet wanted 20 sets of sleigh bells for a session, when there were only enough musicians to play 14 sets—"We'll overdub them," Van Vliet said of the others. Overall, Winner's story paints a portrait of a fascinating and original genius, a man too full of mysteries to ever fathom, and too full of musical integrity to compromise. This article surely did much to spread the legend. But Winner's piece was not gush-journalism; he also attended to another side of his subject:

> Most of the Captain's relationships with those close to him [vacillate between two extremes:] Everybody's a despicable villain one day, a marvelous hero the next. . . . During the writing of this article, for example, Van Vliet became convinced that I was public enemy number one. For days he brooded about the crimes that I was supposedly committing against him.[2]

If Van Vliet's suspicions about Winner were unfounded, and his treatment of him, as the above quote suggests, a touch paranoid, his relationship with the musicians in the Magic Band went through even more violent attitude swings. At this late date there are still a number of former Magic Band members who don't care to go on record about their experiences. Some have lives so unrelated to this part of their past that they don't want to relive it, others are wary of the possibility of legal action if they tell their stories.

But Bill Harkleroad and John French have both come forth with details of life as a member of the classic Magic Band. Their accounts present the unsettling revelation that Van Vliet was—particularly during the intense nine months when *Trout Mask* was being written and rehearsed—a "Mansonesque" (Harkleroad's word) manipulator of the gifted young admirers who gathered together to make up the Magic Band. He was a totalitarian who was not above verbally, even physically attacking band members.

This is naturally a difficult picture for Van Vliet's fans to have to confront. The self-mythology of rock and roll has always declared it to be a vehicle for and a product of freedom. The freedom most thought they heard on the album when it was first released was not there. In interviews he gave at the time, Van Vliet made no secret of the fact that every line of the music was played note-for-note as he dictated, that he allowed no improvisation. Nor, as has been revealed only recently, was there much if any personal freedom for the musicians. The man who once declared, "I've always been disgusted with no choices. I want to breathe with all my holes open. Anything that closes off possibilities is dangerous,[3]" allowed his band almost no choices at all—musically or personally.

When Harkleroad joined the band in June of 1968, he already knew the other band members. But "the vibe was strange," Harkleroad noticed. "John and Jeff were not the same guys I used to know. They both had a seriously dire look in their eyes, yet on occasions would flip into an almost over-the-top excitement."[4] Harkleroad is open about the fact the he was using quantities of marijuana and LSD during the period immediately before joining the Magic Band, and during his first weeks with them. But while the other members of the band, Van Vliet included, had used drugs in the past, they were by this time collectively trying to move beyond drugs into "Maharishi 'OM' stuff" as Harkleroad puts it. And Harkleroad himself soon tapered off drugs as well. This was to be only the first of many, sometimes forced, modifications of his behavior.

Once work began on the *Trout Mask Replica* material the pressure on the band increased exponentially. Van Vliet would write the music, either on the piano, or by whistling or picking out sounds he liked on the other instruments, taping these parts while the others watched. He would speak in metaphors similar to his lyrics, and expect the band to follow these oblique instructions. The same kind of metaphors were used in attempts to try to coax players into producing parts Van Vliet could hear in his head but could find on no instrument. The band members were to learn their parts, as dictated by Van Vliet, and play them without deviation, in the manner of chamber music. John French was responsible for writing out the actual parts once they were decided on, and for teaching them to the players. Arrangements were worked out as much by what was possible as by what Van Vliet might suggest. After a while, in fact, he stopped telling French which instruments were to be assigned which parts, saying only, "You know what to do."[5] Van Vliet would only sporadically sing with the band. Instead, he spent his time sleeping or watching television.

The band practiced up to 16 hours a day. The music was incredibly demanding, in large part because *Trout Mask Replica* is music composed for a standard guitar-centered rock and roll band by someone who doesn't play guitar. In creating new music for their instrument, guitar players tend to let pieces emerge through "muscular composition," through letting the fingers find their way over the fretboard in new combinations of familiar physical moves and positions. Van Vliet created his music by reversing this: by turning to the physical unfamiliarity of playing the piano his fingers had no familiar patterns to fall into. The untutored patterns they found created music totally unrelated to guitar-playing technique. The piano was not Van Vliet's sole composition instrument—as in the past, he also might whistle one part, sing another, play another on the harmonica—but the most intensely "Beefheart-sounding" parts came from taped or transcribed piano parts. The guitarists then faced the formidable task of reproducing the raw unfamiliarity of these piano inventions on their very different instruments.

Van Vliet even insisted that they reproduce exactly the sometimes hesitant and awkward rhythms which resulted from his unfamiliarity with the piano. A transcription of "Peon" (from *Lick My decals Off, Baby*, the follow-up album) points out the difficulty of notating the simply human: Van Vliet's hands speeded up or slowed down as he played, and executed whatever rhythms struck him at the moment, a simple emotional effect which needs some exotic time notation to capture: a bar of 11/32 followed by one of 6/16. Learning such music was difficult for the band, because their body rhythms were of course different from Van Vliet's. For the music to succeed, their nervous systems had to, in effect, be colonized by Van Vliet's own.

One necessary step if this goal was to be achieved was the partial dismantling of his musicians' hard-won personal styles. Richard Snyder, guitarist/bassist in the 1980 - 82 Magic Band spelled it out quite clearly:

> Occasionally the musician part of my mind gets in the way and I won't be able to play exactly what Don's after, and when that happens I just have to drop my musician's armor and play it the way he asks. . . . [To] play Don's music, you have to drop your preconceived ideas about playing. You don't drop your *abilities* but you do drop your concepts.[6]

In listening to the music Van Vliet made over the course of his music career, it is clear that the music succeeded in "sounding like Captain Beefheart" on a sliding scale directly related to how successful Van Vliet was in taking over the hands and minds of the players. Musicians in the Magic Band, particularly those in the 1968-69 incarnation, were pushed beyond the usual composer to musicians relationship toward the ideal of becoming unthinking prostheses—extensions of Van Vliet's body, attenuations meant to help him overcome the limitations of being one man, with only so many limbs, sinews and synapses.

It is certainly no surprise that, practicing this difficult music every waking moment, having his nervous system colonized by the body rhythms of Van Vliet, Harkleroad soon began to see himself as a "slavedog," and Van Vliet as the band's domineering "overseer."[7]

As difficult as the effort to arrange and learn the music might have been, life could be even harder for the band when they weren't practicing. In addition to learning the music, the musicians were meant, even forced, to leave their own identities behind and to become extensions and reinforcements of the Captain Beefheart image. They were given stage names, told what clothes to wear on stage, even how to hold a cigarette. They were to become, as thoroughly as possible, the Captain Beefheart Players, in the theatrical sense of the word. And because Van Vliet was more and more "in character" as time passed, the band was subject to more and more pressure to conform to his vision of their behavior. To this end, he would exert either psychological or physical pressure, or both. Harkleroad doesn't feel that Van Vliet was trying to brainwash them in the "military" sense of the word, but that he was certainly aware that he was pushing the band to extremes, psychologically. He would keep the band up and talk to them for twenty hours straight, then tell them he had done all this arguing *for them* despite the exhaustion it had produced in him.

At the same time Van Vliet sought to take over and colonize the nervous systems of his musicians, he was, in a real way, being taken over and colonized by his own music and persona. As reported by one interviewer after another, and by fans fortunate enough to encounter him on a one-to-one basis, Van Vliet can in unguarded moments be a friendly and attentive conversationalist, one who takes pains to make the other feel comfortable, to coax them through awkward moments, and who makes every attempt to make contact on a very human level. Which is not to say that he has shown himself willing to reveal deeper aspects of himself; but most other subjects, especially (as with all of us) those things he finds of interest—art, animals, cigars, what have you—might bring out the almost unguarded Van Vliet. On a recording of a radio interview done in the early 1970s Van Vliet even answers the phones and takes telephone requests as the "interviewer" continues vaguely trying and failing to find his ass with both hands. And according to one account, Van Vliet once was restricted from using directory assistance because he would engage the operators in 45 minute conversations.[8]

And yet Van Vliet has more often used the ramparts of his Captain Beefheart persona to keep those closest or most able to help him—members of his band, sympathetic critics—uneasily off-balance. Van Vliet's friend, critic Lester Bangs tackled this seeming contradiction, without success, in an interview Even in this short excerpt, Van Vliet can be seen trying to ward off Bangs's attempts at making contact as friends and equals:

> *Why do you almost always talk elliptically?*
> Due to the fact that probably it's very difficult for me to explain myself except in music or paint. . . .
> *Well, don't you think you're missing something you might get from other people by being that way?*
> Sure, but they won't accept me anyway. I'm comfortable talking to you. Not many people seem to have things in common with me. I guess what really intrigues me the most is something like seeing somebody wash my windows—that's like a symphony.
> *But if you and I are friends, and you trust me, we should be able to have a reciprocal conversation.*
> We're talking without talking. . . . We're saying things that can't be put into the tongue. It's like good music.[9]

But Bangs clearly found these limited interchanges irritatingly unmusical.

It seems clear that Van Vliet chooses when to be "on" and when to relax based on how challenging his environment or company was at a given time, whether or not he feels challenged in some way. A spacey interviewer, or telephone operator would offer no challenge to his artistic superiority. But, while Bangs might have seen himself as a "friend," Van Vliet would never have forgotten that Bangs was a critic, someone who would pry into his personal thoughts if he could, and someone who not only could have an effect on his career but also as a writer was a rival artist. So he stayed "on" almost full time with Bangs. And did the same with the members of the Magic Band. While they had come to him as enthusiastic fans, they were excellent musicians in their own right, with no shortage of ideas of their own, and no challenge from that quarter could be allowed.

So Van Vliet stayed in character, and stayed in control: harangued, bullied, verbally mesmerized and amused them, made demands to the point of psychologically damaging them. Van Vliet would at times single out a member of the band, saying this person "had a thing," had done something that threatened or betrayed the goal they were all supposedly striving toward. He would also speculate about the band members' relationships to their mothers. Band members weren't allowed to leave the house without Van Vliet giving the OK; once a week one member was permitted out to go get provisions, what little they were able to secure. At times all the band had to eat for a day was a single cup of soy beans each. Some resorted to stealing food. The band was broke and lived off various kinds of assistance, governmental and parental. Van Vliet's mother and grandmother, as well as Harkleroad's mother, sent money for the rent.

On the positive side, Van Vliet would also at times expound at length on his ideas and concepts, something the band enjoyed, and from which he got reinforcement for those ideas. And he talked about other artists, at least in the early days. Innovative jazz musicians and singular musicians such as Harry Partch were for a time offered up as models, only to be dismissed later in favor of a narrow concentration on the superiority of what the group was creating. He also spoke at length about painters, including Warhol, Rauschenberg, De Kooning and Klein. (Band members' accounts are the sole source for stories of Van Vliet visiting museums in this period.) He clearly went into his ideas about other artists to a much greater extent to the band members than he ever did to interviewers, again probably to avoid any distracting publicity about "influence."

When talking, either negatively or in a way meant to fire up the band with the glory of what they were creating, failed to achieve the desired effect, Van Vliet could turn physical. The usual pattern was that Van Vliet would single out a culprit and attack him. Other times he would get the band members to attack one another. After Jeff Cotton was beaten badly enough by another band member that he had broken ribs, he left the band.[10] Harkleroad himself was once crammed into a garbage can by Van Vliet, a much less drastic action than he had earlier been threatened with. The result, predictably, was that the young guitarist went from feeling like a "slavedog" to feeling like he was "only worth trash."[11]

At different times, Cotton, Boston and French all tried to escape, hiding their clothes and sneaking out, or simply crashing through the door and running down the street with others running behind them.[12] Like Cotton, French was only able to detach himself from the group after an act of violence: Van Vliet threw him down a half flight of stairs.[13] A phony Drumbo was installed, but didn't last long.

Some outsiders knew about what was happening in the band's Woodland Hills house, but no word appeared in print until years later, and then only obliquely. In 1989's *The Real Frank Zappa Book,* for example, Zappa says of the band, "we could use the word **cult** here."[14] Zappa doesn't mention anything of violence (it is impossible to be sure that he knew about it, but it seems likely that he did), but the word "cult" inevitably calls up the mass organizations of Rev. Moon and Jim Jones, mass weddings or suicides, armed camps, and tales of forced de-programming. To compare the experience of Van Vliet and the Magic Band to cults of this kind would be ludicrous, but there was, at least on Van Vliet's part, both a cultural siege mentality and an urge toward total control. The necessary dynamics of a rock and roll group, be it the Magic Band or any other, cloud the question of how "cult-like" the Woodland Hills period should be viewed, just as the personality and needs of an artist have enough in common with those of a full-fledged cult leader to make impossible any simple characterization of Van Vliet's role. (Van Vliet, for his part, has responded to accusations of opportunism and intimidation by insisting that the only way he has ever used people is the same way he uses paint, a comment which is not a denial.[15]) Cults and charismatic leaders have become so common in America that a number of studies have now been done of their inner workings. Looking at where actual cults and the experience

84

of the *Trout Mask Replica* Magic Band overlap and where they diverge may illuminate some of the murky corners of that experience, and, less reliably, of the men who shared it.

Psychotherapist Gerald Alper, in his book *The Puppeteers*, lists a number of elements characteristic of cults. These include: Those who join cults are most often young adults or older adolescents struggling with their insecurities; cults favor the isolation of their members, often with a denouncement of the outside world; grandiose claims are made on behalf of the cult and its leader. A "psychic numbing" occurs, which detaches the members from the outside world and leads them into a more closed symbiotic relationship within the cult circle. Threats are made against those who would step out of line or try to leave. The leader of the cult creates a mystique which says to his insecure followers, "Share my madness or I will abandon you." There is often a turning to reckless behavior or drugs—anything which helps cover the fact of an inner deadness caused by the member's detachment from the world and his or her former self. There is a combination of us-against-them and exaggerated flattery of followers, who are told that they are idealists, living by great principles and turning their backs on conventionality and economic security.

Several of the items here—the age of those most susceptible; a bonding together and disdain for the conventional world; reckless behavior and/or drug use; and, often enough, grandiose claims and self-images, often centered in one or two "leaders"— are not just common to, but almost *essential* to, the formation and success of a rock and roll band. Other characteristics above— that of a "psychic numbing," and threats made against those who want to leave the group—may occur in some musical groups. Yet to read that Van Vliet would at times single out a member of the band and, by cajoling, or sleep deprivation, or violence, compel him to conform to the line of thought Van Vliet wanted certainly supports the view that something beyond normal band dynamics was at work within the Magic Band.

Grandiose claims made within a cult—or a rock and roll band—function as a defense against the centrifugal forces which would destroy the group. Alper points out that this group aura of greatness is often tied "to the symbolic but deeply personal expression of a single extraordinary individual."[16]

> This individual will likely treat the members of his group as an audience; he will be obsessed with being not simply a self but a "personality," to be not larger than life but larger than himself. . . . [We may] fear that to suppress the charismatic persona would . . . unleash a predictably violent counterreaction. . . .[17]

This might have come from an article about Jim Morrison, Jimi Hendrix, Kurt Cobain, Prince, Elvis . . . the list goes on. And the list would certainly include Van Vliet.

But the most interesting passage in Alper's description has to do with the feeling such a personality conveys of being "primitive," meaning more in touch with some unconscious personality.

> [Even] if he is acknowledged to be brilliant, the cognitive process is perceived as having a correspondingly weaker hold on the more dominant unconscious personality, and to be mainly in the service of channeling an insatiable surge of psychic energy.[18]

This is indeed very close to many people's first hand experience of Van Vliet. On the other hand, there is not enough evidence to support any suggestion that he shares the damaged psyche of the classic cult leader Alper describes. Such a leader is pushed by childhood deprivations, and while Van Vliet has often complained about his parents ruining his art scholarship chances, he has also said he had to purge himself of all the attention his parents gave him as a child: "I wasn't neglected enough," he has said. A classic cult leader denies the existence of a personal unconscious, while the opposite seems to be true of Van Vliet, with his statements about turning himself "inside out." A cult leader will feel that his or her genius has little to do with intellect but with a mystical power to bring forth a dormant historical trend. Van Vliet has never claimed to do this. (I recognize this even as I will point out below how his approach to making music might best be understood in the light of a theory of mind which was emerging even as Captain Beefheart was emerging from Don Van Vliet.) A cult leader will often see him or herself as an incarnate symbol of something, and as a messenger of cultural salvation. By all accounts, Van Vliet fits these last no better than you or I on a day when we are feeling particularly full of ourselves.

Still, there is no doubt that at least some members of the Magic Band feel their experience in the Woodland Hills house was much the same as that of being in a cult. During this period, at least two of the group fit the classic profile of a cult follower even closer than Van Vliet fits that of a cult leader. Years after this period, John French wrote a letter to his local paper. Included were comments about having worked with a man who filled him with self-doubt for personal gain, who had criticized his every motivation and crushed his dreams. For a time, French wrote, he could not escape this man, but when he did he found he had lost much of himself. And because of the physical violence this man had done to him, for a long time after he would duck when people talked with their hands.[19]

Whether French was here referring to Van Vliet or to another authority figure in his life matters less than his characterization of the insecurities of his younger self. Twenty-five years later French would say that he stayed with the band because he had "gotten twisted enough where I felt more at home [in the house] than I did in the world—about 51 percent more. Just enough."[20] And Harkleroad has characterized French as being the one who was most resistant to Van Vliet's machinations, in part because of his Christian beliefs.

Harkleroad has characterized his younger self (he was nineteen when *Trout Mask Replica* was being rehearsed) as being "too insecure to be real free . . . being a tall skinny kid, I was trying to hide." As a nineteen-year-old in the age of the

Vietnam War and the draft that served as its cattle drive, Harkleroad was letting himself drift. Speaking of the photos on the album he has said, "I'm nineteen years old, coming down from taking acid two or three times a week—like *I gave a shit* .... Black fingernail polish? That's cool. Lipstick? That's cool, too. I'm breaking it all away at that point. Nineteen years old—who had brains at nineteen?"[21] "The Sixties" had many such drifters, moving toward they knew not what. And many of them attached themselves to charismatic figures who could offer a direction they could follow. In his memoir he returns several times to the fact that before he joined the Magic Band Van Vliet was his hero, and later felt sure that Van Vliet was taking him toward many of the things he wanted from life at that time—money, fame, integrity—and so he was willing to submit to the circumstances. This mindset, "Any direction is better than none," is guaranteed to produce a great number of victims.

If it is unclear how close the experience of being in the Magic Band was to being in a true cult, it clearly was not that elusive ideal of so many 1960s crowded houses, a commune. The ideal of the communal experience is that everyone, while treating one another as equals, joins in a single experience. (Van Vliet has never expressed any enthusiasm for this kind of communal experience, not with other humans—communion with other species, however, does seem to interest him.) Where other bands might have tried to live a communal ideal, what Van Vliet sought to create was something quite different.

Van Vliet sought to establish might most accurately be viewed as an ecological system (in a larger, rather than simple "save-the-earth" sense), based on his own ideas and, in the form of his music, his most basic personal rhythms. Everyone involved would not be equal: Van Vliet's sensibility and personal rhythms would be at the center of everything which was created. His personal experiences to this point—the initial rejection of the first album, several of its songs being altered by another writer, its musical innovations resisted by some of the musicians, Krasnow's manipulations of contracts and music, and the resulting collapse of his musical career plans—all would have suggested to Van Vliet that the forced march of his musicians was the only way in which the music and experience of "Captain Beefheart" could come into being. However low it ranks on the scale of "man's humanity to his fellow man," Van Vliet's bullying of the Magic Band was likely done out of what he felt was personal and artistic necessity.

Thus he created an ecological system based on, and meant to nurture, the music of his physiology and the visual and verbal elements which supported it: Van Vliet as Gaia in microcosm. "Gaia" is the name given to the idea that the earth's biosphere, its air, water and living organisms, is self-correcting; that the biosphere will alter itself for self-preservation—a preservation the conditions of which would not necessarily favor the survival of humans if they should come into conflict with the survival of the planet itself. (For trivia fans: the man who originated this theory, James Lovelock, had it come to him in building on the grounds of NASA's Jet Propulsion Laboratory just outside Pasadena in the Fall of 1965. If it was a clear day, Lovelock could have seen all the way to Glendale. And as Lovelock stood there, "Diddy Wah Diddy" had only recently been released and could, in fact, have been in the radio waves that were passing through the building at that very moment.) Like the earth considered in its self-defensive Gaia persona, Van Vliet's artistic/dictatorial ecological system made few if any allowances for human limitations, needs, self-expression or personal happiness.

The "Gaia" metaphor, the timing of its emergence, is useful in making another point. As singular as the music produced by Captain Beefheart and the Magic Bands undeniably is, he and they were still very much of their time and place. Van Vliet came to artistic maturity in a historical moment that put forward new ideas in both social philosophy and the science of mind, many of which (while not consciously appropriated) can be seen reflected in the creation of *Trout Mask Replica* and its immediate successor. Van Vliet's approach and the ways in which he acted out these ideas show both the great human potential which might be tapped through "ecological consciousness" and the new conception of mind, as well as some of its overlooked, darker aspects.

Gregory Bateson (quoted above on the "segmental") was one of those formulating this new view of mind. In Bateson's view "mind" includes not just the brain but everything in its environment which affects it. The mind, therefore, is that which is doing the thinking, and that which is being thought, as well as that which is being seen and being felt through any of the senses. Bateson used the example of a blind man's cane, asserting that the hand holding the cane, the cane itself and all it touches, being integral to the decisions the blind man makes, should all be recognized as being part of the blind man's mind. In this view, Van Vliet's hands, his piano, the musicians in the Magic Band, even their instruments, were all part of his "mind" rather than discrete, autonomous entities.

This complex new conception has been extended into new ways of thinking about the organization of human biology—including a new way of looking at the human hand. When neurologist Frank R. Wilson asks, "Should the parts of the brain that regulate hand function be considered part of the hand? The perspective of *physiological* or *functional* anatomy suggests that the answer is yes."[22] Wilson writes that the ups and downs of his learning the piano convinced him that:

> Inside me, it seems, there was *already* a plan for being a musician . . . the protocols of music had simply set the specific cognitive, motor, emotional, and social terms according to which hand and finger movements that were initially unsure and clumsy would gradually become more accurate and fluent.[23]

But what if someone with a plan for music inside him approached the piano but refused to bow to any of the social terms to which music and composition are usually subject, while unavoidably still being subject to motor limits? Van Vliet presented one answer to this question by way of his use of the piano in the creation of his music.

Members of the Magic Bands agree with Van Vliet's own characterization of his approach to music as being that of a sculptor. What neither Van Vliet, the band, nor any critics have pointed out is that this is evidence of another kind of "brain-washing"—one Van Vliet himself underwent from his earliest years, one lacking the overt violence he visited on others, but no less thorough. That Van Vliet began sculpting at an early age would have permanently, and deeply, affected his way of interacting with the world. Again according to Wilson, the way the hand begins to engage the world is tightly bound with the way language develops and with all of the body's basic rhythms:

> The brain . . . defines its own procedures for regulating the flow of information generated by all the interactions that are taking place, and it models its processes and its formulations of the world on the narrative principle. It even, I suspect, creates an internal perceptual biological clock scaled to and calibrated by observable changes in the extra-personal world—which means the brain acquires, and tunes itself to, the rhythms that the legs, shoulders, arms, hands, chest, tongue, and lips invent in their responses to the world.[24]

Which helps explain why Van Vliet looks at everything as a sculptor might: he was self-programmed to do so by his precocious artistic efforts. And Van Vliet was programmed in other, less-physical ways by his life-long interest in animals and nature. What may not be readily apparent is that Van Vliet's ecology-mindedness is a part of what allowed him to drive his musicians as relentlessly as he did, and how his actions highlight some of the overlooked contradictions inherent in such an orientation.

Some of the ideas involved in the above had been around for a century. They first emerged in the U.S. one hundred years before Van Vliet's birth, most notably in the Concord circle centered around Ralph Waldo Emerson. Van Vliet, the life-long non-reader, likely knows little of Emerson's writings, but he is a born Emersonian none the less. Emerson too, for example, was a believer in avoiding the deadening effects of comfort: "People long to be settled, but it is only as they are unsettled that there is hope for them."Emerson also faulted history for concerning itself with only one race, one species, even for restricting itself to living matter:

> I hold our actual knowledge very cheap. Hear the rats
> in the wall, see the lizard on the fence, the fungus
> under foot, and lichen on the log. What do I know,
> sympathetically, morally, of these worlds of life? . . .
> What connection do the books show between the fifty
> or sixty chemical elements, and the historical eras?[25]

Emerson's attitude (he inspired and supported Thoreau) set the first American foundation for the ideas which were to become ecological consciousness—more specifically, "Deep Ecology." Standard or "shallow" ecological thinking remains anthropocentric; man is still at the center, and shares with the non-ecologically concerned the view that nature should be seen as being of "use" in various ways, even if these ways are very idealistic. "Deep Ecology," on the other hand, does not put humans on a separate, superior level. The entirety of the environment, including humankind, is seen as one network or web, interdependent, with man no more important than any other element.

One difference between Emerson's conception (and, as I say, Van Vliet's) and that of the modern Deep Ecologists is that modern thinkers tend to romanticize this idea, to see it as "spiritual or religious . . . in which the individual feels a sense of belonging, of connectedness, to the cosmos as a whole. . . ."[26] Emerson saw it differently:

> If there were good men, there would never be this
> rapture in nature. . . . [Our] hunting of the picturesque
> is inseparable from our protest against false society.[27]

By "society" Emerson primarily means individuals he encounters. This complex view—at once democratic, levelling, disappointed, idealistic, stubbornly misanthropic —is one

Emerson shares with Van Vliet. Van Vliet has made it clear on many occasions that he has more admiration for a honking goose than for any but the most exceptional people. Van Vliet is profoundly disappointed in his fellow man, and so can only be pleased with himself when he is least tied to their society. This view leads to identification with animals (or is it the other way around? In the end the direction of the arrow makes no real difference), to his pre-1984 art which shows human and animal figures merging, and contributes to his willingness to use other people as extensions of himself. He wishes to be no part of any "them," and only cautiously part of an "us" beyond his relationship with his wife. The simplest way to achieve this is to see people only as tools or as hindrances, and their separate existence as irrelevant.

Van Vliet's example highlights an overlooked short-coming of Deep Ecology-style philosophies. These include no suggestions for ways in which extraordinary individual goals, particularly those which need other hands to help realize them, might be achieved within such a system. Fritjof Capra, in his book *The Web of Life*, supplies a table of thoughts and values grouped as Self-Assertive (bad) or Integrative (good). This includes

Self-Assertive	*Integrative*
rational	intuitive
analysis	synthesis
linear	nonlinear
expansion	conservation
domination	partnership[28]

Van Vliet's character includes elements from both sides.

Clearly, the ecological approach, in systems such as Capra's, presumes a community of like-minded individuals *willing and able* to cooperate with one another. What does such a community do with the genius, with the wholly unexpected individual, with the original and individual artist? Such a person must work according to the dictates of his or her art, by self-created rules— or produce no real art at all. And an artist will make sacrifices to achieve artistic ends; everyone accepts this. But, in ecological thought, if everyone else is part of the greater "self" or "mind," then goals (including any artistic ones) will justify the sacrifice of the autonomy of another—who is, after all, one with the artist. If a band member fails to execute or agree with one of Van Vliet's musical dictates, Van Vliet would have felt justified in driving the musician as relentlessly as he would a hand which failed to manipulate the brush as he wished, or, as he himself remarked, as he would paint itself. For a painter or a sculptor, the resistance of the chosen material is something to be dealt with and overcome. It is that simple, that necessary, and that harsh; as harsh as Van Vliet's treatment of his musicians.

Whether or not a listener chooses, with me, to see in the experience of the creation of *Trout Mask Replica* larger historical concerns, the knowledge of the reality behind the creation of the music compels us to face some difficult questions. Can we separate our enthusiasm, even awe, for the best of Captain Beefheart and the Magic Band from the unsettling reality behind it? If we had the keys to the Way Back Machine would we return to 1968 and, knowing what was to befall them, turn French, Cotton, Boston and Harkleroad away at the base of the drive to the Woodland Hills house, allow them to get on with their lives, make their own music? Unmake *Trout Mask Replica?*

If the most dedicated fans among us are honest with ourselves. many of us might well choose to have the music, and allow the psychological damage to be inflicted upon these men. (Many of us would even choose to take their place, and endure what they endured for the sake of being part of the moment of *Trout Mask.*) And if so, what right have we to disparage Van Vliet? At some level we fans must finally share in any charges of selfishness and lack of fellow-feeling we choose to level against him.

Out of the House
and On the Road

The moment of *Trout Mask Replica* couldn't last. Van Vliet's artistic curiosity and restless ambition (as well as simple economic necessity) would not allow it. But, more importantly, the shanghaiing of the Magic Band's hearts, minds and bodies, their part-volitional, part-forced detachment from the outside world could not be maintained indefinitely. Captain Beefheart and the Magic Band were not, finally, a closed system. Van Vliet had long been critical of people who, as he phrased it, "breathe in and don't breathe out"; takers who give back little to the people around them, or to their world. Without true interaction—without "breathing out" after "breathing in"—even an artist remains an isolated individual, unable to grow. Van Vliet's ideal was to operate on the "breathe in *and* out" principle. (The answer to how he rationalized his treatment of his musicians as means rather than men may well be found here; it may lie in his feeling it was justified by the importance of accomplishing the end of "breathing out" the music.) In releasing the music into the world Van Vliet let in some much needed fresh air.

The moment had to pass for other reasons, as well. Because the individual band members grew personally, or because they had been hurt in one way or another by the experience, none of them were the same man they had been when the cloistering began. While the Magic Band was in a very real sense an expanded and multi-textured replicator of Van Vliet's body lingo, it was also very similar to one of the album's polyrhythmic compositions. Like the separate phrases and melodies of *Trout Mask's* music, each with its own internal logic and harmonies, phrases which lined for a unison "one" only at long intervals, each of the musicians had come to the band with his own needs and ambitions, history and tastes, which were combined to create the enormously powerful but unstable "one" that was the moment of the album. This was the enforced, months-long "one" of the greater composition known as Captain Beefheart and the Magic Band. But, just as in the music, the players soon began moving out of sync again, their composite music harder to keep together. Van Vliet, too, changed: he married. He and his new wife, Jan, would have wanted more privacy than had been available when the band all lived together.

John French left—or, more accurately, escaped—the Magic Band just as *Trout Mask* was being finished. (He fled to Wyoming and worked on a cattle ranch.) He can be seen peering out from under the bridge in the photo on the back of the album, but his name was left off the credits, so great was Van Vliet's displeasure. Jeff Cotton had moved out after the beating which broke his ribs and would not play with Van Vliet again. Harkleroad and Boston were now living apart from Van Vliet as well, though not in as estranged a circumstance. Harkleroad soldiered on in part by retaining his detachment, by being not quite in the world. In *Lunar Notes*, he repeatedly writes of not knowing about events in the outside world, or even in the world of music. Playing with Van Vliet wasn't for Harkleroad anything to think about as separate from his existence—it *was* his existence. He and Boston were given the task of fulfilling Van Vliet's wishes, which could mean anything from being awakened in the middle of the night to learn a new guitar line, to being sent out for art supplies. Boston has for some years now insisted on flying below the Beefheart fans' radar (as has Cotton), so it is more difficult to say what his attitude was in his six years with the Magic Band.[1] His marginal appearances in the interviews of the time suggest that he chose to play the role of loyal sidekick or majordomo to Van Vliet, helping jolly interviewers along, remembering facts,

96

cheerleading when Van Vliet was in a modest mood. It would be 1974 before Harkleroad and Boston would finally leave Van Vliet's side.

After the departures of French and Cotton, Van Vliet moved to replace the missing limbs of his musical body. Art Tripp III, a classically trained percussionist and sometime Zappa band member, auditioned to replace French. Van Vliet sought to counter Tripp's academic training by way of an erector set. He bolted a few of the girders together, to make a small square-cornered construction and handed it to Tripp and asked him to squeeze it. "How does it feel?" Van Vliet asked. Tripp apparently got the message: he became Ed Marimba, the Magic Band's new drummer and marimba player. A second guitar player was harder to come by. Pianist/saxophonist Ian Underwood tried to learn the parts, but he soon came down with migraine headaches and had to stop. (Ex-Mother Elliot Ingber would soon join as second guitarist, but too late to play on the album.)

But the unique balance of talents and personalities which had allowed Van Vliet to create unprecedented music, the combined brilliance and weakness which had created the moment of *Trout Mask* could not be replicated by plugging in other players. If the sculptural shapes of the rhythms and melodies came from Van Vliet's body, the larger body of the *Trout Mask* band was the material which gave them convincing form. When it came time to record the next album Tripp had trouble learning to play the drum parts for the music, most of which were developed by French during the *Trout Mask* cloistering. To come completely to life, the music *needed* the touch and sound of "Drumbo." So, for a time it was as if the needs of the music forced themselves onto the musicians; almost as if the music itself refused to let the moment dissipate.

So Harkleroad and Boston drove to Lancaster in search of John French. They found him sleeping, woke him, and when they returned to Los Angeles, French was with them. In the end, despite his desire to escape the band and its situation, French played all but one of the drum tracks ("Japan in a Dishpan" being the exception) for the album, with Tripp adding percussion and tandem drumming with French on some compositions. French was to leave, return, tour, leave . . . repeat this pattern at intervals for the next dozen years. No replacement for Cotton had yet been found, so Harkleroad overdubbed all the guitar parts. Tripp's marimba also did duty as a second-line instrument, its timbre fitting beautifully with Harkleroad's guitar. Because the album was planned before French was coaxed back, Harkleroad also did arranger's duties for the album. The music here has much more of a normal guitar shape to its parts as a result. But the album is clearly an extension of *Trout Mask Replica's* ideas and techniques

Even here, a year after the release of *Trout Mask*, the question for fans was already a topographical one: if that album was seen as Captain Beefheart and the Magic Band's Mount Everest, then everything else would be a lesser peak or a foothill. The music on *Decals* is very similar to that on *Trout Mask Replica*, but the sound of the record is much smoother; there are fewer songs, and the lyrics are for the most part more sparse than the year before; the instrumentals are much more consonant here than on the earlier album. And nothing could replicate the shock of hearing a totally new music for the first time. For a combination of reasons, then, *Lick My Decals Off, Baby* was heard as a more listener-friendly take on *Trout Mask*-style music.

The title track begins with romping percussion and a warm sounding slide guitar. Harkleroad throughout the album plays with a less aggressive tone than the razor-like one employed on the previous album, his sound evoking the texture of the strings' windings rather than their solid steel core. The music enters at a very fast clip then breaks for a slower, tail-dragger rhythm when the singing begins, an effect which is repeated for each verse. (Van Vliet will use this same technique for a later song, "Dirty Blue Gene," written circa 1972 but not released until 1980.) The lyrics inform the singer's lover that rather than hold her hand he wants to lick her everywhere it's pink. The music seems to produce a red light, lit by the tango master in Van Vliet's heart: notes in the accompaniment quickly cluster and move toward resolution, only to hesitate . . . then slide down, like the body of a man in love, loose with delight, dancing to a romantic ballad. Sex and romance are both here, united as they ideally should be, one in the lyrics and the other in the thick-fingered squeezes of the music. This is rapturous music for a pair of dancing bears, musky and romantic.

Much of the music to "Doctor Dark" is onomatopoeia of the Doctor's horse's hooves "makin' sparks." Tripp and French both play trap sets here, and the doubled drum sound and constantly shifting cross-rhythms are thicker than any of the percussion on earlier Beefheart albums. Who Doctor Dark may be is unclear, as is the identity of the "black leather lady" mentioned in the lyric. But the sound of the track, even when it shifts to a passage like boxes falling down wooden stairs, is among the tightest and most united on the album. Harkleroad's antiphonal guitar has such a ringing blues tone as it responds to the lyrics that it can be mistaken for a harmonica. There is some feel of an urgent bugle call to it as well. When the accompaniment changes to a rocking-horse rhythm, the guitar sound is even thicker. Harkleroad considers this track to have been influenced harmonically by Coltrane's work. The lyrics, while no more linear than usual for this period, still manage to convey a strong feeling of sentimentality.

The music for "I Love You, You Big Dummy" was constructed from a number of Van Vliet's piano fragments. This song shows both the new strengths and surprising weaknesses of the material here. The cantering rhythm is compelling, and this is the only track to include Van Vliet's harmonica playing. (On chromatic harmonica, a larger instrument which makes the player feel like he is running his mouth along the top of a car radiator.) The scat singing is inventive, but the lyrics to the song are so slight as to be a one-joke routine. Other songs share this lyric shortfall. "Woe-is-uh-Me-Bop," for example, offers nothing more than the title, sung in a variety of emphases. The track is successful nonetheless. Tripp's dark-carny marimba and French's drums carry much more of the weight than does Harkleroad's guitar, offering a series of textures for the ear. Van Vliet's voice does the same.

"Peon" is a guitar and bass duet. Here, more clearly than anywhere else on record, it is possible to feel how the notes came from Van Vliet's body rhythms. The first lick in the piece (which recurs with variations throughout the pieces) is a quick snap from the guitar's topmost "g" down almost a full octave to the "a" below, and its quirkiness produces an oddly friendly feel. The repeated chords that follow have a harmonic simplicity that allows the warmth created by the clear humanity of the irregular rhythm patterns to shine through. This piece has such a potential for interpretation that, despite the rancor the Magic Band members would feel upon the split from Beefheart in 1974, Harkleroad would record a lush reworking of this on an album by the Magic Band spin-off group Mallard.

"Bellerin' Plain" is an underappreciated masterpiece, a train song for our less easy-riding society. "The kettle leaped fire 'round the belly-o" and other lines here are among Beefheart's best lyrics. The guitar/marimba passages with Harkleroad and Tripp (who coaxes such a lovely timbre from his instrument that you can almost smell the rosewood), are Beefheart at his compositional best, Harkleroad's arranging ear at its sharpest.

"Japan In a Dishpan" is an instrumental, with Van Vliet blowing free-form reeds over a complex overlaying of several, individually mostly melodic, guitar and bass lines. Of the horns on "Japan In a Dishpan" and "Flash Gordon's Ape," Jeff Morris Tepper (guitarist with the Magic Band from 1975 to its 1982 dissolution) speculates,

> That's [Van Vliet's] ego. He wrote this music and then he hears the band do the track and he doesn't feel he's part of it. I think he covered up a lot of great music, but at the same time, watching him take out his big fire hose and spray was real boss![2]

For the musicians to work so hard to perfect their difficult parts and then have them almost buried beneath Van Vliet's wriggling-finger saxophone must have been a trying experience.

"I Wanna Find a Woman That'll Hold My Big Toe Till I Have To Go," has one of the least integrated accompaniments of the songs on the album. Boston's tone here is rubbery. The doubling of voice with guitar brings the melody briefly to the fore, and Van Vliet's voice is set trekking across a rubboard of bass and marimba. "Petrified Forest" steams and clatters, guitar and marimba and bass all distinct, joining together for the last tag of the title.

"One Red Rose That I Mean" is another instrumental, this time a solo arrangement played by Harkleroad. The architectonics of the piece are fascinating, with notes played as if they were slurs on a brass instrument, single lines giving way to bracing dark chords even while the modal feel remains. Hearing Harkleroad play this piece in concert inspired 1980s Magic Band member Gary Lucas to want to play with Van Vliet.

"The Buggy Boogie Woogie," an over-population warning song, features a single eccentrically syncopated guitar part, with Tripp and French playing brooms as percussion instruments. Van Vliet's vocal is fierce and insistent most of the way, but also drops down for gentler notes, vocal winks to invite the listener in. "The Smithsonian Institute Blues (or the Big Dig)" is more conventionally syncopated, with the instruments running alongside one another, not like horses in harness, but like wobbly-kneed colts running over rocky ground. The lyrics warn us that we are becoming the new dinosaurs because we are walking in the old dinosaur's shoes—headed for extinction.

"Space Age Couple" has some fierce guitar chording and clattering, propulsive drumming. The lyrics—"Space age couple, why don't you flex your magic muscle?"—suggest that love-making may be the best answer to the question of how to make our way through the craziness of the modern world. (At a later date Van Vliet would suggest that by "magic muscle" he also meant the imagination.) "The Clouds Are Full of Wine (Not Whiskey or Rye)" features an insistent 3/4 base rhythm, with Harkleroad and Tripp playing 4/4 over the top. The result is a wobbly pogo-stick feel—which may be the best overall characterization of the music on the album as a whole. Van Vliet was trying to ride the same path he had ridden on *Trout Mask Replica,* but things were already wobbling.

A one minute black and white film was produced for the album, with the idea that it would be used as a television commercial. The film, most of which was conceived by guitarist Elliot Ingber ("Winged Eel Fingerling"), is in the tradition of surrealists' short features. A hooded man plays an egg-beater, Van Vliet kicks over a bucket of batter, and a smoothly professional announcer suavely recites "It's *Lick My Decals Off, Baby!*" with perfect enunciation.[3] The commercial aired a few times on a test basis, but there were so many complaints (mostly about the album's title) that the commercial was pulled and didn't air nationally.

As Langdon Winner tells it, Van Vliet's booking agency was busy with an Ali/Frazier fight, and no tour was being planned to promote the album. So, in the second half of 1970, Van Vliet took it upon himself to speak to Warner Brothers merchandising director Hal Haverstadt. "I want to start playing for people, why don't you put me on tour?" and Haverstadt decided it would be an interesting experiment. With the record company taking on most of the financial risk, a tour was quickly arranged. Captain Beefheart and His Magic Band were paid $1000 per concert.

Warner Brothers paired the band with Ry Cooder, and sent them off on buses. The tour began in January of 1971, in Detroit. They played small halls, movie theaters and college auditoriums, twenty-some dates in all. It was on this tour that Van Vliet began responding to encore calls for "more!" by whistling "More," the theme from the film *Mondo Cane,* a practice he would follow through the *Clear Spot* tour.

Two weeks into the tour, in Wilkes Barre, Pennsylvania, Ingber quit the band. His temperment was a much more distant and darker one than the others in the band. Ingber did not join in the hi-jinks the other members enjoyed on stage. The others glad-handed anyone they encountered, fans or uncomprehending middle-aged women, bought silly souvenirs, and generally behaved as if this tour had finally freed them from the entrapment of The House. The core of the band—French, Boston and Harkleroad—must have felt a common psychic release in being on the road at last, something in which Ingber did not share. He gave various reasons for wanting to leave, including that it was too difficult to find organic food on the road, but the decisive reason was that he simply did not feel comfortable playing within the tight strictures of Van Vliet's music. He wanted more freedom to improvise, to solo. (When he rejoined the Magic Band for the next album, Van Vliet granted him solo space, a move which angered Harkleroad, who had yet to be given the privilege.) Art Tripp tried to put the best face on the situation, saying that if Ingber was not comfortable, then it would be best for all if he left, and no hard feelings. Ingber left, some hard feelings lingered, and the band carried on as a quintet.

Van Vliet, too, must have been feeling some release. He certainly seemed to be enjoying himself. After his set, he would venture out into those of the audience who remained, and talk with anyone who approached him. In March, the Magic Band played forty minutes on a Washington, D.C. television show. In the middle of the host's introduction, Van Vliet came up behind and tickled him so that the man broke up on camera. He sat through as many interview sessions as could be arranged, some lasting hours. His playful, Escher-prints-in-language style of responding to questions sometimes left interviewers frustrated, but he refused to pretend that straight lines were more important that circles of language and how they float. Interviewers who persisted in trying to get blunt-object answers were told by Van Vliet, "You keep trying to get me to hit you, but I'm not going to do it."

Van Vliet also enjoyed what sight-seeing the combination of lumbering busses and busy schedule allowed. In Washington, D.C. he took a limo to the Smithsonian Institution, a place he had long wanted to visit. Van Vliet did the requisite gawking and admiring of the preserved and simulated animals, and bemoaned the fate of the extinct. One thing which caught his attention was the "poetry" of the descriptions which accompanied the exhibits. He admired the succinct and vivid way they reeled off each animal's distinguishing features. The evocation of the lives of animals, so different from that of men, was a poetry he could appreciate.

Winner watched as Van Vliet investigated a sign which read, "Press the button to see the wonder animal that has survived vast environmental changes for thousands of years." Van Vliet pushed the button, and a trapdoor opened to reveal ... that the Smithsonian has a sense of humor. Van Vliet found himself looking into a mirror.

Van Vliet would indeed soon have need of this survival skill.

Running Hard to Find a Clear Spot

The cover of the next album, *The Spotlight Kid,* says a good deal about the music on it. Van Vliet faces the camera directly, watchful but calm, his stance loose. There is no mask, no disorienting light or scenery, nothing stagy here. His desert-rat-Dali look has been smoothed out. He wears a fancy Western-cut suit. He looks at ease, a man with no message, artistic or otherwise, to force on anyone.

The music is less challenging, less disorienting here. The rhythms still change in the course of a composition, but the changes are less jarring, and each part is more conventionally coherent both harmonically and melodically. The disappointed whispers about Captain Beefheart and the Magic Band going commercial began immediately. But Van Vliet didn't agree:

> "It's not a compromise" [he told an interviewer]. "I got tired of scaring people with what I was doing. . . . I realized that I had to give them something to hang their hat on, so I started working more of a beat into the music. It's more human that way."[1]

Gone are the wriggled-finger saxophone parts. The hands here have largely turned the composition of the music back over to the voice, and to the harmonica. The reappearance of this little instrument makes a big difference, as Van Vliet pointed out at the time:

> *The Spotlight Kid* only sounds different on account of the use of harmonica: on that instrument you can play scales, melodies. I've realized, playing the songs of *Trout Mask Replica*, that—for a young audience— they were too intellectual. [The harmonica releases] the feeling that should come loose. [2]

In addition to the return of the harmonica, the music differs in that much of it is based on guitars and their strengths, rather than on Van Vliet's piano parts. Van Vliet listened to Harkleroad and Ingber warming up at rehearsals and heard things he decided to use. The way Van Vliet expressed this was by saying that he had absorbed rhythms from the band members: "I've watched their walk, I've watched their talk—and not just watching. It's more like I've been a sponge and soaked up all their water."[3]

Water of another sort also had a direct effect on Van Vliet's music: the Pacific Ocean. In the early 1970s, Van Vliet and the band lived much of the time in rented houses in northern California. The area impressed lifelong desert-dweller Van Vliet so much that he bought ocean front property near Trinidad, not far from the Oregon border. While he would later be so destitute as to move into his mother's trailer in the Mojave (she moved out), he held on to this piece of property, hoping to build there. (He was not to have his ocean front home until 1983.) The idea of commercial success must have grown more attractive with the ocean front prospect in mind.

Van Vliet's voice, which had always been a focal point, is here pushed even more to the fore. At least one of the band members, used to having equal aural space, felt crowded into a corner by the prominence of the vocals. Bill Harkleroad has been very open about his dislike of *Spotlight Kid.* In addition to hearing the vocals as overpowering, he feels the entire album was played far too slowly. He writes that this was, in part, because Van Vliet was being even more bullying than ever, if less physical now that the musicians were no longer the same insecure young men he had gathered together in Woodland Hills. By this time, according to Harkleroad, the music was suffering due to Van Vliet's tactics. The band members had been "beaten into submission and played like mummies."[4] But Harkleroad also concedes that the music had been slowed in part because Van Vliet wanted to concentrate more on his singing. And taken solely on the basis of vocal technique and variety, this is the most impressive of all Captain Beefheart recordings.

Van Vliet's vocal range has been reported as being anything from "3 1/2" to "7 1/2" octaves. This likely began as a kind of one-upmanship: "You've got 3 1/2? Well, I've got. . . ." (A good vocal range is generally about three octaves.) While examining his recorded output does not settle the question of his range beyond appeal, *The Spotlight Kid* includes what sound to be his comfortable limits—from the low rumbles on "I'm Gonna Booglarize You, Baby," and "Ain't No Santa Claus On the Evening Stage," to the high keening "don't knows" of "White Jam," and the falsetto scat near the end of "When It Blows Its Stacks." Van Vliet's voice here extends from "E" in the second octave below middle "C" up exactly three octaves. His vocals are loose and breathy at the bottom and slightly strained at the top, suggesting that this may well be his full range.

Van Vliet plumbs the depths of his voice for much of "I'm Gonna Booglarize You Baby," the first song on the album. The guitar-based nature of the new music is announced immediately and loudly. The track opens with returning member Elliot Ingber playing a monster-metal E7 chord. Behind this Harkleroad creates metallic landslides on steel appendage guitar. Both Ingber and Harkleroad make their guitars snarl. Boston can finally be clearly heard on this album, his bass given a open space down at the bottom where he can be heard booming through his lines like a set of tuned cannons. This song includes one of Van Vliet's best lyric lines: "The moon was a drip on a dark hood." He also does his best scat singing on record here.

"White Jam" begins gently, beautifully, with a unison guitar and marimba line taken from one of Van Vliet's piano recordings, a line that alternately hesitates and glides. (Harkleroad notes that there was already a good deal of reshaping of *Trout Mask* era material done during the recording of this album[5].) Van Vliet sings the lyrics describing the overpowering effect of a woman's love in a voice loaded with longing, as if he cannot believe such a wonderful woman could want to be with him and afraid that he could lose this grace at any time. This same tension is in the music of the first section, where the guitar and marimba waver between E and F, adding an uncertainty to the sound. Some wonderfully chiming chords signal the end of this uncertainty. For the second half the key changes to E-flat and the music becomes a wheezing, harmonica and tambourine driven blues machine celebrating how she makes him feel. The song chugs away into a fade with French's chunky hi-hat powering it and Van Vliet's wonderfully robust falsetto floating above it like white smoke. "Blabber and Smoke," a straight-forward ecology song, has lyrics by his wife Jan Van Vliet. The music is a simple, loping riff played with a very wiry tone by Harkleroad. The drums, marimba and bass add the colors to this minimal outline. Boston's bass dips and rises like a dancer's shoulders, and French's drums are as exuberant as a cantering horse.

"When it Blows Its Stacks" is a snaking voodoo hex, a bluesy declaration of male power and independence: "He don't bow to bad water!" Van Vliet again sings in his river-bottom voice. The song is guitar-riff driven for the most part, but there are breaks for synchronized guitar and marimba parts, and Ingber solos frantically in several places. His solos also power the instrumental "Alice in Blunderland." This was composed during the interregnum between *Trout Mask* and *Decals*. It is the most segmented piece on the album, and it works beautifully.

"The Spotlight Kid" is another reworking of an older piece, and features Americana-style lyrics and a guitar line adapted from one of Van Vliet's more relaxed piano parts. This song is both charming and cheering, with its loping drums, chiming marimbas, and lyrics about "mud-cat ponds" and "rockin' chair moanin'." Van Vliet lets out with a number of exuberant falsetto whoops, while the guitars growl beneath. Slightly different shadings of instrumental combinations are used to shadow the bright ascending and more ominous descending scales of the melody.

"Click Clack" has all the elements of a classic train song: a woman leaving, a mournful whistle evoked by harmonica and slide guitar, a man left standing in the gravel. But this is definitely a train on the Beefheart line. The music opens with piano and bass playing a three note cut-time riff while French lays a 3/4 time high-hat pattern over it. The result is a swirling polyrhythm as insistent as a steam locomotive. Midway through the song, the band all move into straight time and build up more and more power, Van Vliet alternately bellowing and playing harmonica. As the track fades, the slide guitar plays a riff more and more slowly over the steady rhythm section, a dragging, bluesy sound that tells us the woman isn't coming back.

After this comes "Grow Fins" which achieves its power through sheer insistence. A guitar with heavy tremolo playing a single six-note riff—a sound like John Lee Hooker in a vengeful mood—provides the backbone for the entire song. Van Vliet's belief that all beings are intertwined adds a completely new dimension to the traditional "If you don't do me better, I'm leaving you woman" blues theme. Here, if she doesn't do better, he's going to grow fins, return to the sea and take up with a mermaid, leave "land-lubbin' women" behind. The harmonica sound here is enormous, what Harkleroad refers to as a "big as the Empire state Building" sound.

"There Ain't No Santa Claus On the Evening Stage," is a murky, sawtoothed composition which Van Vliet again sings at the very bottom of his register. As Gary Lucas once pointed out, the title phrase can be taken to be about show business. The album's closer, "Glider" is a trifle, with an awkward but insistently contagious rhythm pattern. A studio drummer plays here, and the drum part follows more closely in the tracks of the other instruments than French likely would have done.

The relative simplicity of the music here leads us back to questions about the tyrannical way in which the more difficult music was created. If the most difficult question to be dealt with in considering Van Vliet's career as Captain Beefheart is whether the Mansonesque control of the musicians was a necessary element in the creation of the startling and brilliant music of *Trout Mask* and *Decals* albums, it may in part be answered by seeing what happened to the music once he began to relinquish— or have taken away from him—this absolute power.

Looking at the changes in the music from *Spotlight Kid* through the next three albums takes us into a cat's cradle of interconnected, contradictory threads. The easiest way to make the music more commercial, Van Vliet knew, was to move it closer to more conventional guitar-based rock and roll. But to do this, both because he didn't play the guitar and because his own musical tastes sought quirkier sounds, he would have to release some of the responsibility for creation of the music to the players. This worked well enough for the songs on *The Spotlight Kid* and its follow-up album, *Clear Spot*, but left Van Vliet with less and less of the greater body and mind he had created with the Magic Band in the months of seclusion, a loss which, coupled with his desire to achieve commercial success, soon caused his music to go slack and dull.

But in the latter part of 1972, Van Vliet and the band released *Clear Spot,* an album which seemed to promise the *Trout Mask* and the commercial sides of their music could successfully coexist. The album was originally to be titled *Brown Star*, a Van Vliet nickname for the earth. The lyrics to the title song were written, but no music was never recorded. Instead, the album was retitled *Clear Spot* and released in a clear vinyl sleeve. (Van Vliet had wanted the record company to press the record on clear vinyl, but they declined to take on the enormous cost this would have entailed.) It only takes listening to the first few bars of the opening track to know that there will be a great difference between this album and its predecessor. The guitars here have a clean, springy sound. Where on *Spotlight Kid* the guitars had all the grunge of alligator wrestlers, here they bounce around one another like gymnasts in shiny tights. For the first time guitar parts were being stacked up in the studio with definite tonal effects in mind. Song structures are more conventional, with clear verse, chorus and bridge parts. These differences were due to a number of things.

First and foremost, Van Vliet announced that he was seeking to expand his audience once again, this time in a definite direction—toward women. He had come to the realization that almost no women listened to his music. His audience was, as guitarist Gary Lucas has good-naturedly pointed out, "weirdos and intellectuals, mainly nerdy boys. Not your surfer types—it was more Beatniks."[6] Van Vliet deliberately set out to capture this huge potential audience. He announced that *Clear Spot* was music "for the ladies," and asserted that women understood his music better than men did. So the clean sound and simplified structures are, in part, the musical equivalents of flattery and seduction.

A second reason for the change was that the other musicians, particularly Harkleroad, were now shaping the structures of the music. The piano music Van Vliet had created in the Woodland Hills house and had mined so frequently for the past three albums is almost entirely absent from the compositions here. Van Vliet's personal rhythms here begin to give ground to those of the band members. Ingber had left again, and Boston takes over rhythm guitar chores, while the bass is played by yet another ex-Mother, Roy Estrada (dubbed "Orejon"). Parts created by the band play a much larger role, to the extent that Harkleroad would soon begin to feel that he should be given co-composers credit. Van Vliet never went that far, but he did begin to give the band more credit in interviews, pointing out that the billing was now "Captain Beefheart and *the* Magic Band," rather than "*his* Magic Band." He even went so far as to claim that he had "never wanted to" run the band, only to sing and play his harmonica.

The third major factor in the change of sound and direction of the music was that the absolute control that Van Vliet had always sought to have over the recording process was denied him by producer Ted Templeman. Band members recall the times Templeman told Van Vliet, in these words or others, to "shut up." Templeman worked to keep the music shapely, convincing Van Vliet to delete some of the stranger tangents the songs had originally gone off on. (Several were reworked from earlier versions arrived at during the *Spotlight Kid* sessions.) Van Vliet bristled, resisted, but in the end he and Templeman arrived at a sound with which they both could be happy.

The first track, "Lo Yo Yo Stuff," has a happy-sounding guitar, with dancing marimba and cowbell. The lyrics concern themselves with a nonsense dance craze, mixed with a little light-hearted sexual innuendo. There are stops and starts here, but they are playful rather than challenging, and add to rather than subvert the "pop" feel of the song. On an album aimed at women there are naturally going to be very few attacks on "the Mama heartbeat."

"Nowadays A Woman's Gotta Hit a Man" opens as a variation on the "Bo Diddley" rhythm over Art Tripp's Neo-New Orleans drumming, but the hard-edged guitar lines multiply the cross rhythms until the music takes on an identity all its own. A reed section adds some swaying, punchy soul to the mix, and a minimalist but charging slide solo adds more fuel. This is one of the Magic Band's most energetic performances, and one of the best of Van Vliet's "pop" compositions.

"Too Much Time" is slow-groove soul. The playing guest guitarist Russ Titleman suggests a Stax sound, that of Steve Cropper with Otis Redding. The melody is conventionally romantic, with the lyrics retaining enough of Van Vliet's individuality that they don't sink into bathos. Still, Van Vliet's voice is a little too controlled-sounding for the performance to be completely convincing. In Harkleroad's opinion, Van Vliet had been changed too thoroughly by the experience of singing *Trout Mask's* fragmented songs for him to be able to sing this kind of sincere torch song convincingly:

> Sometimes, you can be working on something for years, and then when you go back to trying something you did earlier, you don't have the spark or naivete or whatever it takes to do it . . . I think too much time had gone by for Don to sing just straight R&B.[7]

"Circumstances" has legions of fans among guitar players, for its angry wasp guitar sound, but it is one of the lesser songs here. The lyrics are vague, but ominous-sounding. The guitars here do their most frantic work on the album, and Van Vliet's singing is for the most part an unmodulated bellow. Tripp's drums do a fine imitation of a train approaching from a distance.

"My Head Is My Only House Unless It Rains," is another gentle love song, with swaying guitar arpeggios and straight, lounge-style drumming. Some low string playing by the second guitar has the feel of gentle nudging. The music has a lot of warm air and moonlight in it. "Sun Zoom Spark" has standout drumming from Tripp, a complex pattern that jumps back and forth between snare drum and cowbell with absolute precision. Van Vliet sings in a choked voice here, and his harmonica is at its wheeziest.

Harkleroad's guitar on "Clear Spot" is soaked in tremolo, a sound the band thought of as being "swampy" at the time. The bass part is thumpingly insistent and holds the music too still in places. Tripp plays very sparely here, leaving a lot of space for the guitars to come through. The lyrics concern themselves with the idea of the world being a swamp, and Van Vliet having to run through its dangers to get to a "clear spot" where he can live like he wants to live, and be with his kind of folks. Van Vliet seems to run out of ideas before his harmonica solo here ends.

"Her Eyes Are a Blue Million Miles" has a beautiful pillowy sound, created by Harkleroad's layered acoustic and electric guitars and mandolin. The accents are unexpected, but natural-sounding and friendly; sleigh bells move through the background. The stark simplicity of the lyrics, the romantic puns, are perfect for the gentle but insistent dance of electric string parts. On the minus side, there are too few lyrics and Van Vliet repeats verses to the point where the words begin to lose their affect.

"Big Eyed Beans From Venus" is considered by some to be Van Vliet's best composition. The sound of the guitars swell like steam boilers about to burst, and the parts are played so fiercely that the strings might have broken and whipped the notes into space with the ferocity of their release. The lyrics are both apocalyptic and nonsensical. At the famous instruction, "Mr. Zoot Horn Rollo, hit that long lunar note and let it float," Harkleroad lets loose with a solo that sounds as if straight-razors were scraping the windings off his strings.

After all the commercial touches on the album; after all the thought about appealing to ladies, the album ends with a raw blast of uncompromising Beefheart poetry: "Golden Birdies." (Much of this piece was arranged by Ingber from fragments of Van Vliet's piano music, according to John French.) Boston returns to bass here, and he punches out the tricky bass line responses, its flutterings and collapsing cadences which form a perfect counterpoint to Van Vliet's spoken obi man poem. An entire album of pieces such as this—compelling, angular music with undeniable human warmth in its stops, starts and hairpin turns, irreducible word strings which convey the power of hoodoo, recited in a voice like a fire-eater's exhale, all in just over a minute-and-a-half—would have made all the other albums sound like warm-up exercises.

Instead, the next album would mean the end of the Magic Band, and stop Captain Beefheart's career cold.

Rock and Roll's Evil Doll

On the two 1972 albums band members, Bill Harkleroad in the lead, began making musical decisions. They would take Van Vliet's ideas and arrange them in more manageable musical structures. For a number of reasons Harkleroad had by this time become the bandleader, cuing the other players on their parts, and even cuing Van Vliet as to when to sing. With *Clear Spot*, Harkleroad and Templeman had effectively broken Van Vliet's iron grip on the music. By the time of the recording for the next album, Harkleroad recalls, he was telling Van Vliet to "fuck off!" when they disagreed. The system Van Vliet had bullied into being, his dictatorial control over the tight and powerful mind/ body musical machine, were no more. And as the band won more musical input and freedom, as the music began to move toward collective rather than individual composition and arrangement it also—as is inevitable with group art—began to sound less individual, less unique.

The glee some of the band felt upon seeing Van Vliet forced into a direction not entirely his own, in being "driven away from his own steering wheel," as he sings in "Upon the My-O-My," quickly turned to dismay as Van Vliet chose to turn control of the music over not to the band, but to outsider producers, and to follow a commercial trajectory far beyond the point any of them could have imagined. After *Clear Spot*, Van Vliet said, he began working toward a sound which would appeal to more people. "I must admit I feel I was being quite selfish about that other music

I was playing."[1] This time around, rather than resisting a producer's suggestions, Van Vliet said he wanted someone to give it a "specific form." The producer he chose to do this was Andy DiMartino, half of a production and management team with his brother Augie. Van Vliet's long-time manager, Grant Gibbs, reportedly had quit the music world, and the DiMartino team took over completely. They signed the band to a new label, Mercury, and, with Van Vliet's blessing, attempted to take the music in an even more commercial direction. Van Vliet said of Augie DiMartino, "He's the right producer; the cosmic mitt." Of the band's new sound he said, "The other was the other and this is this. I like the other but I like this too."[2]

The music, particularly on the first of the two Mercury albums, is a departure from Van Vliet's earlier music, but not as abrupt a change as is commonly portrayed. It is, undeniably, worlds away from *Trout Mask Replica,* but *Trout Mask* was five years in the past by the time *Unconditionally Guaranteed* was released in 1974. Five years is a very long time for any artist who values development and change in his or her work. Still, direct links are easily heard between the more pop-styled tunes on *Clear Spot* and the songs here.

The Magic Band was drastically overhauled for this album. Van Vliet added keyboards, played by Mark Marcellino, and woodwinds, by Del Simmons. There were otherchanges: Roy Estrada and Elliot Ingber had gone; Art Tripp and Alex St. Clair returned (his name here spelled "St. Claire"). Boston was back on bass full time. Andy DiMartino played acoustic guitar on the record, his thin strumming more like a washboard than a guitar.

Van Vliet, too, underwent a drastic personal transformation. The link between his physical and his musical presences remained intact. His Van Dyke was trimmed back to a simple moustache; his hair had a razor-cut, Rod-the-Mod look; his weight had dropped. His interaction with the press changed character as well. His responses to interviewers were much more straightforward, as he patiently explained his change in orientation. He insisted that he had not altered the message of what he was saying, that the new sound was "just a friendly extension."

Van Vliet never tried to hide the fact that economic considerations played a part in his change of style. Part of what he wanted the money for, he said, was for art supplies. Van Vliet would at times go so far as to say that painting and music were equally interesting to him, but for the most part he was always open about preferring painting, with music being a poor second. And, as he pointed out to more than one interviewer, oil paints are expensive.

The cover for *Unconditionally Guaranteed* was done by a design team, but Van Vliet must have told them what the album was about. The front shows him grasping handfuls of dollar bills—the bills are crumpled, as befits "filthy lucre." But the back of the album features a pensive portrait of Van Vliet, whose gaze is very much elsewhere, and beneath this is "Love Over Gold—Don Van Vliet." How much clearer could he make it? There were two sides to his motivation, money and love—love of music; love of painting; and, certainly, love of his wife whom he would not want to live in the less-than-genteel poverty toward which his uncompromising music was moving them. It's also possible that whatever illness Van Vliet has developed was making itself known at this time; or it could have been the desire to build a home on the ocean front property he had purchased in Trinidad. Many saw only one side of this album, saw only the bid for money, but not the flipside, the love and the unavoidable needs (which, as Van Vliet's gaze should have reminded us all, lay "off the record" in more ways than one) which lay behind it. The band could feel something happening inside Van Vliet, though he didn't share it with them. Harkleroad writes that, "No matter how abusive he was, I was beginning to feel sorry for him. I got the feeling that something was going on with him that I was unaware of."³ For whatever reasons, the time had come after a decade of struggle for Van Vliet to take a breather and build a more secure home base; for the private Don Van Vliet to look out for his simple human needs. The artistic pride of Captain Beefheart would have to step aside for a time.

Van Vliet knew that part of the outrage which met these albums was because he was no longer being the romanticized embodiment of the uncompromising artist, willing to sacrifice all for totally free expression. Others listened to his records and made their own Man-Behind-the-Music, "in some weird fantasy-category out of [their] need to explain what it was that [the band] did."[4] It can be argued that he had done little to discourage this notion in the past, even encouraged it in his more self-important moments, but by 1974 he was rejecting it completely, vehemently. His words make it clear that his turn away from challenging music was an aspect of his personal freedom:

> People always considered me as personal property, like a home poet you could send for whenever you wanted. Someone who—as part of his image—should be poor, too, a recluse who needs chastening to increase his performance. They would not like it if I made much money with my music, and that's bullshit.[5]

And, in words much like those he used to explain his change in direction on *The Spotlight Kid,* he declared to the world that he no longer wanted to be "the Big Bad Wolf of rock & roll," but a kind of musical matinee idol. That there was never any real chance that this would come to be, was in large part because Van Vliet had no idea *how* to make commercial records. What the two Mercury albums most clearly demonstrate is how isolated Van Vliet was from the popular music of the time. He had been so long climbing out on his own individual limb that he had left the main trunk of rock and roll behind, and he didn't know how to find his way back again. Listening to these albums, it is clear that he has had little real contact with the popular music of the time, certainly no love for it. The feather-weight sensibility here is closer to the fluffy pop music of the late 1940s and early '50s, the time of Van Vliet's childhood.

Van Vliet also put his trust in the DiMartinos, more so than was wise: "As the DiMartinos came in [Van Vliet] seemed to get weaker and weaker. . . . I don't think he was in control of the details, I don't think he cared," Harkleroad has written[6]. It is one of the responsibilities of a producer to help an artist find the pulse of his or her musical times. Gauging by the songs they helped create, the producers had little understanding of what listeners of the day were looking for in pop music. As a result, the songs written and recorded with the DiMartinos for *Unconditionally Guaranteed* severely underestimate the aesthetic sense of their intended audience, aim far too low, resulting in songs more bland and simpleminded than any but the most banal album filler material. That one of the DiMartinos could imagine "This Is the Day" from the first of these albums would be Van Vliet's "Stairway to Heaven"[7] (likely becomes some of the guitar fills are similar to the neo-celtic lines on the Led Zeppelin track) shows how disconnected from the contemporary state of the art of rock and roll the entire project really was.

The album opens with "Upon The My-O-My." A descending horn riff, wiry slide breaks by Harkleroad and a passionate vocal by Van Vliet almost save the slight composition. "Sugar Bowl" deflates any illusions that the album will resemble past efforts. It is simple-minded in the extreme, almost a nursery rhyme. The guitars play saccharine lines, and the rhythm seems tailor-made for a soft-shoe routine. The most prominent instrument on "New Electric Ride" is DiMartino's washboard guitar. The rhythm is board-stiff, the lyrics flat and forgettable.

Fully half of the tracks here, "Magic Be," "Happy Love Song, "I Got Love On My Mind," "This Is the Day" and "Lazy Music," are mid or slow tempo love songs, to which Van Vliet's voice seems ill-suited. Most of the lyrics are poor, some downright clumsy. The songs are credited to DiMartino and Don and Jan Van Vliet, but the band's opinion was that her credit was a scam by Van Vliet to get two-thirds of the publishing royalties rather than only half.

"Full Moon, Hot Sun," sparkles and rocks along in a light pop mode, with some nice guitar work. But hearing Van Vliet call his lover "Honey Bun" is unsettling. "Peaches," the last track, zips along, but the spare and inane lyrics ruin any chance it may have had of holding a listener's attention. It is as if in losing his hold over the band which were extensions of his self, he suffered almost complete amputation of his musical judgement.

119

A tour was scheduled, and then, five days before they were to depart for England, the entire Magic Band walked away. Some of the members had already decided to leave, but stayed on to get paid for the recording sessions. Harkleroad, for one, was fed up with supplying guitar parts, being promised he would be credited and paid for them, and having nothing come of these promises. But the primary reason for the complete break was that St. Clair discovered that Van Vliet had been hiding the band's money behind his production company, "God's Golf Ball," while telling them their pay for their last European tour was "tied up in customs." The band met with Van Vliet and one of the DiMartinos and St. Clair laid out what he knew. The other musicians, who had been through so much with Van Vliet, was incredulous at first. But then the truth sank in and the band walked. The core of the Magic Band, with vocalist Sam Galpin, recorded two excellent albums as Mallard before disbanding.

The DiMartinos called in a number of session men and members of the band Buckwheat and created a backing band (known to fans as the "Tragic Band") so that the tour could go on. Perhaps the most bizarre two minutes and forty seconds in the saga of Captain Beefheart is that Van Vliet spent on Swedish television, lip-syncing to the recorded version of "Upon the My-O-My." By all accounts, there was more heckling on this tour than at any when the band was at its most "weird." Van Vliet did his best to talk up the musicianship of the new band members—"I'm a real blabbermouth," he said, "but this new album has got me really soothed out—particularly reedman Del Simmons, who had played with Charlie Parker. He sucked a cosmic particle into his horn and illuminated his brain . . . he demands imagery!"[8] But *Captain Beefheart London 1974*, the live album recorded on the tour, says otherwise.

"Mirror Man" starts out promisingly enough, though the guitars have an underamplified sound that prevents them from ever working up any great power. Soon enough it becomes clear that this is to be Big Note Beefheart, so simplified are the arrangements. But the reduced complexity of the older songs included, and the nursery rhyme simplicity (which, admittedly,

120

is at times inane) is finally the smaller part of the problem with the recording. What defeats the music, give it no chance to succeed with new listeners any more than with old fans, is what sounds like complete disinterest on the part of the musicians. The arrangements continue at a logy mid-tempo no matter how much urgency Van Vliet puts into his voice. He pushes against the dull plodding of the band, but they rarely move with him; there is a decent but very short solo by Simmons, and some melodic soloing by the guitarists, but there are few such moments. Everything fails here, if for slightly different reasons: "Upon the My-Oh-My" fails by its lounge sluggishness, "Sugar Bowl" gets an intro which makes the theme sound like "Taps," and its quirky turn-around riff is made marshmallow by some fatigued, vibrato-hollowed guitar work, "Crazy Little Thing" does not survive its stripped-down arrangement and too-slow tempo despite Van Vliet's most energetic vocal of the set, "Peaches" fails simply by being a poor song. The musicians are all proficient, but it is painful to hear how they fail to understand the way in which the music might be brought to life.

The second Mercury album, *Bluejeans and Moonbeams*, is a real improvement over the first, both compositionally and in the quality of the recording. That Van Vliet's head was a house divided in the Mercury period, as presented graphically on *Unconditionally Guaranteed*, inspired the lyrics to one of this album's best songs. "Rock and Roll's Evil Doll," the first track on the second side, once again lays the cards on the table. Rock and roll's "evil doll," its incarnation, is huge and is chasing Van Vliet, who runs from her. Rock and roll makes him feel small. He does not like running away from her, but he does not want to "fall." So, after hearing doors slam he too begins running down rock and roll's "rainbow hall." Then he gets big, too. At least, this was the plan. One track here, J.J. Cale's "Same Old Blues," reportedly did get some FM radio play, but this album was no more successful at making Van Vliet "big" than was its predecessor.

The Magic Band on this album included three of the musicians who were in the touring band, as well as Ira Ingber on bass. Van

Vliet would later complain bitterly that he brought Elliot Ingber into the sessions (the best compositions on the album bear Ingber's name as co-writer), but that the producers later stripped off those guitar parts. This album also includes "Captain's Holiday," a pedestrian instrumental track that according to Van Vliet (and as is suggested by its title) was recorded without him. The composers credit goes to four names, none of which are among the musicians credited. It appears likely that this was a ballast track assembled by the producer so there would be enough material to issue the album.

The band that works with Van Vliet here sounds much better than the original Magic Band did with the flat and empty production DiMartino gave *Unconditionally Guaranteed.* Here his production gives power to the music, and the arrangements, most by Van Vliet, display an much more interesting rhythmic complexity. The album begins with a declaration that brings to mind *Trout Mask's* poems and "Golden Birdies" : "The Camel Wore a Nightie!" Van Vliet announces. The occasion for this is a "Party of Special Things to Do," as the first track is titled. Present at the party are Elixir Sue (last heard from on "Tarotplane"), a number of wild cards, distant cousins (last heard from on "Big Eyed Beans from Venus), and that camel in its sleepwear, among others. The music has call and response slide guitar lines, and a *shooping* hi-hat off-accent that creates more rhythmic counterpoint than anything on the previous album. "Same Old Blues" allows Van Vliet to explore blue notes in the basement of his range, and Dean Smith's shimmering slide offers just the right of upward pull to keep up the interest via musical tension. "Observatory Crest," "Further Than We've Gone" and "Bluejeans and Moonbeams" are mid-tempo love songs that make syrupy romantic sounds and then are gone.

"Pompadour Swamp" (a title once attached to a different piece of music) is one of four songs (the others being "Party of Special Things to Do," "Rock and Roll's Evil Doll" and "Twist ah Luck") which suggest that Van Vliet could have forged a successful style out of the pieces he was exploring here had he continued along this line. Keyboards and chunky guitar rock the music back and forth between them, then smooth out as if Van Vliet has suddenly walked into a clear spot in the swamp, then return to their original gaits. Some beautiful images float through the lyric, as when "wafer thin" shadows dance in "nostalgic meadows." Aside from a feeling of being padded for time in a corner or two, this is an almost entirely successful track.

"Rock and Roll's Evil Doll" opens with some fierce slide playing, including a run-up-the-incline sound that almost equals some of Harkleroad's playing. When the guitar settles into a two-chord see-saw, the drums take a few turns around the toms to keep the rhythm alive. Lead guitarist Smith achieves the feel of two guitars playing complementary lines in his solo. While not as inventive as "Pompadour Swamp," the music is again very strong. "Twist ah Luck" is riff-driven, more conventional than the other three in this group, but has some nice harmonica work—which is buried too low in the mix, as is all the harmonica playing here.

Despite these strong moments, this album made even less of an impact than did *Unconditionally Guaranteed*, which attracted long-time fans because of the presence of the classic Magic Band members. Van Vliet urged buyers of the Mercury albums to return them and ask for their money back. If not many did it was because so few bought the albums in the first place. There was no tour for *Bluejeans and Moonbeams*; Van Vliet again broke with his manager/producers; was again entangled in contractual difficulties; and was again without a band. It would take him several years to regain the ground he lost in trying to "be big, too."

Driven Away From His Own Steering Wheel

What is known of Van Vliet's arts and his life suggests that it has proceeded in a series of approximately decade-long cycles. From age 3 to 13, he painted and sculpted. From 13 to 24, he gave up art. Counting ahead from age 24 (1965), when he began working on his Captain Beefheart persona and his unique musical style, to age 34 we arrive at 1975, a year of drastic transition for him, musically and personally. The two 1974 albums, Van Vliet's double-shot at commercial success, failed, both in that regard and artistically. He had tried following his own taste, and never rose above a barely middle-class poverty, but commercializing himself destroyed what career and artistic momentum he had. One musician described Van Vliet as "an almost broken man"[1] in the wake of these failures.

After the Mercury records, Van Vliet told one writer that he had quit music and taken work as a choker-setter. This is among the most outrageous of Van Vliet's claims. As anyone living in California above Sacramento, or in Oregon or Washington knows, a choker-setter is low man on a lumber cutting crew: when the trees are felled and partially limbed, someone (the setter) has to clamber down from the logging road and tie a special cable (a "choker") around the trunk. With this, the logs are winched up to the logging truck, tearing their way through plant, animal and mineral matter alike. It is almost impossible to imagine natty Van Vliet climbing up and down gullies tying steel cable, even more so because of his love for trees. But if this was not black humor, if Van Vliet did take this job, or even consider it, this is an indication of how desperate he became after *Bluejeans and Moonbeams*. He was desperate enough, as it turned out, that just before Halloween 1974 he called Zappa and asked him for work.

It had been a long time since the two had spoken. Six months after *Trout Mask* was recorded, Van Vliet had done a guest vocal for Zappa. This was "Willie the Pimp," recorded at a September session at TT&G studio for the *Hot Rats* album. The melody of "Willie the Pimp" just barely deserves the term. It is a repeated ten note riff which does not modulate, played by Zappa on guitar and Sugarcane Harris on electric violin. But Van Vliet's voice provides more than enough interest; his notes-from-a-cauldron scat singing here, which winds around the beginning of Zappa's wa-wa guitar solo, is better than any he had recorded up to this point. (He would not surpass it until "I'm Gonna Booglarize Ya, Baby," on *Spotlight Kid*.)

Van Vliet's vocal is so fierce and convincing that it almost overpowers the comic element on the lyric, adding a dimension Zappa could not have intended when he wrote them—unless he had Van Vliet in mind from the very beginning. His respect for Van Vliet's singing never diminished even as the two continued to clash over many other things. But even as he was adding this jewel to the album, Van Vliet was trying to distance himself from the proceedings. While Zappa was overdubbing a new ending on his guitar "improvisation," Van Vliet sat so still in a corner of the control booth that he may have been sleeping.

(After the session, after Van Vliet had gone, Zappa told his wife that two weeks earlier Van Vliet had burned the only copies of hundreds of his songs. This horrified Zappa, who never discarded even the smallest of his musical ideas.)

But "Willie the Pimp" was to be the last collaboration of these two uneasy friends prior to a six year period of estrangement and public name-calling. *Trout Mask Replica* was not an overnight sensation, and Van Vliet blamed Zappa for its failure. Though some buyers bought the album because they knew Zappa had recorded it, Van Vliet felt that the album had been promoted as if had been done by drug-crazed freaks, rather than as the art statement Van Vliet felt it to be. His entire career, Van Vliet expressed the belief that his music would be accepted by ordinary music listeners if only they were given the chance to hear it. He felt that the preconceptions of record company executives, radio station owners, record store managers, and others in the music business blocked his way. When asked some years later if his audience were "underground people," Van Vliet denied that such a division existed among music fans: "No, I don't believe in that story about 'underground' and 'overground': it's dangerous, because it puts up a barrier between them."[2] He faulted Zappa and others—most vocally Virgin Records, his label for 1980's *Doc at the Radar Station*—for not seeing this as clearly as he did.

Nigey Lennon, a guitarist with Zappa in the early '70s, writes of witnessing Van Vliet's frustration. Lennon met Van Vliet in 1970, a time when, in her words,

> He'd spend hours chain-smoking evil-smelling Balkan Sobranie cigarettes, listening to "Trout Mask". . . bitching about the production, the art direction, the color of the label . . . shaking his fist at the stereo, and calling Frank highly original names. . . .[3]

Zappa's recollection was that Van Vliet had signed so many conflicting contracts that he was unable to record or tour with a band of his own, and that he was almost destitute. Zappa also recalled that in 1975 even Van Vliet's rhythm sense had deserted him to the point that he struggled to play in time on songs as rhythmically simple as "Willie the Pimp" during the first rehearsal. Van Vliet, in effect, "failed the audition," and had to make a second attempt in order to finally convince Zappa that he could still sing and play. But Van Vliet did convince Zappa, and 1975 found himself working as a lead-singer-for-hire with his on-again off-again friend. Zappa made him one of the singers for a Mothers tour in 1975. The resulting album, *Bongo Fury,* is credited on the cover as a Zappa/Beefheart/Mothers album.

On this recording, most of which was recorded live in Austin, Texas, Van Vliet sings lead on several Zappa songs, and recites two of his own poems over sculpted musical backgrounds. The most interesting of the Zappa compositions is "Debra Kadabra," which must have been written for Van Vliet to sing. The song is made up of in-jokes and references to the California of their youth, the bad Mexican horror movies they used to watch together, the time Van Vliet doused himself with too much Avon "cuh-laag-nuh" and other beauty products (Van Vliet's mother was for a time an Avon Lady) to the point that his hair began to fall out and his skin break out. Van Vliet's voice is strong here, as powerful as ever, a fact which was obscured by the high-sheen production of the Mercury albums. His vocal on "200 Years Old" is especially ferocious when he sings, "She's squatting down and popping up in front of the jukebox like she's got true religion, *boiiiing!*" His harmonica is featured here as well. He sings the satirical cowboy song, "Poofter's Froth Wyoming" with just a hint of a Western accent, but doesn't put much energy into this trifle.

Van Vliet's two poems, "Man With the Woman Head" and "Sam With the Showing Scalp Flat Top" (from which the album's title is taken) are recited to music credited to Van Vliet, and they are reminiscent of "Golden Birdies" in their jagged call-and-response patterns. "Man With the Woman Head" is a forgettable vignette about an effeminate man at a Hollywood drive-in restaurant. "Sam With the Showing Scalp Flattop," however, is a prize for Beefheart fans. In the recitation, Van Vliet tells of playing such melodies as "roughneck" and "thug"; how his music was "thud-like" and "opaque." Fans have taken this to be self-celebration, an artistic self-portrait in poetry.

On this tour, Van Vliet travelled with shopping bags that included his drawing tools, his harmonicas, and whatever personal support items he needed to get through the experience of having to go to work for Zappa. Zappa mocked him for this, telling interviewers that Van Vliet had all his worldly goods in the bags. The album credit for Van Vliet reads, "harp, vocals, shopping bags." One reason for Zappa's needling of Van Vliet during this period was that Van Vliet would sit on stage while he wasn't singing, and drawing unflattering caricatures of Zappa and show them to him during the concert. The BBC documentary includes several brief snippets of Frank Zappa talking about Van Vliet. Zappa, who had the reputation of being able to say anything to anyone without flinching, briefly turns his face away from the camera when asked about the animosity that grew up between them on the tour. When he faces the camera again, he is once again composed. "That was difficult," Zappa admits. "But it only lasted a few weeks." By the time the tour was over, the pair were barely speaking.

But the bond between Van Vliet and Zappa was not broken completely. The following year Van Vliet recorded *Bat Chain Puller*, a come-back Captain Beefheart album with Zappa producing, an album which has yet to be released. This recording featured the return, once again, of John French. In addition to playing drums and guitar, French was again doing duty as transcriber of the music. But before the album could be released, it became one of the hostages in a legal war between producer Zappa and his long-time business manager. For a time Van Vliet wandered from project to project. In 1976, he sang one song for the soundtrack of a film titled *Blue Collar*, backed by a studio band which included Ry Cooder. In 1977, he made a guest appearance playing saxophone on an album by the Tubes.

Then the 1976 album was rerecorded, with some changes in the selection of songs, and released on Warner Brothers in 1978 as *Shiny Beast (Bat Chain Puller)*. The album featured a new Magic Band. Jeff Morris Tepper and Richard Redus played slide guitars; Eric Drew Feldman played keyboards and bass; Robert Arthur Williams played drums, with Art Tripp along to add miscellaneous percussion. Bruce Lambourne Fowler played trombone and "air bass"—his trombone played through an octave divider which put the horn into the bass range.

Fowler is yet another Zappa alumnus: he is credited with trombone and dancing on the *Bongo Fury* album. The inclusion of Fowler in the Magic Band was, theoretically, a logical idea. Like the slide guitar, a trombone can smoothly move from one pitch to another in a continuous slide. But the instrument's tone, which can be flatulent or blowzy by turns, weakened the over-all strength of the notes which had always marked the best compositions. And the broadness of the tone seems to crowd Van Vliet's voice.

Jeff Morris Tepper met Van Vliet during the *Clear Spot* tour in 1972. That Van Vliet had found Tepper simpatico is testified to by the fact that he gave Tepper a drawing at this first meeting. "I don't *ever* do that," he later told Tepper. In August 1975 Tepper was driving in Northern California, looking for a place to live when he saw Van Vliet drive by in a pumpkin-orange Corvette. Tepper walked up to the car and said, "Don." Van Vliet's head literally hit the roof with surprise. Van Vliet showed his phenomenal memory for people he has met, recognizing Tepper and remembering he had given him the drawing. Van Vliet showed Tepper a house for rent, and so Tepper soon became Van Vliet's next door neighbor. Tepper had been playing guitar, but with no serious plans. When he figured out and played both guitar lines from "Dali's Car," their composer was impressed. After the *Bongo Fury* tour ended, Van Vliet called Tepper to play on the original *Bat Chain Puller* sessions (with guitarist Denny Walley, from Zappa's band). Van Vliet tried to drive what he saw as the influence on Tepper of the Beatles by making him listen for hours to "Red Cross Store" by Mississippi John Hurt.

In the early 1970s, drummer Robert Williams had gone to a club where Van Vliet, then in his commercial period, was to play for a seven-day run. Augie DiMartino was arguing with the club's manager over who would lug the equipment around between shows. Williams asked for the job, and got $20 for the week's work. On the last night of Van Vliet's stint, Dr. John (Mac Rebennack) was in the audience, and Williams heard that Rebennack was looking for a drummer. Williams auditioned for the job and failed, but a few years later Williams got the call to play with Van Vliet, who had remembered the audition. Williams played with the Magic Band through *Doc at the Radar Station*.

Van Vliet often claimed to like the new Magic Band more than the old because they "wouldn't work"—they sustained a feeling of play, where the earlier bands had had the attitude that the music was work. For the tour to support *Shiny Beat* (a tour which helped reestablish the Captain Beefheart reputation), the new Magic Band learned more than fifty compositions, playing live great earlier works such as "Bellerin' Plain," as well as the new pieces.

As much as these players admired the genius of their leader, they were not impressionable young 1960s-types. Nor, of course, was Van Vliet the same man he had been a decade before. He was no more willing to once again go through the Herculean labor ("animal training," as he sometimes would unkindly call the experience of working with musicians) that had led him to the great achievements of 1969 to 1972 than the new players were to be wholly taken over. At this same moment, a moment when it would have become clear that there was no possibility of ever again creating a personal ecosystem like that he had once forced into being in the rundown two-story in Woodland Hills, Van Vliet began to run out of new music.

"I think there's an order on this planet, and that order is not to look back," Van Vliet once said. But he began disobeying this order with *Shiny Beast*. At least one of the songs dates from the *Safe as Milk* period. Others, at least lyrically, are if not leftovers from the Mercury albums, then products of some of the same musical impulses which formed those songs. Music-starved fans welcomed the album as a return to the classic Beefheart style. But only the title track, "Owed T'Alex" (a decade old or more) and the instrumental "Ice Rose" would have been at home on any pre-1974 album. The songs "Tropical Hot Dog Night," "Harry Irene," "Candle Mambo" and "Love Lies" would not have been out of place on *Bluejeans and Moonbeams*. "You Know You're a Man" and "When I See Mommy I Feel Like a Mummy" have a transitional feel---whether from the older style to the commercial one, or an attempt to move back is not clear.

That both of these styles—one admired, one reviled and denounced even by Van Vliet himself—should have coexisted

130

almost in equal proportions on this album should have given Beefheart fans more pause than it did. Comparison of the track list for the original *Bat Chain Puller* and *Shiny Beast*, two years later, show that Van Vliet removed the most difficult material— "Brickbats" and "1010th Day of the Human Totem Pole" in favor of less challenging compositions. It seems clear that Van Vliet was still convinced that a commercial simplicity could be his path to success. But the album did offered enough encouragement that those who wished for a return of the classic 1969 - 72 Captain Beefheart could tell themselves that it was about to happen.

The album's opener, "The Floppy Boot Stomp," is a ground-pounding variation on the theme of Charlie Daniels' rowdy country-rock hit "The Devil Went Down to Georgia." Its stops and starts, its helium-high slide licks, are reminiscent of the *Decals* album, but with its pop-counterpoint guitar lines and deliberate silliness of its lyrics—the devil rousted by a square dancing farmer—it could have been written as a companion piece to "Party of Special Things to Do."

"Tropical Hot Dog Night," part of its music recycled from 1975's unreleased "Odd Jobs," brings to mind visions of brightly-colored drinks with little plastic umbrellas. Fowler's trombone bleats a peppy riff that leads the music in concert with an equally peppy guitar and marimba line. This is a blowzy rock-calypso, happy and slight. "Harry Irene" is a joke lyric set to a faux tack piano sound and asthmatic accordion. The real treat here is the inclusion, finally, of some of Van Vliet's legendary whistling.

"Ice Rose," an instrumental which is placed between these two pop trifles, dates from late in the *Strictly Personal* period.[4] It is segmental, but with an insistent beat. There is no avoidance of the dreaded "Mama Heartbeat." Fowler solos at length here, but runs out of ideas before its three-and-a-half minutes have run their course, making the track seemed padded. "You Know You're A Man" has a throbbing beat, and a stand-out slide solo.

"Bat Chain Puller" stands far above the rest of the material here. Van Vliet wrote this sitting in his Volvo with John French behind Frank Zappa's studio, using the Volvo's windshield wipers as his rhythmic base. French had transcribed Van Vliet's parts on a matchbook. The drums do indeed evoke windshield wipers. Over this basic rhythm, twin guitars play shifting lines in eccentric harmony; at times Van Vliet's harmonica joins in with them. A burbling synthesizer part dives through the music like a whale sounding. The technique of gradually slowing the slide guitar part over a steady rhythm, which was so effective on "Click Clack," is used here again. All in all, this is Van Vliet using his full palette, and succeeding beautifully.

"When I See Mommy I Feel Like A Mummy" has a hopping rhythm and chuffing trombone. Musically, the composition is closely related to "Tropical Hot Dog Night," but the guitar is much more raw-sounding. The lyric is slight, but the music holds our interest.

"Owed T'Alex" has more Neo-New Orleans second-line drumming and a slow drag bass riff. A chiming guitar rides over the top and Fowler's trombone sways in the mid-range. A wonderfully dense track, with a sound that suggests *noir* but doesn't go too far up that alley. Van Vliet recites rather than sings the words here; he scats and plays unamplified harmonica. After "Bat Chain Puller," this is the most successful track.

The instrumental "Suction Prints" (another of the recycled tunes, dating from the same period as "Ice Rose") is the most frantic track here. This is a rhythmically regularized take on *Trout Mask*-period music—though not *too* regularized. Fowler is at his most effective here, and the guitars are sharp-edged and relentless, and the active bass line for once suits the sound of the synthesizer bass. Van Vliet blows soprano sax in his familiar finger-waggling style. The album ends with "Apes-Ma," a poem about an aging ape in a zoo. Van Vliet recites this gently, but insistently, trying to get the ape's attention; we are only eavesdropping on their exchange. This is a nice, personal-feeling moment, and with this moment the album ends.

With *Shiny Beast*, Van Vliet's Captain Beefheart career slowly began to regain its momentum. The follow-up album would be seen as a return to his classic form, even as the Captain Beefheart part of Van Vliet was steadily dwindling away.

John French made a final encore appearance for the recording of the next album, *Doc at the Radar Station*, released in 1980. Significantly, French plays guitar and marimba more than drums. But he again left before the tour to support the album, and Jeff Morris Tepper held auditions for a new second guitarist. This slot was filled by Richard Snyder. Snyder thought of himself as primarily a bass player, and believed himself more likely to be hired as a roadie than guitarist. The 22-year-old Snyder had been working out parts from *Trout Mask Replica* and *Lick My Decals Off, Baby* since his early teen years. He passed the audition, and played with the Magic Band on the *Doc at the Radar Station* tour, then moved to bass for the recording of *Ice Cream for Crow,* when Gary Lucas joined on guitar. Snyder was such an avid fan that he was willing to accept the nickname Van Vliet wanted to bestow on him—"Midnight Hat Size" Snyder—and even let Van Vliet dictate his haircut and stage clothes, where the others in the band insisted on keeping their own names and making their own personal decisions. This diminution of Van Vliet's reach is reflected in the slightly cramped feel of the music here.

Van Vliet may or may not have been aware that the rhythms of the opening guitar part on "Hot Head" are nearly identical to the opening of the Marcels' doo-wop classic "Pretty Little Angel Eyes." But there's nothing old-fashioned about the song. Robert Williams does a fine impression of the "Drumbo" drum-style. The rhythm rows like a steel galley slave. This is a hard-chugging, call and response return to Van Vliet's heavy-Americana style: "She's a hobo wire-toaster," refers to the loops hobos used to make out of old coat hangers so they could make toast over an open fire.

"Ashtray Heart" starts and stops, the scrubbing sounds of the guitars thick over French's nimble, thumping drums. The lyrics include some of Van Vliet's most quotable fragments. Many of the words turn on the similarity of the language used for dealing with cigarettes and with love: "crush me out," "brush me off." The phrase "open up another case of the punks" was taken by a number of reviewers at the time to refer to the "punk rock" movement, many bands of which claimed they continued on paths opened up by Captain Beefheart and the Magic Band. But, in context, the words more likely refer to other senses of the word: as in "feeling punky," for feeling sick, or "punk out," meaning to be overcome with fear.

"A Carrot Is As Close As a Rabbit Gets To a Diamond" is a lovely instrumental duet of guitar and electric keyboard. Its primary motif is a 4-note major scale lick that is reminiscent of "Peon." The intervals here are much smaller, however, and the piece as a whole is less chordal, more pointillistic. "Run Paint Run Run" is thin, the music an up/down see-saw, the lyrics not progressing far beyond the title, the vocals an unmodulated shout. The middle section includes a trombone part reminiscent of "Long Neck Bottles," but this is almost the only point of interest here.

"Sue Egypt" features one of Van Vliet's most unusual accompaniments. A single slide guitar plays a dirty-sounding chord pattern, over which swoops a melody on the mellotron. Van Vliet said this instrument had for him a merthiolate sound, and that is very much present here. At times the guitar drops out and the merthiolate continues unaccompanied. There are no bass or drums on the track.

"Brickbats" is known to date from the original *Bat Chain Puller*, but is a very 1969 - 70 sounding composition in how the guitars wander and clash. Van Vliet's astringent alto saxophone playing is down in the mix further than usual, however. He sings full-throat, deliberately trying to force the edges of his voice to fray for effect. But here, as is true of all the vocals on the album, some of the resonance is missing from Van Vliet's voice. In its stead there is a hoarse cloudiness, a new hollowness in the lower range, making his voice a less powerful instrument than just two years before.

"Dirty Blue Gene" starts out at top speed, then stops and becomes a frantic badminton game with the rhythm and riffs flying from one instrument to another every couple beats. The track never resigns itself to any groove, but continues as a series of sudden changes in tempo and texture. The pieces are filled with all the jagged beauty of Van Vliet's music at its best.

The music for "Best Batch Yet" is ominous, heavy as hot steel in a rolling mill. The dissonance of the guitars gives way at times to happy-sounding, thickly noted ensemble riffs, like a western swing 45 that's been broken and glued together all wrong. The lyrics tell of the creation of beautiful pearls, done "from the inside"; a parable of creativity. "Telephone" is a throw-away song. Van Vliet sings in a high strangled voice, cursing the instrument he calls a "plastic-horned devil" for the way an old-style receiver looks when set upside down in its cradle. "Flavor Bud Living," the solo by Gary Lucas, is antic, more fragmented than such pieces as "Peon" and "A Carrot," but its Asian-tinged overtones float nicely above the pounding-nails attack Lucas uses (per Van Vliet's instructions).

French plays both bass and drums on "Sheriff of Hong Kong," and this makes a magical difference. The track has a density that none of the others even approach. Despite the excellence of many of the compositions on the album, this is the only track recorded after 1972 to equal the gripping strength of performances such as "Doctor Dark" and "Click Clack." This song is colored by Van Vliet's enthusiasm for Chinese music. On the tour, a recording of Chinese opera was played as intermission music before the band came on. On this song, Van Vliet plays a pair of gongs (considered "male" and "female") such are used for Chinese opera. The force with which he plays them. however, make them sound like the ricochets of shells bouncing off his hull. This song includes Van Vliet's only lyrics in Chinese: "er-hu," he sings, and "zing-hu." These are the names of Chinese violins. These names and the genders of the gongs may in fact have been the inspiration for the lyrics: they tell of a man and woman struggling for dominance, and whoever is temporarily dominant is "the Sheriff of Hong Kong," all of which could be the story of the two instruments sounding one after the other, each tone dominating in turn.

"Making Love to a Vampire With a Monkey On My Knee" is another poem-and-music track. A cartoon steam engine-sound created by a tootling synthesizer and drums powers the opening section of the music. A series of dramatic-cue sound sculptures make up the middle, and the steam engine returns before the track abruptly ends—and with it, the album.

The tour for *Doc At the Radar Station* featured Van Vliet playing the small Chinese opera gongs, and substituting a new sign-off gag for his "More" whistling. With all the publicity being given "New Wave" rock and roll bands, Van Vliet would produce a firefighter's hat and say, "Keep up the new wave. That's what the hat is for."

Van Vliet's physical movements on this tour were noticeably stiff and restricted-looking. He moved like a man just recovering from a major series of muscle pulls: gingerly, disjointedly, turning slowly from the waist, his feet for the most part anchored. His arms seemed to have a shadow of palsy on them as he raised them.

The band's November appearance on *Saturday Night Live* was in support of an album which was virtually impossible to find. Only weeks after *Doc at the Radar Station* was released, the distribution contract between Virgin, based in the United Kingdom, and U.S. Atlantic Records ended. And so Van Vliet's best album since *The Spotlight Kid* eight years before suddenly vanished.

But circumstances weren't all working against Van Vliet. It was in this same period, as Van Vliet was struggling to rebuild his career despite the undependability of the record companies and while Zappa was too busy with his own battles to be willing to help, that he connected with a young guitarist named Gary Lucas. Lucas was to have an enormous part to play in what was to come for Van Vliet. He had been acquainted with Van Vliet for a few years by this time. While music director for a radio station at Yale, he had interviewed Van Vliet over the phone. Like Tepper, Lucas was at first reluctant to even tell Van Vliet that he played guitar, not believing he was good enough to play Magic Band music. But he eventually auditioned. Van Vliet said he wanted to use Lucas, but had a band at that time. When he was forming the original *Bat Chain Puller* band, Lucas was travelling out of the country. When Van Vliet was preparing to record *Doc at the Radar Station* Lucas was once again available, and was asked to learn "Flavor Bud Living." The composition had already been taped, by John French on guitar. But Van Vliet felt that French played the piece "like church music," and wanted Lucas to up the attack, which he did.

Lucas and his first wife also became Van Vliet's managers for a time. They placed the band on *Saturday Night Live,* and Van Vliet solo on the David Letterman show. In the end, it was Lucas who was finally able to give Van Vliet what he had wanted for years—a way out of being Captain Beefheart.

But before he made good his escape, Van Vliet recorded one final album. After the collapse of Virgin's distribution deal, Lucas deciphered the contractual tangle and discovered that Van Vliet was now signed to Epic records. So it was that this label was able to release *Ice Cream for Crow* in 1982. For this album Lucas became a Magic Band member. But in addition to playing guitar, Lucas still handled business details. It was he who asked Warner to check their vaults for finished music from earlier periods, and it was Lucas who finally went nose-to-nose with Zappa over the original *Bat Chain Puller* material.

This came about because Van Vliet was having difficulty finishing *Ice Cream for Crow.* He was, for all practical purposes, no longer writing music. This difficulty had also figured in part in the recording of *Doc at the Radar Station.* Of the twenty-four tracks on the last two albums, nine are known to date from 1972 or before, and another four date from 1976.[5] Which is not to say that the last two albums are in any way inferior. They are, on the contrary, among the best Van Vliet recorded. They are both vastly superior to the shaky *Shiny Beast* (which also included older compositions). They stand above all but the triumvirate of *Trout Mask, Lick My Decals Off* and *Spotlight Kid*—and some would rank them just below *Trout Mask.*

Van Vliet hoped to finish *Ice Cream for Crow* by including some finished tracks from the original Zappa-produced *Bat*

Chain Puller. So Lucas called Zappa's manager. Zappa initially agreed, but then his manager stopped taking Lucas' calls. So Lucas took the direct approach: he and Van Vliet drove to where Zappa was rehearsing on a soundstage at Francis Ford Coppola's Zeotrope studio. Zappa was onstage with a fifteen-piece band, and the audience included a number of ex-Mothers, all hoping once again to link up with Zappa. In front of so many current and former sidemen he could not allow anyone to get the idea that he could be wheedled financially. Gary Lucas has described the scene:

> From the corner of his eye, Frank saw Don and he kind of whirled around to confront him. Don said, "Frank, you know what we want, don't you" in an authoritative voice. Frank said in a hostile voice, "No Don, what *do* you want?" I was like, "Oh, man . . . I thought these guys were childhood friends." Don just said, "Gary?" and I went into my schpiel. . . . [Frank said] "I changed my mind. Unless you buy all the master back from me, it's not worth it for me to split up the set. It won't be worth that much out there in Beefheart land." I was thinking, "What a disrespectful thing to say, 'Beefheart-land.' He looks at it like a freak show." I said, "Look, you promised us those tracks. . . ." Frank wouldn't look me in the eye. . . . Meanwhile Don is chanting the lyrics to "There Ain't No Santa Claus Onthe Evening Stage," which is a song about, among other things, show business.[6]

In the end, Zappa did not let Van Vliet have his music. And as it turned out, this was to be the last meeting of the former friends. Lucas was discouraged by Zappa's refusal, but Van Vliet remained positive. He congratulated Lucas for standing up to Zappa for him—"That's the best thing any manager ever did for me"—and that night went into the studio and wrote music for "Skeleton Makes Good." "He took a hit of pot," according to

Lucas, "which is something I didn't see him do too much, and he just came up with all the music. . . ."

Problems remained, however. According to "Midnight Hatsize Snyder," the band, which comprised Lucas and Jeff Morris Tepper on guitars, Snyder on bass, Cliff R. Martinez on drums and Eric Drew Feldman on keyboards, had only a short time to rehearse together and there was insufficient time for the band to find its chemistry as a unit. And even after fifteen years of working with relatively more linear-minded musicians, Van Vliet still chose to—and let this be differentiated from being "unable" in any sense other than being unable to betray his own basic orientation—instruct the musicians in the same opaquely metaphorical way. Drummer Cliff Martinez was instructed to play as if he were "juggling a plate full of B.B.'s."

The album was finally finished by rerecording some of the compositions from the original *Bat Chain Puller*. "The Thousand and Tenth Day of the Human Totem Pole," for example; French recalls transcribing this in Van Vliet's trailer in 1975, and it was recorded the next year. The original version remains unreleased.

Jeff Morris Tepper had by this time been playing with Van Vliet for seven years. He told an interviewer that over that space of time the music had become

> even more abstract and broken up. His singing is less
> melodic—there's more talking or yelling—and the
> music has become more rhythmically fragmented. . .
> I think the music feels less oriented.[7]

The cover photo of Van Vliet was shot by Anton Corbijn, who was later to make the short film *Some Yo-yo Stuff*. The photo was in black and white to harmonize with the image of black crows and white ice cream that inspired the lyrics of the title song. It was while taking Van Vliet's photo that Corbijn first saw Joshua trees, which later became the center of photos he shot of the band U2, as well as the title of one of their albums.

The title track here is a tight, John Lee Hooker-style open tuning boogie. The lyrics pivot around a pair of black and white opposites—ice cream and crow, day and night—but are no more restricted to these images than any of Van Vliet's free-form poem-songs. Musically and structurally, this is the most straight forward composition on the album, and was its video single. The only cacophonous moments in the music are at the end where Van Vliet has overdubbed himself playing harmonica, and the two clash violently.

Lyrically, as the title clearly suggests, "The Host the Ghost the Most Holy-O" is Van Vliet's take on a spiritual. This is not a song as such, but a poem, recited over music which recalls *Trout Mask Replica*. The parts here are more shapely, however, as is the overall structure. A clanging guitar chord and unexpected off-accent cymbal mark off the cycles of the main riffs, while the other repeating section features a simple, descending guitar line which calls the background singers to their part. This is only one of several compositions here which present poems recited against *Trout Mask* style music. "Hey Garland, I Dig Your Tweed Coat" is a full dose of Van Vliet's piano composition music. The words were in fact printed in *Rolling Stone* in 1970, so it seems likely the music dates from that period as well. The way Van Vliet's voice is mixed miles in front of the band rather than even with it is the only thing which differentiates this from the *Trout Mask* tracks. Almost exactly the same things can be said of "Cardboard Cutout Sundown," except that the music is more fragmentary than either of the two above. This Neo-*Trout Mask* group also includes "Ink Mathematics," which includes a vocal closer to singing than the clear recitations of the other tracks, though at times Van Vliet has to stop and carefully enunciate the tongue-twister tangles of the poem.

"Semi-Multicoloured Caucasian" is an instrumental played by the full band. Despite the oddly syncopated drum part (much like those which were to figure in the music of such "acid jazz"-tinged players as Steve Coleman ten years later), this is nearly a march. The guitar parts are fairly melodic, and the full-stops in the music are more likely intended to coax smiles than to deliberately short-circuit a listener's enjoyment of the complex, pleasing rhythms. "Evening Bell" is a two-minute guitar instrumental, played by Lucas. The lines are twitchier than usual, and no clear melodic ideas emerge. The music flirts with a walking-bass line in places, but always veers off.

"The Past Sure is Tense" resurrects the music from 1972's "Little Scratch," a song recorded for but not included on the *Clear Spot* album. The words here are language-centered and playful—based on a series of dumb-sounding puns that Van Vliet's dead-pan delivery almost slip past us—and much more fun than the penniless playboy verses of 1972. One shortfall is that the sections of "Little Scratch" music which included a rhythmically tricky unison guitar and harmonica line are absent here. This track includes, instead, some of Van Vliet's wheeziest and weakest harmonica playing.

The music to "The Witch Doctor Life" creates an easy-going yarn-spinning air, like a laconic 6/8. Some deliberate guitar-string squeaks and marimba lines add a playful skipping feel in places. This is the most beautiful music on the album. "'81 Poop Hatch" is a poem, recited in a very scratchy voice, without musical accompaniment.

"The Thousandth and Tenth Day of the Human Totem Pole" is Van Vliet's most successful ecological metaphor.[8] The pole is a stack of people, all standing on one another shoulders, all having to maintain their balance together, all affected by the fallout from those above them on the pole ("It hasn't rained or manured in over an hour"). The pole, Van Vliet also observes, is taking on "a reddish-brown cast," as the races intermingle. The music here, which was composed for the original 1976 *Bat Chain Puller*, is dense and warm, and proceeds by way of a series of wonderfully unpredictable rhythm changes, and open spaces. Toward the end, Van Vliet has recorded himself playing both soprano saxophone and "prop horn" (which sounds like a musette), and the reeds fill in these spaces between the other instruments like mortar between bricks. This is as original and dynamic a piece of music as any Van Vliet ever composed. It is certainly not incidental that this was assembled with John French's help.

The music for "Skeleton Makes Good," as noted above, was composed during the sessions for the album. The track is so dense that in many places its rhythms cannot readily be sorted out. Each piece is, again as is the rule with most of Van Vliet's Neo-*Trout Mask* compositions of the 1980s, more melodic and more similar in length than those of his earlier period. This is demanding in the way much of the 1969 - 70 music is demanding, but lacks the feel of an overall shape, the touch of the sculptor's hand, that marks the best of Van Vliet's work. Nonetheless, it shows that when he summoned himself to make the effort, Van Vliet could still assemble the kind of music which marked his most ecological period, and without the totalitarian elements. But, as Lucas' account makes clear, it was a great effort for Van Vliet to do this. So great was the effort, that "Skeleton Makes Good" marks the last time he would force himself to make it.

After *Ice Cream for Crow* was released, Van Vliet declared himself uninterested in appearing before an audience:

> . . . I'm there doing what I do and it has nothing to do with an audience. I'm not enough of an exhibitionist or a voyeur to enjoy audiences and they're actually more a distraction than anything.[9]

He chose not to tour, going out into the desert to make a video for "Ice Cream for Crow" as a substitute. MTV declined to show this, but Gary Lucas managed to get Van Vliet onto *Late Night with David Letterman*, where the first minute of the video was aired.

Morris Tepper's recollection is that Van Vliet couldn't get a offer for a record contract except from small independent labels, and so gave up and chose to concentrate on his art. But Gary Lucas recalls that Van Vliet had a contract for a follow-up to *Ice Cream for Crow*, but that he simply did not want to do another record.

Having to resort to recording old music, playing songs he had set aside years before, Van Vliet couldn't have felt the same about what he was doing as he had in the past. It would have been not quite a question of self-impersonation, but it must have had some of the feeling of having prematurely slipped out some back door of creativity and onto the Oldies Circuit. Under the circumstances, it was inevitable that Van Vliet would choose to shut down the Captain Beefheart Players at some point, to set free all the musicians—himself included.

Van Vliet never made a formal announcement of his retirement from music, but this was in effect what he did. The video (shot by the cinematographer who had done *The Texas Chainsaw Massacre*) was taped on August 7. Unbeknownst to any except perhaps Van Vliet himself, and excepting only a few interviews, this day was to be "Captain Beefheart's" last day on the job.

Exuding the Ground He Walks On

When the man who had been Captain Beefheart for more than seventeen years walked away from that name, he remained Don Van Vliet. He didn't drop his adopted name and go back to being Don Vliet. The name Captain Beefheart had been both an alias and a conjuring. Through it, Van Vliet summoned up and channeled those parts of his makeup which could create music. In just this same way the "Van," which had been added by way of tribute to Vincent Van Gogh, marked the channel through which the parts of his makeup which could produce visual art could make their way into the world.

But if this addition was meant as pointer referring to the example of the Dutch painter, it also (conveniently for purposes of looking at his life, though this certainly was not intended by Van Vliet) points toward both a French pun, and a related literary work. By inserting "Van" into his name, Van Vliet gave himself a double V in his initials. In French "double-v" is the name of the letter "W," ("double-u," in English). As "vie" is French for "life," a pun emerges: "W ['double V'] marks a double life." The late Georges Perec used this pun in the title of his book *W or the Memory of Childhood*, which is both autobiography and fiction (and which reminds us how close each is to the other). The text is made up of two alternating stories, of which Perec wrote,

> [You] might almost believe they have nothing in common, but they are in fact inextricably bound up with each other . . . only their coming together, the

distant light they cast on each other, [can] make apparent what is never quite said in [either], but said only in their fragile overlapping.[1]

Van Vliet's double V's are reminders of his double life and arts—musician and visual artist—and their overlapping. Where they overlap is in Van Vliet's environmental (again, in the larger sense of the word) relation to aspects of the world around him, and how they shaped both his arts.

While cautioning that Van Gogh is only "one drop of water which makes up the ocean" of what he feels about art, Van Vliet goes on to say,

> I think Van Gogh almost improved the natural sunshine. He got into alchemy, he got into feeling his feet on the ground and feeling the colours up from the ground and the metals and the salts and everything to such a degree that he was able to exude the ground he walked on into canvas, into paint—which I think is what an artist can do and should do.[2]

Which tells us very little about what the historical Van Gogh may have thought, but much about Van Vliet and what he wants to do with his painting—exude the ground he walks on, express the ways in which he feels about his contacts with the world. And this is what he has been doing since taking up art again in the mid-1960s, after a ten year hiatus.

Few sightings of the Van Vliet from 1965 on are without mention of his ever-present sketch books. He is said to draw almost constantly, compulsively. It seems clear that this drawing helps him think, helps him maintain contact with his own ground for feeling, the same reason guitar players so often hold tight to their guitars while being interviewed. Van Vliet has made thousands of such sketches over the years, but his gallery states that Van Vliet never sells these, and few have been reproduced.[3] We enthusiasts of these drawings find ourselves virtually standing on our heads to view the page he is working on in a photo on the inner sleeve of *Shiny Beast* ("It's a cat!"), or tacking up the finished drawing on the other side of that sleeve, or the beautiful intermingled-group portrait included inside *Doc at the Radar Station*, or clipping the piece of the old *Rolling Stone* magazine page which reprinted a letter from a California man who chanced on an early (pre-1970), undated but signed Van Vliet drawing—resembling an ant wearing a tailored suit—which he purchased at a Lancaster garage sale for seven cents.

All these images, and similar drawings reproduced in 1970 and in 1976, allow us to be fairly certain that Van Vliet has never been a traditional realist in his art. Still, it must be said, he has created a number of "near-realist" works, nearly all of which might be categorized as belong to his "rock and roll portfolio." These paintings and drawings convey, with great insight and wit, the kind of effects and information to which observant realism is so well suited. Reproduced on the back of the 1972 album *The Spotlight Kid,* for example, are portraits Van Vliet did of four members of the band. (When the album was reissued on CD, several other line drawings done in 1971 and '72 were also reproduced, but these are little more than doodles.) Van Vliet has characterized Mark Boston ("Rockette Morton") as the least rigid member of the classic Magic Band and the portrait reflects this. The image here refuses to "set up" with any finality, remaining fluidly expressionistic, even while being undeniably realistic. Open rectangles of red and two blue chevrons refer to a body, above which some briskly brushed black, which widens to a loose broom at the right edge, comprise both a suggestion of Boston's hair and face as well as some swift movement. One eye appears clearly, but the other and the nose and mouth and jawline are less resolved. A red wing at Boston's temple supports the overall suggestion of speed and fluidity.

The portrait of Art Tripp ("Ed Marimba") is done with fauvist-extreme color displacements—Tripp's hair, face and arms are rendered in dark grape colors, purples and wines, with a flat look that gives back little of the light it absorbs. His eyes are piercing, almost demonic, and a deep bottle green. The portrait as a whole depicts a sober and cerebral individual.

The last of the painted portraits is that of Bill Harkleroad ("Zoot Horn Rollo"). This seems at first glance to be entirely concerned with the guitarist's physical size (Harkleroad stands well above six feet). His legs begin at the bottom edge of the paper and rise up three-fourths of its height; his arms appear to hang down to his knees; his long jaw extends below his shoulders. This seems the least inspired of the portraits here, a knock-off, until we consider the overall air of the figure Van Vliet has painted. He is not active in the way the two portraits above are active. He is inert, slack, smiling blankly; his slightly stooped posture is that of a puppet waiting to be moved. If, as Harkleroad himself suggests, Van Vliet chose his classic Magic Band members both for their musical abilities and for the kind of character which would allow them to be dominated by his musical vision, then this painting is a portrait of the Bill Harkleroad that Van Vliet thought he saw at the moment of selecting him for the band.

The likeness of Elliot Ingber ("Winged Eel Fingerling") is not a painting, but an ink drawing on a lined page torn from a notebook. Between the stalagmites of his hair and the stalactites of his moustache and beard, there is only the outline of his forehead and nose, and a single seed-like eye. The leanness of the portrait suggests an attempt at elegant simplicity, but it also suggests what is known of Ingber's musical character. He was always uncomfortable with the music because it was not the conventional blues rock he favored. He left the band not long after joining, and thereafter came and went time and again. The straight-line look of the portrait, then, mirrors the conventionality of the musician; the ephemerality of the medium suggests Van Vliet hurrying to catch the guitarist's likeness before he was gone.

The drawings and caricatures of Zappa (which have never been exhibited or reproduced) Van Vliet did on stage during the *Bongo Fury* tour need to be considered in the light of Van Vliet's attitude toward his art. In the BBC documentary he can be seen answering questions about a large black and white painting in front of which he is standing. (This appears to be 1972, as he is wearing his *Spotlight Kid* suit.) He is subdued and stiff, speaking quietly, if no more seriously than usual. He is clearly uncomfortable with being asked for explanations as to why he paints. He seems to involuntarily shrug toward the painting more than once, as if trying to shift attention from him to it—in some ways the opposite of his stance toward his music. In a later clip in the same documentary, he works on a drawing in a sketch pad while talking with an interviewer. When the drawing is finished, he turns it toward the camera. But it is more interesting to watch Van Vliet himself when this is done: he grows still, he seems to be trying to blend in with the tree behind him as he shows the drawing. If his art is indeed a way of "turning himself inside out," then he naturally has more of himself exposed in his art. He clearly is more shy about it than about his music, which comes from elsewhere in his physical being. His drawings of Zappa, and his exhibiting them to their subject *was* a kind of "gotcha," though perhaps not the aggressive kind Black took it to be.

To have to go to Zappa must have been an embarrassing act; to be saved by the kind of musical/industrial complex mind that he had so often ridiculed must have been a coming down for him. His drawing on stage would have been a way of keeping an important part of himself whole, of putting a little dignity-by-distance between him and this come down. Showing the works to Zappa would have been a way of declaring that, whatever his external circumstances, inside himself he had not lost his personal bearings. Whether or not Zappa understood that Van Vliet was using his art as a shield and a comfortable familiar is impossible to say. Some who saw the drawings have said they are excellent, and Van Vliet would have been striving to make them so, for his own sake, and not—as some have understood it—exclusively in the interest of needling his temporary leader.

Van Vliet had long since come to feel that Zappa was one of the people who "breathe in and don't breathe out"; takers who give back little to the people around them, or to their world. (For Van Vliet, this was the explanation for Zappa's striving toward being a truly innovative musician and failing to do so.[4]) And doing and showing the drawings to Zappa while on stage would have been a way of showing that Van Vliet could still do both.

This respiratory philosophy is clearly visible in the best of Van Vliet's art. And this is why the realistic drawings and paintings ("realistic" here meaning they refer to actual people, and are concerned with their subjects' character), as insightful and at times brilliant as they may be, must be seen as among the least interesting (because least formed by his own inner being) of his works.

Again, this is true because of those elements Van Vliet's music and his art at its best have in common, elements which can quite rightly be thought of as having the kind of "fragile overlapping" Perec sought, elements of which the rock and roll drawings show us almost nothing. Rather, this overlapping lies in how the ecological impulse in Van Vliet, the same impulse which channeled in very different ways led to his acting as a "Mansonesque" band leader, enters and shapes the art he creates when he thinks on a larger scale than that of realistic or expressionist portraits.

As he showed in his creation of an extended physical system during the *Trout Mask* period, Van Vliet's ecological orientation is more basic to his character and his creative impulses than can be accounted for by any conventional "love the earth"-style definition of the word. And while an alliance with such movements has been part of the rhetoric he has employed, he has consistently sought to extend this narrow definition. In 1972, for example, he told a Dutch interviewer,

> I want to help the animals and the people. All I can do to help the people is to try and raise the level of art. Actually, when the level of art is raised it helps everyone, so the sea and the animals, too. [By the word] "art" I mean real art: without words, without a real meaning, only feeling.[5]

If Van Vliet is correct, the ecological benefits of his art increased steadily after a period in the late 1960s when he was experimenting with a number of techniques, with mixed success.

The first work by Van Vliet made widely available was the cover of *Strictly Personal* in 1968. This is atypical in that here Van Vliet experiments with collage, the only such example he has shown the world. For the cover, Van Vliet altered (or directed to be altered; an art director is credited) some foreign postage stamps, replacing the original center images with photos of the band—he becomes a Costa Rican stamp, while John French is surrounded by Cyrillic letters. The front and back of the sleeve reproduce a large manila envelope, complete with string clasp at the flap. The address and the return address are in Van Vliet's spiky hand, with fanciful street, city and state names (including as part of the address "5000 mg.", which certainly helped spread the idea that this was drug inspired music), and "Strictly Personal," "Fourth Class Mail," and "Photographs Do Not Bend" are stamped on it in red. Van Vliet's thumbprint appears on the back in blue, as befits the record label name: Blue Thumb. There are indeed photographs inside this mock envelope, but they are the opposite of the revealing photos the cover is meant to suggest: the band is not uncovered, but covered so completely, in long coats, masks and bizarre headgear, that they are totally unrecognizable. The satirical humor causes us to smile, but little more. The cover is more of its time, the heyday of Pop Art, than it is of Van Vliet as an artist.

But Van Vliet is telling us something important with this cover, as well. His music (and his art) may be strictly personal, but that does not mean that they will be revealing; he will dress up his personal expressions in any costume, use any prop, as he sees fit. He means what he says when he uses the word "strictly."

The year before he designed the cover for *Strictly Personal*, Van Vliet did a painting titled *Ghost Red Wire*. This is a two-foot-square study in yellow gold and dark brick red. The title comes from the way the paint is applied, in wire-thin dribbles that look as if the oil paint had been poured onto the primed masonite through the eye of a swiftly moving needle. In the center is a brushed white burst that gives the title its first word. The red suggests both manmade and natural strands: jellyfish, old style radio antennas, topographical maps. The yellow forms

150

a pasta-thin fringe across the top. This is a painting by an artist dipping into the Jackson Pollock technique manual to see if there is anything there of use to him. This is not a lead Van Vliet chose to follow.

In this same period, Van Vliet was also doing paintings on old window shades. For one such untitled painting from 1967 (SU 47), the blind is used inverted, so that the pull-cord appears at the top of the painting, jaunty as a tassel on a fez. This is primarily painted in black, an irregular oval with the cracked-lake-bed look of industrial enamel spilled on heavily and allowed to dry unthinned. A circle above this brings the painting up to the edge of being a figure, without forcing it over. Sweeping black and blue lines suggest a hat in the same uninsistent way. A gold swath, like a leg bent at the knee, slides behind the circle, adding depth, and a deep blue slope at the bottom (which shows the traces of something beneath the shade when this was applied) adds a tipped-back, penguin-poise life. This is a sad sack dressed as a dandy, out for an Uncle Wiggly-style escapade. The painting as a whole is light, delightful.

Three other paintings (all from 1969) on shades are painted with the shade right side up, the tassel at the bottom. More clearly than the first, these three show that the shades were not brought straight from the shelf to studio. These were once working shades; all show signs of fading. The shades for the 1969 paintings once were a light robin's egg blue; the top quarter remains blue, a convenient sky. The remainder of each of these shades shows degrees of fading, ending in a grubby tan where they spent years at standard daytime three-quarters retracted. One of these three (also untitled [SU 48]) is also primarily black. The wide, blocky lines are almost calligraphic, like Chinese characters or the Hebrew alphabet. The black here was applied and then run through, apparently, with some sort of (probably metal) gear. The result is areas dark as a wet crow, contrasting with black and white (and to a small degree orange and white) barberpole streamers. A small orange circle buttons the right side of the painting to the left. A very active painting, this could be a busy birdfeeder seen against harsh light.

The other two shade paintings are more colorful, and show signs that Van Vliet recognized the similarity of his window shade works to Chinese scroll paintings. Yet another "Untitled" (SU 49a) even includes traditional Asian elements: a bamboo stalk runs up the left side, and a red chrysanthemum appears in the center—with a yellow face with sharp black eyes half-hidden behind it. Stabs of the same red nestle under the crook of the bamboo stalk like floating petals, and a small knobbed form (a walking stick?) stands between. Many "Dharma Bums" travelled up and down California in the late 1960s; this painting may be in part a nod to them in their passing.

The last of these shade paintings is titled *When She Dropped The Flower*.[6] The "she" of the title is an unearthly-looking creature (although, alternately, it may be very earthly indeed: she shares some of the look of a ladybug) with a quietly beautiful dark green, blue-haloed head, and eyes as black and round as in any sentimental puppy portrait. Her four or five long tapering legs reach out toward a clover-green flower at the lower right. She still carries several personal treasures. The fuzzy line marking the soiled lowest quarter of the blind stands in for a horizon, and the pale blue at the top is the sky. Van Vliet has painted this singular being's portrait gently, almost lovingly.

When She Dropped the Flower has much in common with the painting on the back of *Lick My decals Off, Baby* from 1970. But there is a crucial difference, one that marks this latter painting as the beginning of Van Vliet's mature art. This difference lies in how the shape in the former painting maintains the sovereignty of its personal boundaries, where that on the album cover playfully and lovingly opens and shares such boundaries. So it is with this latter painting that Van Vliet's deeper concerns come to the fore, that his personal ecological view of the world first makes itself known in his art. Here a domed shape appears to have a long tongue flickering out, reminding us of the title of the album. The two streamers that descend in kinked lines below it are like those in the "calligraphic" blind painting. The poem which shares the title of the album—and which is not the lyrics to the song—refer to a "bouncing ball" of beehives, wings, legs and many other things, a ball that may be the vitality of life itself. This poem also refers to a child this ball accompanies. The child sticks her tongue out at the sun and licks three decals. The shape in the painting—and this is what I mean when I refer to a surrender of boundaries—seems playful enough to be simultaneously ball *and* child. And this blurring of boundaries, this sharing of outlines and forms, will be a constant in Van Vliet's approach to art for years to come, a way of seeing he will abandon (or—and I will show that this is a real possibility—be driven away from) only after 1984.

Everywhere in the best of his art in this period, Van Vliet portrays humans and animals intermingling; not just sharing the same space, but sharing the same biological system, the same body. (This effect has more often been a part of his drawings than of his paintings; but this also changed after 1984. A 1994 visit to his gallery to view unpublished drawings only reinforced this opinion.) Animal and human forms merge: an animal's head might grow from a woman's side, as in the captivating drawing (dated 1976) which is reproduced on the inner sleeve of *Shiny Beast (Bat Chain Puller)*. This drawing combines normally discrete beings into a symbiotic whole. The foreground figure is for the most part a human female. She is sitting cross legged, and she has a beautiful, almost Egyptian-antiquity style profile, high breasts, smooth legs and a solid body with a suggestion of pubic hair. But growing out of her side is what appears to be another head, perhaps that of a catfish or other marine creature, and a suggestion of fins (?) under her raised right arm. There is nothing grotesque about the image, no more than a mermaid is grotesque. The beautiful face bears a serious expression as she gazes down at the other "self" she may be protecting. Behind her is a wonderfully expressive cat, with impossibly long legs borrowed from some much taller creature. It is flicking its tail and looking quite pleased with what it sees.

On the back of this same album is a red and black drawing on a paper bag. This too is some kind of composite being. While it may at first appear to be one person carrying another on its back (possibly a mother carrying a child, papoose style), the red lines which outline and connect the black conte crayon or chalk features unmistakably unite them as one. Chevrons in the middle of the figure may be ribs or gills. This may well be a mother and child after all—this kind of intermingling would not be an unlikely metaphor for such a relationship. Behind the double figure is what appears to be a dog, and another (which is so faint it may go unnoticed) in the hands of the front figure may be a bird. However many individuals there may be here, and whatever their species, this group is commingling quite happily.

This, too, is part of what I mean to suggest when I write that Van Vliet is an environmental artist—he knows all things are connected, that nothing is isolated. He knows that even a lone individual is accompanied by, immersed in, air and sound and light. And Van Vliet's paintings are full of intense, vibrant light.

This bright immersion is very apparent in the painting*Green Tom,* which is reproduced on the cover of *Shiny Beast (Bat Chain Puller).* This shows two partial-humanoid beings out for a walk, holding hands. One of these figures has a green head and appears to be dressed in traditionally male attire; the other has a pink head and is wearing a dress. Each has some sort of headdress or feather or plumage on their heads. These two figures may be husband and wife, artist and muse, or any other happy couple. Everywhere behind them is a golden glow; the entire painting glows, in fact. Colors which should not be complementary—a thin hot pink and a dark green—vibrate in an attractive (if admittedly alternative) harmony.

The deep glow and cake frosting density of this painting's ground serves to illustrate the unexpected way in which Van Vliet's ecological world view also shapes one of the most basic elements of his (or any other artist's) art: the depiction of space. This seems directly connected to Van Vliet's experience of the vibrant light of his home state.

Van Vliet shares this experience of the sun-soaked California light with others from his coast, San Francisco area painters Richard Diebenkorn and Wayne Thiebaud, to name only two. Both of these men also paint with a luscious surface, whether they are painting abstractly or figuratively. It is true that, unlike

Van Vliet, these Bay Area painters have painted landscapes, but these have most often been either slices of terrain chosen for their geometrical patterns, or vertical cityscapes so little foreshortened as to resemble tiered perspective; horizon lines are either very close to the top of the frame, or absent entirely. It is no accident that Van Vliet paints no great vistas, no open range, includes no perspectival depths in his work. In looking at Van Vliet's paintings, as varied as they may be, nearly every one of them exhibits depth but no horizon, no solid back walls. Even when a painting is set in an interior, the background is most often a deep glow of color which seems to begin at or not far behind the figures or shapes of the foreground and saturate the space behind to an indefinite distance. This is what the experience of living under-water must be like for a fish; or how we would see ourselves in the world if we were constantly aware of the air which surrounds and stretches away from us all in directions. So, even while the figures intermingle, share their boundaries with one another, they are part of a continuum of solids and liquids and vapors and light. This is one reason Van Vliet's open spaces are built up so thickly: for him, "emptiness," when it is in contact with life is never really empty.

This very painterly emptiness and indefinite space, shares an outline with other aspects of art which are ecological in the sense in which I am using the word. In her book *On Not Being Able to Paint*, British psychologist Marion Milner uses her attempts to learn to paint as a investigation of the psychology of the painting process. She writes about the fulfillment she felt in creating a painting with "incorrect" perspectival space: "It was as if one's mind could want to express the feelings that come from the sense of touch and muscular movement rather than from the sense of sight." This could easily describe Van Vliet's piano compositions bypassing his ear, and seems a good fit for his approach to painting as well. According to Milner, this painting by being attentive to sense of touch and muscular movement avoids the almost universal point-of-view of single point perspective, which she describes in terms such as "an observing eye... perched upon a sketching stool. . . . It seemed one might want some kind of relation to objects in which one was much more mixed up with them than that."[7] An ecological relation, in other words.

And this would not be limited to a new relation to objects, but, as pointed out above, to space as well. How a painter handles space, Milner writes, "also [has] to do with problems of being a separate body in a world of other bodies [and] with ideas of distance and separation and having and losing." Milner also speaks to the subject of outlines in a manner consistent with her other ideas. An insistence on clearly defined outlines, she writes, indicates "a fear of losing . . . the boundaries between the tangible realities of the external world and the imaginative realities of the inner world of feeling. . . ."[8] All this is apparent in Van Vliet, whose works, even when it is not clear what kinds of beings inhabit them, are clearly about relationships.

An example of this is an untitled painting from 1976 (SU 53). This depicts two "beings," whose forms are not limited to one known species. One may be a cat, while the other has something human about it, but could as easily be part-bird or even a mollusk freed from its shell, but both bodies are fluid or smoke as much as they are flesh. Whatever these are, they are certainly happy. In each case their mouths are smiling—though the larger (who appears to have a moustache) less so than the smaller. These are open, friendly beings, their bodies are white, bare-flesh pink, and light gray, all the colors we show when we are at our most unprotected. The background is a light adobe or beach sand color, but the figures fill nearly the whole of the small space (24 by 18 inches). They fit together in it like best friends or lovers, the arm and chin of the larger dovetailing with the face and legs of the smaller. This is a non-anthropocentric love song in oils.

Other more minor works formed by these same ecological impulses include a striking bumblebee-in-disarray abstraction reproduced on the cover of a 1982 issue of *Conjunctions* magazine, and three drawings inside. The drawings, two of which are dated 1980, are all spikier than those discussed above, but still exhibit the blending of forms and the primacy of the personalities of animals over the concerns of humans.

Like any other artist, Van Vliet has created works which fall short of what his best have to offer. One such paintings is a small "Untitled" (SU 54) from 1977. This is little more than a joke painting. We are looking straight down into a bloody ocean. Filling the right-most quarter of the painting is a white shark, as lifeless and stiff as a tongue depressor. The rest of the painting is of a dismembered, bloody body, probably a woman's. The film *Jaws* was released in 1975, and this painting seems a clear reference to the film's advertisement image. The painting is not a throw-away, however, because of the way the female figure is painted. The red and white and bruised-looking blue all sweep through one another to create a "face" which is almost featureless yet looms out toward the viewer, lifting up from the dark background. The body is smeared white with yellow and reddish-purple and blue slashes, the arms blur at the ends rather than form hands. The effect is of dismemberment without any horror. Except for the severity of most of its outline, this figure could have come from a Francis Bacon painting.

The painting on the cover of *Doc at the Radar Station*, from 1980, is a variation on the idea of the interconnectedness of all beings. This painting is a stark look at the distance that can grow between people. A woman and a man intensely look toward each other, but all the space between them—and even part of the space their expressions should occupy, are blotted out by wide black strokes. More of the man's tie shows than of his face. Still, and this is what is important to notice here, they are looking toward one another, they are trying.

The drawing reproduced on the inner sleeve of the album is a study of togetherness, done with beautiful simplicity. The drawing shows a group of three, two women and (probably) a man, accompanied by a simple animal shape. The woman in the center, who has the animal pressed to her, looks toward the woman on the right while the man behind her (and who also seems to merge with one or both of the woman) watches her hand. The figures are formed by simple black lines, but the women's faces and the man's hair are all painted in. Once again, this group portrait is formed by Van Vliet's insistence—and his experience—that all beings, whatever their form whatever their species, are at their best when they choose to intermingle, when they strive to become as one.

Not everyone who looks at and thinks about Van Vliet's art will agree with my judgement that Van Vliet's best works have been shaped by his ecological view of life. Others have lumped him in with either the abstract expressionists, or, more simply, with "primitive" or "outsider" artists. And it is true than Van Vliet has something in common with the kind of "primitive" artist that, for example, critic John Berger describes in his essay "The Primitive and the Professional." Berger offers a composite portrait of the self-taught, outsider artist, some of which Van Vliet fits and some he defies. First of all, these primitives (a term by which Berger intends no negative shadows) begin alone, learn their skills alone. This certainly fits the portrait Van Vliet offers of himself as a pre-school sculptor, and education *refusenik*.

Secondly, according to Berger, such painters don't learn the "pictorial grammar" of the tradition they paint in—which is to say that their work is noticeably clumsy in execution. If gauged against the standard of the tradition of realism, this would certainly apply to Van Vliet. (But he has never been interested in joining himself to the tail of any traditions, so it is impossible to say how much, if any, of this "clumsiness" is by choice.)

But it is Berger's comments on the social context in which primitive painters arise and work (Berger's Marxism informs his criticism) which raise the most interesting questions when we read them with Van Vliet in mind. Such a primitive keeps his distance from the fine art tradition, avoids museums, refuses instruction of any kind, all because

> he knows already that his own lived experience which is forcing him to make art has no place in that tradition. . . . He knows it because his whole experience is one of being excluded from the exercise of power in his society, and he realizes from the compulsion he now feels, that art too has a kind of

power. The will of primitives derives from faith in their own experience and a profound skepticism about society as they have found it. . . . [The] "clumsiness" of primitive art is the precondition of its eloquence. What it is saying could never be said with any ready-made skills. For what it is saying was never meant, according to the cultural class system, to be said.[9]

Questions about how extensive was his museum-going or any other fraternization with art history are, finally, no more than the question of "influence" in yet another form. That Van Vliet could be aware of artists such as Kline, Van Gogh, Mondrian, and more and yet could assert that he had learned only from himself finds support in a statement by a very different kind of painter, Edward Hopper:

In every artist's development the germ of the later work is always found in the earlier. The nucleus around which the artist's intellect builds his work is himself . . . and this changes little from birth to death. The only real influence I've ever had was myself.[10]

This has certainly been Van Vliet's ideal, one he lived for years. Yet, the evidence of the art itself suggests that this changed when he finally found a way to leave at least part of his "outsider" status behind. When Van Vliet entered the art world, I suggest, his personal ecological view, which shaped much of his art before this time, was either forgotten, or deliberately pushed aside. I would further suggest that the larger ecology of the world of galleries, international patrons and commercial valuations—the "cultural class system" which only allows certain art statement to be "said," as Berger puts it—took its place. In my opinion, that which Berger warns of proved true for Van Vliet. From 1984 on, his work—in its increasing fragmentation, its isolated elements, the almost complete change in how the paintings are organized—shows the effects of his joining this system and becoming subject to what it allows to be "said."

Julian Schnabel and Don Van Vliet (Cologne, 1985)

"I Fool Myself Gracefully"

While the *Doc at the Radar Station* band was touring and during the recording of *Ice Cream for Crow*, Van Vliet repeatedly told then-manager Gary Lucas that he wished he could give up music and devote his time to being a painter. He had been saying this for years, but either no one took him seriously or no one knew how to help. Lucas was more resourceful. Living in New York City, he knew people with connections to the art world establishment, and he set about trying to find Van Vliet an "in." Lucas couldn't have timed it better. In 1982 the economics of the art marketplace were almost ideal for Van Vliet's entry. It was in this year that the art world began enjoying a commercial boom the likes of which had never before been seen. An influx of new collectors caused a demand for new art and artists, with preference given to those with something shocking or eccentric about them. Such was the art world atmosphere at the time Van Vliet first breathed it in.

The specific "in" Lucas found was Julian Schnabel, one of the foremost painter-cum-celebrities of the 1980s. Lucas heard that Schnabel was a fan of the Captain Beefheart albums, and after seeing the art on the album covers, the more famous artist wanted to buy one of Van Vliet's paintings. Lucas was able to reach Schnabel by phone and arranged for he and Van Vliet to meet. Schnabel then used his considerable reputation to get Van Vliet a major gallery affiliation.

The two painters grew to be friends, as well. In his 1987 memoir *CVJ Nicknames of Maitre D's & Other Excerpts from Life* Schnabel discusses the work of several artists, most of them well-known (Barnett Newman, Clyfford Still), some of them lesser-knowns who have been friends. Schnabel does not discuss Van Vliet's work, but Van Vliet is included. A short chapter about Schnabel's encounters with other artists begins with a quote from Van Vliet, dated 1985: "Some I let drink their own tears, some I would not allow until they came to my studio."[1] There are only three photos of Schnabel in his book, one of which shows Schnabel, and old friend, and Don and Jan Van Vliet, all sitting around a patio table in Bridgehampton in 1984. The photo quality is very poor, but Van Vliet is recognizable by his hunched shoulders and his favorite hat of the 1980s. Jan is only an oval-faced blur with long dark hair.

Schnabel also accompanied Van Vliet to his first one-man show in Cologne in May, 1985. An interview with Van Vliet in a Dutch magazine provides this glimpse of Schnabel:

> [The interview is] interrupted by a loud American voice: "Don! Donnie!" The man in the mustard-coloured suit storms in. He's outraged he is taken for the manager of Van Vliet. "I'm his friend. I'm just another fucking character of the street." What is more, he turns out to be Julian Schnabel. . . . About Van Vliet he says, "I think he's terrific, his heart is so great, he's so moralistic, the quality of the headwork behind his art is so good and accurate. Technique? Technique isn't important."[2]

The translations from English to Dutch and back to English have clearly introduced some static ("of the street" is more likely "off the street," for instance), but Schnabel's points are clear enough. The reference to technique being unimportant may be true, but in the quote above it comes off as dismissive (or are we just ruffled by Van Vliet being referred to as "Donnie"?), and even contradictory to the assumption of intellectual decision that Schnabel asserts. Schnabel's statements would more closely fit the work of another Werner Gallery artist (and friend of Schnabel) A.R. Penck, whose stick figures are said to be in part organized by way of his knowledge of cybernetics.

The lack of technique which Schnabel endorses comes, for his part, from a conscious decision to reject such technique or "style" on the basis of its supposed dishonesty or insincerity. Schnabel's works mine kitsch art, include scribbled letters and deliberately anti-fine art elements. So, it is natural that Schnabel would think it a compliment to assert that the "headwork" (whatever words Schnabel actually used, he certainly meant something intellectual) behind Van Vliet's paintings is "good and accurate." Nothing Van Vliet has ever said about his work ("I try to . . . turn myself inside out on canvas, to freeze the moment so that the person seeing it can observe what I froze," is representative) implies such an intellectual intermediary between eye and hand. It is likely that Van Vliet would agree with the dismissal of the importance of technique, but none of his statements about his art suggest that he consciously "dumbs down" anything for effect. If his own opinion of his art technical skills is anything like that of his music compositional techniques, then he is more likely to be of the opinion that his technique is precisely what he needs to create what he wants to create. Van Vliet would likely recognize no lack of technique at all. Schnabel, while well-meaning, has here fallen into the error of applying one of his own decals to the work, something Van Vliet always struggled against as Captain Beefheart.

At the time he took up Van Vliet's cause, Schnabel was himself relatively new to the world of art renown. He had studied art for four years at the University of Houston, studied at the Whitney Museum, and travelled to France, Italy, Germany and Spain to study art and architecture. Four years after graduating from Houston, Schnabel had his first major one-man show. His experience along the path to artistic recognition and that taken by Van Vliet could hardly have been more different. And, not surprisingly, their very different experiences, as well as their decade difference in age have resulted in Schnabel and Van Vliet having very different philosophies of painting. Schnabel began his work as Pop art was fading, but he shares some of Pop's enthusiasm for appropriation. Art works are, inevitably, relics of past experience; nothing is new; "Everything has existed before." (Schnabel, who has done drawings on old maps, would certainly have appreciated that the painting on *Ice Cream for Crow* was done on an old window blind.) He also explicitly rejects the notion that art should be "self-expression." For Schnabel, there's "no achievement" in creating a graphic depiction of his personality on canvas. "Using used ideas," as he refers to his appropriations, is the direct opposite of the idea of creating the sort a specific, original signature which marks a work as uniquely belonging to a specific artist. The recycling of materials establishes, Schnabel feels, "an ethnographic level in the work." Schnabel wants to create a deliberately antiheroic art, whose tasks and acts are ordinary.[3]

Van Vliet, on the other hand, comes from the far side of the art philosophy divide, works very much in the consciously heroic spirit of the Abstract Expressionist in the 1950s. These artists felt the point of art is to present in some medium the deeper, subjective emotions and responses of the artist to the world as he experiences it—thus Van Vliet's, "I'm just trying to turn myself inside out." And, for all his seriousness about his art, his moments of artistic self-analysis are cut with touches of humor: "I do what I'm doing," he said just before being taken up by Schnabel and the Werner Gallery, "and I try to make myself believe that what I'm doing always is something completely new. So I fool myself gracefully. I think that that's art."[4]

And Van Vliet is already on record about appropriation, with the protests he has made about musicians playing blues or other kinds of music from the past—that it is "war-like," in that it is a kind of "shield." It would be unthinkable for Van Vliet to quote images from art other than his own.

Finally, Schnabel's use of the word "ethnographic" triggers something in our memory: it recalls Zappa's wish to record *Trout Mask Replica* as "anthropological" field recordings, as if Van

Vliet and his music were not really part of the civilized world.

None of this is meant as an attack on Schnabel, who certainly must have more thoughtful things to say that these few off the cuff remarks, and whose work is not so easily wrapped up as I have done here. But the conversation in Amsterdam serves to point out the difficulty of talking about Van Vliet's work in the context of the history of art or of the philosophy of art without reducing either the art or the man. While Van Vliet remained an outsider, a denizen of the alternative art universe of rock and roll, he was not subject to these kinds of judgements and pressures. Being totally overlooked by the established art world was an extra measure of freedom. His being absorbed through the cell walls of the art history organism clearly affected his art.

Van Vliet's first New York show was affiliated with the Michael Werner Galleries, but it was held at the "trendy" (as at least one article called it) Mary Boone Gallery, on West Broadway. Van Vliet showed eight paintings, with titles like "Eye Whine" and "Gum at the Bottom of the Grocery." When Ms. Boone was interviewed by the *New York Times* she was enthusiastic about the entire body of Van Vliet's work to that time, saying, "For the last 20 years, he has been doing figurative painting, with a very steady, consistent vocabulary of forms and images."[5] But Ms. Boone's opinion was not held by those who would come to direct Van Vliet's art career—and, for me, this raises a few unsettling questions.

Van Vliet is represented by Michael Werner, an international dealer based in Cologne. Werner had been showing advanced German art there for years, giving the now well-known A.R. Penck a show in 1969, for instance, while Penck was still living an underground artist's life in East Germany. When Werner opened a New York City gallery it primarily showcased German artists making similar kinds of art. Werner's expansion, which was to be so fortunate for Van Vliet, was a result of the art bubble, which nurtured and was in turn sustained by a new, business-wise approach on the part of the artists themselves.

Another of the differences between the philosophies of Schnabel and Van Vliet lies in the fact that there was an enormous change in art world economics between the mid-1960s when the adult Van Vliet reasserted himself as a painter, however isolated, and the late 1970s when Schnabel emerged on the New York scene. Schnabel began exhibiting in an art world which, taking Andy Warhol as its model, freely admitted that its artists were interested in getting their names in the paper and strategically manipulating their output to attain and keep high prices. Renown and acclaim were the measures of success. Art, in short, was learning to love the business side of itself. Van Vliet had matured in a much more idealistic art world, where how true an artist could be to his own vision was the ultimate measure—or this was at least the accepted rhetoric. (This stance was in fact already passing away when Van Vliet returned to painting; his relative isolation from the art world's currents may have helped him keep this idealism.)

In the opinion of Robert Hughes, the often cynical (and therefore most often on-the-money) art critic for *Time* magazine, by the late 1970s increased demand for art in the galleries had created "a market structure that resembles, and parodies, that of the multinational corporation," a structure into which emerging artists were "apt to get locked." Associations of galleries sell "one product" in all the major art markets, a situation which favors artists who "work on an industrial scale. . . ." To supply, preferably to "supersaturate," this network an artist might need to paint two paintings a week. Georg Baselitz and A.R. Penck, two German painters, are singled out by Hughes as artists who produce at this level.[6] And Werner's gallery, which quickly acquired a reputation for representing "some of the hottest, most controversial American and European artists,"[7] represents both Penck and Baselitz. Schnabel reminisces about Polke visiting New York and engaging in such hysterically funny antics as photographing and ridiculing tired subway commuters. He characterizes Polke's art as possessing "a craziness, a nonchalance," as well as "the texture of poverty. [A] way of notating inarticulateness,"[8] all of which Schnabel celebrates. Baselitz once characterized his own art as "ornaments in a climate of disharmony," with no implication that they were meant as antidotes.

Baselitz, Penck, Sigmar Polke and other Werner Gallery artists are often grouped as practitioners of German Neo-Expressionism. The original German Expressionism flourished from about 1880 until Germany's defeat in World War I. The influences which fed into its philosophy were not primarily visual ones—the most important exceptions being Van Gogh (whose style was more enthusiastically received in Germany than in his adopted country, France) and the Norwegian Edvard Munch. Non-visual influences include Nature Philosophy (echoed in Munch who said of his most famous painting, "I hear the scream in nature"), mythology and various kinds of archaic symbology, the theories of Wagner and philosophy of Nietzsche, and a number of poets, as well as what have been called "the extreme mood swings"[9] of politics and historical fragmentation in Germany at that time. All this led to an art which had as its homeland "'the Germany of the soul,' neurasthenia, melancholia, a rationality tragically disposed toward superstition and the supernatural,[10]" all served up with an anti-intellectual bias.

When Expressionism rose again in a divided, post-World War II Germany, other elements were added. Most crucial was an admiration for collections of *art brut* (art by the certified insane, often made while they were institutionalized), and for "outsider art"—naive art, often done by solitary compulsives and social outcasts. Influential sources were Karl Jasper's book *Strindberg and Van Gogh*, which discusses two late nineteenth-century Swedish schizophrenic artists, a collection of *art brut* gathered by Jean Dubuffet which was first exhibited in Paris in 1967, and what is known as "the Prinzhorn Collection." This last was a collection of *art brut* made by the patients of a psychoanalyst named Hans Prinzhorn, who practiced in Heidelberg from the mid-teens to the early 1930s. Prinzhorn gathered them as part of an inquiry into creativity, but they survived World War II because the Nazis used them as examples of "degeneracy" in their attacks on modern artists working in Germany. Selections from the collection were exhibited in a Heidelberg gallery in 1967, and a book Prinzhorn wrote about the art was reprinted soon after.[11] A number of German Neo-Expressionists have taken images from this collection as models for their own art, in the service of creating a fresh visual vocabulary.

Clearly, Van Vliet, who (as Mary Boone noted) has had his own consistent vocabulary of forms and images, wouldn't need outside sources to refresh his visual vocabulary. And his intentions and goals have little or nothing in common with the philosophical ground of such artists. One critic, Kristine McKenna, explicitly rejects any suggestion that they are even visually related: "[You] can't lump him in with the Germans," she writes.

> In his startling use of color, his playful approach to pictorial space, and his hermetic vocabulary of private signs and symbols, he is above all else an American primitive, and the mythologies of this country—rusted and twisted beyond recognition—are at the heart of his work.[12]

Yet he hangs side by side with these men. (A 1998 group exhibition of works on paper grouped Van Vliet with Georg Baselitz, Marcel Broodthaers, A.R. Penck and others very much of the German Neo-Expressionist school.) What can we imagine is happening here? From all reports, Van Vliet's works sell well for the gallery. As of 1993, Werner had sold between 60 and 75 paintings, at prices ranging from $10,000 to $35,000; and many more drawings, which sold at that time from $500 to $5,000. So there is the simple fact of commercial viability.

But a shadow remains, an uneasiness which has its root in the fact that Van Vliet has more in common with the "outsiders" that the younger artists romanticize, even enthuse over in a patronizing way, than with the others Werner represents. Werner once characterized Van Vliet as being an outsider artist "in a sense," because, "He's not connected with any school or movement and he never looks at paintings. . . ." Werner also feels that "Some of [Van Vliet's] work has a fragmentation and a crazy sense of space that reminds me of the drawings of Antonin Artaud, but mostly his work exists in a different universe. For me, that's what makes him so important."[13] Artaud was a poet and actor, who spent much time fighting mental illness. Most of the visual art he produced was created as part of a therapy regimen imposed by the doctor who subjected him to electroshock treatments.

Michael Werner is also on record as lamenting Van Vliet's "fame" as Captain Beefheart. "It's very hard because he's famous," the dealer has said. "Many people know his name as a musician. It's very hard to make a career as a painter, and that's a big obstacle."[14] Yet the gallery's own Van Vliet exhibition catalogues never fail to mention the fact, and the large "coffee table" style *Stand Up to be Discontinued*, which Werner Galleries had a role in putting together, opens with four pages of reproductions of Beefheart articles, and the critical pieces included also look at this aspect of his life. Does Werner mean us to understand that his own exhibition catalogues include material that puts obstacles in Van Vliet's way to success? Clearly, we have to take Werner's protests with a very large grain of salt.

Werner takes it as a truism that "Very few of the music lovers buy his paintings, because most of them don't have money." Others have a different opinion. At the time of Van Vliet's 1990 show at the Free Hoffman Gallery in Santa Monica, Hoffman expressed enthusiasm for Van Vliet's musical work, but then quickly said that he was not trying to play the crossover card, even though he "knew it would being out an audience. . . . I know one of the buyers of one of the paintings was somebody from the music industry."[15]

Werner also makes it clear that he dismisses the art Van Vliet made before coming into the Werner stable. Van Vliet's new (that is, art-savvy and monied) fans "take him as a young artist," which Werner feels is correct:

> They act as if he's a young artist, because he's been painting now for 15 years or so, and the first three or four years don't even count, because he was also making music. It only counts from the time when he

painted exclusively. . . .[16]

The director of Werner's New York Gallery, Gordon Veneklasen, echoes this opinion, though more subtly. At the time of a 1995 New York exhibit Veneklasen complimented Van Vliet by saying, "He's *become* a really incredible painter."[17] (The emphasis is mine—though perhaps not mine alone.)

In short, Van Vliet's gallery is willing to cash in on his past as Captain Beefheart, but not to credit the art he made before he signed up with them.

Ishmael Reed's poem "Dualism" is relevant here. "Dualism" was inspired by Ralph Ellison's *Invisible Man*, which is certainly what Van Vliet the painter was for many years. The poem begins with the narrator standing outside of history, wishing he had some peanuts—because history looks hungry inside its cage. The poem ends with the narrator trapped inside of history: "it's/ hungrier than i/ thot."[18] The title of the 1992 "Alternate Beefheart" CD is *I May Be Hungry But I Sure Ain't Weird,* a line from the song "Safe as Milk," a song written at the same historical moment as Reed's cautionary poem. History, hungry and weird, has now swallowed Van Vliet's art, begun the process of homogenizing it by way of conceptual colonization, assimilating it into art history. And whether this was wholly voluntary or, as the above comments seem to suggest, in large part due to the influence of his gallery (which would parallel his foray into musical commercialism under the guidance of the DiMartino brothers a decade earlier, though with much more successful results), it is clear that Van Vliet has left behind his outsider status and entered into the art historical continuum. The artists and the galleries, even if they have had all the good will in the world—and they have made Van Vliet happy, let him live by doing what he has wanted to do all his life—have also begun the (inevitable) process of reducing his work from a magnificent singularity, a brilliant and mysterious "sport of nature" in the world of popular culture, one suggesting a fascinating alternative approach to the life of a popular artist, to a sidebar to 20th century neo-expressionism, a footnote to art history.

But my main concern here is not with questions of Van Vliet's place in art history. Rather it is with how changes evident in his paintings suggest that, once again, he was driven away from his own steering wheel in order to achieve success. To see this change clearly, we have only to look back at the art he was producing just before he was taken up by Michael Werner, at the paintings he created even while still making music, and follow some very visible changes which occur in his art (and imply changes in Van Vliet as well) over the next several years.

The space of time between the release of the last Captain Beefheart and the Magic Band album, *Ice Cream for Crow* in early 1982, and Van Vliet's first one-man show as a painter in May 1985, is largely uncharted. We can be certain that a number of things would have had to have happened over this period. After Lucas introduced Van Vliet and Schnabel, Schnabel would have gotten to know Van Vliet and his art, then approached his gallery on Van Vliet's part. Once an exhibit had been agreed upon and scheduled (Van Vliet would have had to "get in line," with the gallery's other artists) more time would have passed, allowing him to prepare more new work for the show—a period of time up to as much as two years. If his exhibition was to be in 1985, it certainly would have been agreed upon no later than 1984.

The 1984 paintings which have been reproduced include several of solitary figures, some of which are accompanied by animals. There is, for example, a joyous, long-limbed female painted in two-tones like a fancy saddle shoe (SU 66). Her body is heavily outlined with India ink, and her skin is an even-all-over light sand color. The wide, viscous-looking lines unexpectedly add lightness and energy to her upward-extended arms and a ballerina's graceful legs. Her black hair is gathered on top of her head, and her eyes and the shadow of her chin also are black, as are her nipples, navel and pubic hair. She has two non-human companions, both also black. One is a silhouette, and the other an outline lightly filled in with more black. These may be dogs or fawns, or . . . ?

In *Pet Surprises—Pet Surprising Pet* a feline figure scratches the back of a seated, light- green-and-yellow skinned woman. The cat-like animal is a simple but graceful arc, with a smoky tail. The woman appears to have her hand raised to her hair, so is possibly seated at a vanity mirror. Grooming is an act basic to the social life of all mammals, and this appears to be a caprice on that fact: the woman is grooming herself—treating herself as her own "pet"—and another of her pets comes up behind to give her a surprise grooming. Crammed into the corner above and behind them is the reddish brown schematic of a second animal. This one has a dirty gold face the shape of a garden spade. It is out of the grooming loop, looking out at the painting's viewer.

A third painting, *Boat and Blue Bodagress* is more dramatic and puzzling than anything seen to this point. The "Blue Bodagress" is again a nude or semi-nude female. She is black and blue and her hair crackles with energy, her face (as fully realized and character-packed as those on the back of *Spotlight Kid)* is stern with concentration. Her legs, black with green highlights, look powerful, and support her as if she were seated in the air before the royal red background. The suffix of her title is the same as that in "lioness," et al. What, if anything, the first half of her title means may depend on how it is pronounced. If pronounced with a long o, it could be a send-up of the vacuous compliment "bodacious!" If pronounced with a short vowel, it could simply come from "body." Either way, it is clearly meant to be a superlative—simply looking at the figure we understand Van Vliet means this to be a powerful, intelligent woman. This Bodagress occupies the lower right half of this diagonally divided painting. The left side is some kind of curtain or drape, perhaps of cloth or even of some exotic foliage, painted in a more translucent red than that behind the figure. The suggestion is that this woman has just drawn out the object in her hand from within this concealed place. The shining gold object she is holding is a puzzle. The title of the painting identifies it as a boat, but on first and even second glance it still looks to be the kind of lamp Aladdin used to rub. A rectangle and triangle of white keep insisting it is indeed a boat, but the suggestion of magic lamp will not relent. In the end, we will come away feeling that it is both at once.

The last of the female figure paintings is *Japan In the Dishpan.* The figure here has the same blue and white flesh as the swimmer in the 1976 shark painting. This figure is folded over to fit in the space of the picture. This is a roughly painted portrait, and the figure is surrounded with clashing strikes of highway-yellow, red, deep green and dirty brown, surroundings as unsettling as a constantly changing mind. The title is also the title of a 1970 instrumental, one of Captain Beefheart and the Magic Band's most cacophonous recordings. The title may have been floated free and reattached to this painting in reference to the single visible eye, which is almond shaped and painted at an angle to what we perceive to be the plane of the face. Or, it may refer to the black ridge and curl (a glossy black being one of the definitions of "japan") that tops the skull and extends down to sketch a nose, similar to Picasso's bronze *Head of Woman* from the early 1930s. The tone of this painting is claustrophobic, agitated; something beautiful is caught in a room where the walls are closing in on her.

The above paintings and those which will follow are not discussed in the order in which they are found in the large Van Vliet catalogue, *Stand Up to Be Discontinued.* Instead, they have been arranged to highlight a larger progression I am trying to suggest. It is impossible at this point to determine the exact sequence of these works within the year, and the arrangement here has admittedly been done for dramatic effect. With this in mind, I would suggest that the last of the 1984 paintings included in *Stand Up* may well have been painted before *Fire Party for Boomerang Man.* This painting is a singularity in Van Vliet's work, and a chilling one. It is titled *Dylisheus.*

The spelling insists that the title of the painting is to be pronounced with "die" as its first syllable, and dying—or more properly, killing—is what the work is about. This is a portrait of ferocity, made more insistent by the work being a triptych. In each of the three paintings a wolfish predator is leaping onto the back of a fleeing animal. The wolf appears in the same pose in each of the paintings, as does its prey. Despite the fixed positions, there is a drastic change across the space of the triptych, as the prey is progressively stripped of its flesh. In the left-most paintings, the animal resembles some sort of stripped-down pig—it has a pig's long nose and pointed ears. The wolf's claws are tearing at its haunch as it runs. The wolf's paw and its snout are out-sized in comparison to everything else in the painting. Its green body is dwarfed by its enormous white claw. Above the scene the sun is a torn-pomegranate red, mercilessly beating down. The sky is painted in streaks of clean and dirty whites.

In the center painting the prey's pelt has been stripped away, and lard-and-blood-colored flesh is exposed. The wolf's pelt has also changed, it is darker, has become a cobalt and midnight blue shape. The wolf is still outfitted with the same outsized claws, however. His face is stripped down, the fuzzy oafishness of the first muzzle here gives way to a very active-looking brown and ox-blood wedge, without distinct features but with two ragged white strips of teeth still very much apparent. The sun is even more fruit-like, and the air is bleached even whiter. In the final painting the wolf's head and body are merging like plumes of smoke, the sun sends a tongue of flame down into the scene as if it too will feed. (That the sun appears to join in with the wolf suggests Van Vliet is looking at a much larger reality than simply that of animals killing one another for survival.) The prey, which the wolf is still tearing at, has been reduced to its skeleton and a few tatters of flesh. Dark cords show through bars of rib bones; no life shows in the gruesomely puckered eye socket.

A "sidebar" painting to this triptych has also been reproduced. The cover of *Stand Up to Be Discontinued* features a painting titled *Fur on the Trellis and Just up into the Air*, in which the wolf figure appears yet again. The date given is 1985, but this painting (or at least the detail which is reproduced; the chopped-off paint strokes suggest we are given only a small part) is so similar to the triptych that if it was not painted it at the same time, it may well have used the triptych as its "model." The wolf's fierce teeth and rake-like claw are claiming yet another victim.

174

But what this creature—whose fur it must be that is being left on the trellis and thrown up into the air—might once have been is impossible to determine; it is blue and black, amorphous though there is some slight suggestion of a face. This truncated feast, so different from all but one of the works enclosed—and, tellingly, neither the triptych nor this sidebar were exhibited—seems a misleading image to appear on the catalogue's cover. This detail from a larger work (the dimensions given are for a single 7 1/2 by 5 foot canvas) was obviously selected for its shock value. The same impulse may lie behind another singularity: the *Dylisheus* triptych is reproduced twice, once as a two-page spread, and again with all three panels even further reduced to fit together on one of these pages. Clearly, someone on the catalogue design team was very taken with these bloody paintings.

When the rest of us first come upon this triptych and its sidebar we feel a moment of shock. Their ferocity is totally unexpected, unprecedented in what we know of Van Vliet's work. At least since the time of *Trout Mask Replica* and probably much earlier, Van Vliet has been a champion of nature, an ecologist in the most personal sense. A wolf running down and killing its prey is very much a part of animal survival, as Van Vliet certainly understands. But this is not one of the aspects of nature which he has chosen to include in his art previous to *Dylisheus*. Rather, he has chosen to concentrate on those aspects which might serve as models for a more harmonious order of human behavior. He has also gone on record as deploring man's treatment of animals—including the wolf: "Walt Disney gave the wolf capital punishment!" he has protested.

That this has a sequential form, is a triptych, is significant. A sequential work unavoidably suggests a "plot" or "point." And that "point" appears to be that which has the will to devour, will continue devouring long after all life has left its victim. Surely Van Vliet has seen this before—there are a number of scavenger species in the desert, including the crows he if so fond of—and we wonder if there is any reason he suddenly decided to address this, and in such a graphic manner. Was it in part a visual comment on the feeding frenzy he encountered in the art world?

(To be fair, there are other possible readings of these works. The specifics of the title of the 1985 version allow for these arising from something Van Vliet witnessed, perhaps in his own yard, and which left him shaken and wanting to paint. When the first edition of this book appeared, long-time Van Vliet fan Paco [Frank] Hebblethwaite wrote to tell me of the existence of another variation in this series, one titled *Lycanthropes Pigs*. In reproduction the painting is nearly identical to the others. This work was exhibited at the "Chi-Chi Show," a 1985 group show meant as a tribute to a gallery owner's Chihuahua. That Van Vliet would contribute a painting showing the slaying of an animal which could be mistaken for a Chihuahua is surely an example of his sense of humor, and a poke at a silly art world gimmick. Hebblethwaite also bought another unrelated Van Vliet work, but was only allowed to do so after the gallery called Julian Schnabel and Schnabel okayed the deal. He later learned that *Dylisheus* was available, but would only be sold to a "major collector" or museum.)

Dylisheus may simply be a momentary nod toward realism, toward presenting a broader view of a subject area which has been a long-time interest. But the art which follows suggests this triptych marks a more drastic turn.[19]

Other 1984 paintings show Van Vliet beginning to move in a new direction, one in which he will continue to move, a direction not just pictorially different from what had come before, but which reflects an altered relationship to the world. *Egyptian Toss Up* adds generous helpings of indigo and purple to Van Vliet's usual pallet. The title refers to the profile of the cat figure which occupies the bottom third of the painting. The cat has a reddish-brown body, with a sharply delineated belly and front paw. Its head has the long-nose, high-forehead look of Egyptian cat statues. Its head is turned slightly toward us, but its eye socket is an opaque, milky white. Above the cat's back is a woman with a purple headpiece, which has two feather-like stripes rising from it. Her hands are raised as if she were tossing something, but the other objects in the painting are indistinct, though one appears to be an animal she may have tossed. The background is a thick, subtly shaded white that combines with the indigo and purple, and the pearl gray of the cat's face to give the painting the glowing look of a fresco. This painting would not look out of place on the interior wall of some ancient building; it has a definite Mediterranean light.

But, looking back after seeing the paintings which were to follow, we notice that the woman's body ends just under her breasts; that, if we look close at where the cat's ear and her forearm cross, the two do not touch—in fact, it looks as though Van Vliet scribbled in a few small lines to make it clear that the cat was in some space in front of the woman. Whatever it is she is tossing (which may be alive; there appear to be both a human hand and an animal leg in the mix), is at this point somewhere above and behind her. The painting is arranged, then, so that no two living beings touch.

The beings in *Devil and the Deep Blue Sea* do not touch one another, either. The foremost figure is a portly devil with a head similar to that of the lead shape in *Green Tom*, but this devil is most definitely malevolent. His hands are large and meaty, but no palms are visible; the hands are all long pointed fingers. His face is a roughly painted blur of brick red, and at least a half dozen flame-like horns protrude from his skull. His left arm is extended in the traditional gesture of a salesman inviting the viewer in to inspect a display of his wares. Behind him are several more subordinate devils, one white and yellow, another a wiry blur of colors, with sad eyelids like the puppet Lambchop. At the back of the painting, almost hidden behind slashes of flame is a great yellow and red-tinged cat-devil, lying in wait. Its narrowed eyes stare directly outward over the pickets of flame, its brow drawn fiercely down. This is not a role we would have expected a cat to play in Van Vliet's work, considering all the works that feature cats, and his long-time affectionate relationship with his cat, Garland. The devil is present in this painting, clearly; but there is no sign of any deep blue sea or of any alternative to being captured by this group.

The title of *Fire Party for Boomerang Man with Wrought Iron Curls* describes much of its content. There is a fire in the center of the lower half of the painting which divides it in half. In the upper right is a definite Boomerang Man. A Lone Ranger-mask-shaped yellow face has two coral-ringed eyes that look out at us, and a limp beak or bandanna of the same color below. Above his face are two boomerang shapes, one black, one deep mahogany-red, inverted above one another to make horns. From these horns extend long curlicues of black, his "wrought-iron curls." Boomerang Man appears to be bodiless. Below him a black and white dog, one of its legs hidden by smoke or dust, runs through the edge of the fire, directly toward us. The right half of the painting is abstract in the way smoke and landscape can be. A grey shape, like a bass fiddle with one bat wing attached, all made of smoke, centers the space, while a Pepto-Bismol pink and yellow sky streaks past above it. Other colored areas almost coalesce into shapes, but resist, and we are left with a sense of desert revelry but no sense of the revelers themselves. Boomerang Man is isolated from the dog, who is isolated from the smoke fiddle. Only the amorphous intermingle.

Though the transition is not an abrupt chopline, Van Vliet's art will hereafter develop along these general lines, with less definite shapes, each isolated from the others in its picture space. A review of his second show with Werner commented on this:

> Large formats [allow more room] for all those heads and animals and frightened, staring eyes. These figurative elements, which previously were inserted with almost child-like naivety into abstract wastes, are here carefully isolated from one another. This means that they are taken over even more by the increasingly painterly and expanded abstract chaos.[20]

Within two years, figures will disappear entirely from the paintings. But in 1985 figures still dominate, and a number of Van Vliet's most beautiful works date from this time. The paintings from this year show a great breadth of invention, but still there are few instances of any real interaction. We see a confident experimentation with a range of variations on his previous styles—but most are variations on the theme of people turning from one another.

Cats Got His Tail is the primary exception to this. This is one of Van Vliet's more whimsical paintings. Two standing cat-men look out at us. One is spreading his arms wide, while the second and smaller one, is holding the tail of the first. The color scheme here is predominantly 1950s car culture formal, pink and black: pinks make up most of the bodies of these two black-faced felines, and fill a shape like an arm with its elbow bent that runs down the left hand side. Behind the cat-men is a field of squarely brushed daubs on white, a bright indefinite distance. The child-like white outlining and droopy whiskers leave us with no doubt that Van Vliet has here produced a portrait of some creatures he likes very much.

There are also a number of female figure works from 1985. The canvas for one of them, *It's Like a White Onion-Fleshed Pumpkin*[21] is just short of nine feet tall, and its ghostly white central figure stretches to nearly its full height. There is nothing pumpkin-like about this figure, but its flesh is indeed onion-white. The figure is bordered on the bottom by a jagged triangle of fire red, and on its right by a thick, granular-looking black lines that follow the outline as tightly as a shadow. The left side is strikingly dissimilar to the rest of the painting—even its "up" differs from that of the rest.

Where the white figure and even the slashes of the fire red and the crossed x's of the shadow side all share an orientation to the vertical, the face and orange snail-shell that fill the left side of the canvas try to push it over onto that side. The face in particular is painted at a distinct right angle from the white figure. It is no accident that this is one of the most detailed and expressive faces in all of Van Vliet's work. (Another version of this face which appears in *Ghost Gait, Ghost Gate* from 1985, one which is truly terrifying.) For this much smaller turned-on-its-side image to carry a force equal to that of the immense white figure, a force necessary if the viewer were not to simply dismiss it and stay with the simply vertical elements, it had to have be given this expressive power.

Cave paintings exhibit this multi-oriented characteristic, as if at the time they were painted the hierarchy of space had not yet been agreed upon and artists were free to choose their own ups and downs as they saw fit.[22] And, of course, they were, and still are—though so few feel free to exercise this freedom that we are momentarily disoriented, even dissatisfied when we first encounter it. Van Vliet willingly surrenders the idea of formal unity in doing this, but in exchange achieves something like a suspension between major and minor keys by doing so. We cannot settle into a simple reaction to the painting, and Van Vliet does not want us to. We should recall his insistence that his bands should never grow too comfortable with what they were playing, but should remain off-balance just enough to experience the music in a fresh, playful way. This is what we must do here as well. Beauty, after all, is not always restful.

Bromboline Frenzy depicts two reddish-brown female nudes, standing back to back. To their right are two or three snow white vertical shapes: one has llama-like eyes and brows in red and black, while the other is a woman in white much like the one in *It's Like a White Onion-Fleshed Pumpkin. Beezoo, Beezoo* also includes female nudes. One of these is very closely related, both in coloration and in the look of her features, to those in *Bromboline Frenzy*. The later painting includes a second nude (painted in safety-yellow and white) clearly related both to the earlier untitled nude, and to another painting from 1985, *Crepe and Black Lamps*. Resting her forearm on the top of this yellow and white portrait bust is a pensive, gorgeous woman's face, with scribbled hair like cornrows. The name of the painting comes from a bee (image of industry and sexual fertility, among other things) near this beautiful woman's face. The women are almost looking at one another, but not quite. The background of the painting has a scumbled busyness about it that forces us to give it as much attention as we do the women—except that nothing can be clearly seen there. The background is all swirls and stabs. Its insistence on coming to the fore only serves to reinforce the separateness of the women, even the two who are touching.

180

Crepe and Black Lamps is a painting to linger with. A deepest blue and black female nude with spiky hair and luminous-red nipples fills the right side of the painting. This figure reconfirms Van Vliet's lack of interest in perspectival depth. Conventional perspectival clues are present in the way the woman's head and her right hand are enlarged, and her breasts hang pendulously. But the space surrounding her is unsteady and short-circuits these depth clues. This bold figure embodies the "Black Lamps" of the painting's title ("Lamp Black" is also a color oil paint comes in), and she grabs our attention first, but the faces on the left-hand side, faces that suggest "Crepe," are ultimately more intriguing.

The oval face in the upper right tilts down from a starched robe shoulder into the painting's center. Its features are simple, even schematic: mismatched eyes and puzzled mouth, red-brown outlines on creamy white. Below this is a face in curled strokes of burnished gold. Details of the face remain just below the point of complete resolution, as if it were coming up in a hypo bath or approaching from below the white veil of the background paint and has only partially surfaced. The hushed gold and feathery brush strokes bring up the light between the features, giving the face a glow. (A similar, though distinctly feline, face appears in 1988's *Golden Birdies*.) The picket-fencing of brightness produced by the alternating curls of color and white give the face a softness, a papery lightness that indeed suggests "Crepe." This painting is a triptych of depths, not perspectival depths, but of depths of resolution: the dark figure is completely resolved, solid, but the degree decreases as we move counter-clockwise.

Such degrees of resolution will continue to interest Van Vliet over the next two years, both in some of his figurative and in other, almost wholly abstract works. Of the figurative works in this line, *Carp Catcher* (1986) is the least successful, with the resolved pieces—a dog and two other less easily recognized shapes gathered in a cluster on the right side—being too sharply delineated to make any common cause with the less resolved elements, which are amorphous and blurry. *Sea Wig* (1986), the central figure of which resembles a "sock monkey" or a Punch puppet, has a number of differently resolved faces—at least four, depending on how hard you look. The painting itself has a light, playful feel.

Garden Lion and *Candle Powered Rodeo Ghosts* (both also from 1986) are more somber. The central figure in *Garden Lion* is a long-legged female painted in an almost-blinding white. Her features have the crepe-like sheen used in *Crepe and Black Lamps*. Black lines around her head and between her legs once again make the space she occupies an ambiguous one. She is reaching out to touch some flowers which are so yellow as to erase most of their details. Behind her is a bright purple and dusky rose shape that almost becomes a figure (black lines at the curved top of this shape echo those surrounding the white woman's head), but in the end does not. Again there are three degrees of resolution here, but they are achieved largely by manipulation of color rather than by differing degrees of detail.

Candle Powered Rodeo Ghosts is a gorgeous painting, brilliant in flesh-pinks, flat tans, yellows and golds beneath deep Navy blue and black foliage. The taper thin central figure has an elfin face that seems to slip from one amused expression to another as we sort out its arched brows and pointed ears. Her eyes (if it is a her) are sketchy but convey a powerful impression of character and beauty. To the left of her are white and golden tan swirls like clouds seen from space, bordered by a tender-peach flower ladder. On the right is a white shape that might be dog or goat, but is surely looking straight at us with bemused wonder. There are other shapes that rise around and between these two and disappear into the blue and black above. There is great mystery and great tenderness in this painting, all conveyed through figures which never quite settle into their forms.

The more abstract works which are descended from the *Onion-Fleshed Pumpkin* painting include *Striped Light* (1985), which has almost the same palette: orange and black, tan and white. In this painting a pale version of the face from *Onion-Fleshed Pumpkin* floats between an orange-red and black and white rolling smoke. Another clearly related painting is *With Twinkling Lights and Green Sashes,* a much more densely packed and colorful work—pink and green, umber and black on tan— but one which fails to come together convincingly.

Beginning with some of the 1987 paintings, the tendency (which was apparent in *Fire Party for Boomerang Man* and *It's Like a White Onion-Fleshed Pumpkin)* for the elements of a work to appear to be completely independent of one another becomes Van Vliet's predominant style. In that year Van Vliet also continued working with different depths of resolution. A number of 1987-88 paintings combine thin washes of color with vigorous scratchy lines, as if Van Vliet were working in a space between Helen Frankenthaler and Cy Twombly.

These works also bring to mind Larry Rivers. At first glance, he and Van Vliet would seem to have nothing in common. For more than 40 years, Rivers has resolutely remained a figurative painter even during periods when all around him were painting abstractly. River's line is crisp; many of his paintings openly personal, even confessional; his scenes are almost always completely urban—trees and forest animals are rarities. But, if Van Vliet's *Castfat Shadows* (1987), or *Life Walker* (1988) are put next to such 1950s Rivers paintings as *The Accident* or *It's Raining Anita Huffington* (both from 1957), the similarities are immediately obvious—particularly between the second pair. Both artists combine different depths of resolution, both organize their paintings with clusters of images surrounded by large open areas, and even the palette of these paintings is much the same— vanilla white and nail polish reds, sparse touches of metallic blues. The faces and figures in Van Vliet's paintings are much more loosely painted than are Rivers', but each in their own way create images that have to be completed by the observer.

Many of the colors and even some of the same forms used in *It's Raining Anita Huffington* can be found in Van Vliet's *Life Walker* (1988): the red boot or claw shape in *Shadows* has counterparts in almost identical red in the middle of Rivers' work, and again near the bottom edge. Both men are fond of finding shapes which can stand on their own when detached from their source, so it is not surprising that they could independently discover and use some of the same pieces. They ways of rendering these forms may be very different, but their organizational senses are fairly close in these paintings.

Castfat Shadows, like Rivers' works, has the look of decals which have floated free and gathered where the water has taken them; where Rivers' shapes have kept their edges Van Vliet's are surrendering theirs. Two of the faces in *Castfat Shadows* (there are two or three or more depending on your detail threshold) crowd into one another—the dark almost canine face to the left and just below the mid-line has a second, almost invisible companion overlapping on the right—as in so many of Rivers' double portraits. Black, slate blue and reddish brown shapes suggest a bird, insects, fish, but don't rule out the possibility of linking to another shape and becoming something entirely different. A thumb-and-finger of light turquoise and bits of clay blue suggest space behind the white surface, as uneven as adobe, around the shapes.

In *Dry Morning Wind That Jingle Like Fish Bones* (also from 1987) the pieces no longer even suggest that they may have once been part of a unified scene. Nor does the painting itself seem to find a way of being a whole: when we look at a particular form, the rest is forgotten. A black-outline animal figure walks across the top, toward two flower shapes and a deep red cockscomb. Behind and below this are isolated, mostly jointed narrow, lines of green and light purple and black, and a yellow field shaped something like the Indian sub-continent—or is it a dancing chicken? There are no bones to be seen, and if there is a fish in this painting it is to be found near the bottom: what look like pencil lines drawn over the off-white sketch a fish turning toward the viewer's right, a few brown and black touches outline his eye.

Parapliers the Willow Dipped (1987) and *Riding Some Kind of Unusual Skull Sleigh* (1986-87) are as disjoint as the other abstracts from the same year, but they succeed beautifully, in part because Van Vliet creates much bolder forms here, shapes that dominate the spaces they occupy rather than tentatively occupy them as do the smaller shapes in *Castfat Shadows* and *Dry Morning Wind*. The aqua green, many-legged form in *Parapliers* has an undeniable grace, and seems to be move gently to the right, heading out of the painting. A butterscotch yellow field looks springy under this form's many legs. The two black wickets or iron handles to the left attract one another strongly enough that we accept tiered perspective for this area—the two wickets being the ends and the gold-brown stretch lying between them are tilted up like Bosch or Cezanne or Thibeaud. The lower ("nearer") end has the look of having been wiped with a turpentine rag. A wing and oval which is very suggestive of a madonna appears at the top of the space, painted in light purple (it may even be the color called "Las Cruces Purple"). And in the bottom right corner swims a dark blue and Chinese red fighting fish. The painting is bright and mysterious.

Riding Some Kind of Unusual Skull Sleigh has two dominant forms, both figurative, both very different from one another. Down the full length of the left side crawls or falls a deep crimson man. His arm is outstretched and dirty white flares from his hand. His face is made up of a few black rectangles, but it is clear that he is staring out at us, watching us watching him. (Even when painted in blocky shapes as here, Van Vliet's faces all convey strong individual character, are almost always fascinating—often beautiful, and it seems a shame that he stopped painting them after only three years of his works finally reaching the art world stage.) What may be a displaced limb or a tail in a brighter red, sweeps off to the right; small shapes like familiars or attendant demons cluster around him. From beneath the brighter red limb a skull emerges. It appears to be riding on a cushion of egg-yolk yellow. The skull has one black eye and one red, and it, too, is watching us watch it. Van Vliet has given these figures an undeniable momentum; the skull in particular forces itself nearer as we contemplate it.

Unfortunately, the style here, the particular combination of techniques Van Vliet employed in these two forceful and

185

mysterious paintings was a transitional one. They are as closely related to the thick and choppy works (*Tiger Boat*, for example) Van Vliet was also painting at this time as they are to the lighter style of *Castfat Shadows* and its fellows. A few paintings, such as *Golden Birdies* and *Gray Ape* (both 1988) attempt to combine the light and heavy in the compartmentalized manner of *Life Walker*. One of these, *Golden Birdies*, includes the last of Van Vliet's beautiful feathery faces, but the remainder comes off as a blasted cityscape. *Gray Ape* includes some interesting pseudo-figurative shapes—besides the scribbled ape there is a bear (or perhaps an x-ray of one), and something resembling a robed figure—and is marginally more successful than *Golden Birdies*. After 1988, Van Vliet will occasionally revive elements of this style for a single work—the unsprung and lovely *Dragon Gown* from the next year is one instance, and *Black Twig* from 1991 is another. (And again, these are paintings which suggest a space between Frankenthaler and Twombly.) But a heavier style, at times with a thickly applied paint surface over nearly all the canvas, will dominate beginning in 1988.

One of the earlier of these densely painted works, *Copper Diver* (1985) may be the only Van Vliet painting which conveys simple sadness. Against a foliage green background like a jungle by Cezanne sits a deep copper red figure. He sits on what may be a log, a black shape with a single curving line branching from its right side, and which splits in a pair of lines like a snapping beak on its right end. (This form seems to mean something in particular to the artist: similar shapes appear in other paintings—in yellow in *Day Barrette* [1989], in three colors in *Boat and Locks No. 2* [1991], and in black in other works.) beneath the lines is a rolling mass of white. The title suggests that the figure is getting ready to propel himself off his perch; the white may be some turbulent water below. And on second glance, the out-of-focus foliage resembles green thunderheads.

But it is the diver's posture that commands our attention: he is straight-backed, with his head pulled down into his shoulders.

His hands rest tentatively, almost caressingly on the black of his perch. His brow is furrowed, but his eye still gleams cat's-eye-green. The pushed-in nose, the way his chin is impacted into his chest, the black slashes down his back, all suggest a moment of sadness. He is gathering his strength for the dive after some unhappy experience. The lightness of the diver's touch, the straightness of his back, the way the head and right shoulder are twisted almost into one form, all suggest a contemplative sorrow. Few, if any, of the paintings in this style which follow convey any deep emotion, rather they concern themselves with shapes loosely arranged in free and emotionally undefined spaces.

The Green Gambler and *Cage Reservoir* have black and a dirty pea-green as dominant colors. The repertoire of shapes are characteristic of a number of the paintings to follow. Curved right angles in black, near-figurative shapes with blobby contours, a tendency toward the use of diagonals from upper right to lower left. Present here, too, is the more smeary-looking brush work, and overlays that appear as if they were done before the paint underneath had dried.

Dark Light and *Raven Above* (both 1988) mark a return to a more open, white dominated look. *Dark Light* is little more than a few black squiggles up the right edge, and some darkened and flattened white inside thing outlines up the left side. The middle is all white—which is not to say featureless. As art critic Roberto Ort has pointed out, the open areas in Van Vliet's paintings of this period are not bare canvas, but white paint, painted and modeled with as much variety of impasto as the colored areas. *Dark Light* has the look of a first step, as if Van Vliet had stripped everything down, and was moving out on his new path slowly and cautiously. *Raven Above* is little more than a half-step beyond it, with a tangle of yellow and a field of dirty gold added; much of the painting is still uneven white wall. *Tug*, from 1990, is a close match for *Raven Above*, if less energetic.

Tiger Bow and *White Crepe Boot* add color and complexity to this thick white base. As with many of Van Vliet's paintings, the title *Tiger Bow* is as simply derived as the Smithsonian Institution labels he admired for their poetry. In the center of the painting is a deep blue shape which might be a kiss, but is more likely a bow, and below that something which could easily be a tropical fish in section, but could also be a glimpse of a tiger. These two are repeated in the upper left; this time the orange is more clearly a cartoon tiger, and below that is a black shape like a string tie tied in a loose bow. To the right of these is an irregular black and orange triangle, like the fuselage of the Wright's first airplane. It is also very similar to the "bride" shape in the top of Marcel Duchamp's *The Bride Stripped Bare by Her Bachelors Even*. To right of this, dominating the entire right side, is a brick red edifice. This suggests a hydrant, a pot-bellied stove helmeted face—with a phallic shape leaning off toward the upper right, rising to an incandescent white with red corona.

White Crepe Boot is busier, more liquid-looking, as if we were looking down and viewing shapes floating in milk. The colors are lovely, particularly the blue, which is given an icy look by the surrounding white. *Yellow Yap* (1988-89) could have been formed by waiting until the colored elements of *White Crepe Boot* had soaked up and into some of the surrounding white—producing a more pastel blue, and lightening other colors—and then shaking it to stir up its pieces. In places, paint has clearly been squeezed directly out of the tube in thick white dollops. *The Gray Twist* (1988) is closely related to these paintings, but it adds some effective depth effects which make it seem the shapes and colors are actively flowing out of the lower left, moving into a bright day.

But it is *Cage Reservoir* and the open white 1988 paintings that form the basis for what Van Vliet will adopt as his late style. Both *Black Accountant* (who looks like a crow) and *Black Boar*, painted the next year, are dominated by thick black shapes surrounded by the heavy white fields. (Interestingly, the lower left corner of the first includes a bushy black and green-gold area with much the same look as that of Van Vliet's wonderful 1991 "cactus theme" works; the dirty color here makes the area unremarkable.)

One Bent, One Straight (1989) is lovely, a return to the evocation of Mediterranean light surrounding creamy whites and gently brushed peach pink, below bright white (again with streamers squeezed directly from the tube). Gold and copper glitter here and there, while gray and black suggest depth. This could almost be a Renaissance woman reading her prayer book. This may well be the most beautiful painting that Van Vliet has shown. *Boneless Spirit* (1990) uses much the same palette, but is more loosely organized. The effect it produces is of an active and distinctly friendly spirit. *Puzzleloaf* (1990) is a more disordered use of some of the same colors; *Don't Step On Rain Thing* (1990) uses them to create a creamy study in puddle reflections. (The central shape is *almost* a cartoon of a human—almost Mr. Magoo as a merry-go-round figure.)

Day Barrette (1989) includes the recurring oval with beak or fingers or tendrils which appears in several paintings of this period. *Day Barrette* is considerably lighter than *Dark Light* and *Raven Above*, both in effect and in its choice of colors. It marks an arrival a a brighter palette. Yellow gathers itself in the center of the painting and shoots out a tendril to make gentle contact with an Indian yellow wedge, which in turn touches a melon or squash-colored stripe across the top. Two house-like hieroglyphics float or dance below. There is a reprise of the early *Ghost Red Wire* in some scribbled crimson. *Dust Devil*, from the same year, also includes a more geometric version of the recurring shape, something like one half of a dark tunnel entrance—this painting is in fact more geometric than anything which precedes it. 1991's *Boat and Locks No. 2* presents a more colorful and even more severely geometric version of the shape, and produces a much more satisfying effect. Burnt umber, sienna outlined in ocher, and a very dark green form the shape, which here looks very much like the head and jaws of a pipe wrench, perhaps to echo the opening and closing action of a lock. Another strip of green and a wide band of umber form a bank across from this, in which bluish-white water flows. Stretching across this channel is a black schematic of a ship, seen from the side so as to resemble a sextant. Out in the "open sea" more black shapes await their turn. The color combination, the right-angle regularity of the lock, work together to create a compelling image—almost as if we are standing before the flag of an unknown country which calls forth our deepest feelings of patriotism.

Thickly bubbling impasto surfaces continue to dominate in the 1990-91 paintings. Some, like *Gorillacrow* and *Up Sifter* (both 1990) are heavy and dark. The second of these has an unusual color scheme: a thick white to the right, then a deep, nearly-indigo blue, dark maroon and a slightly smokey yellow; all are thick and almost unmodulated, yet, surprisingly, the painting does manage to maintain an upward momentum. Other thickly painted works are light and airy—to the point of defining "a zero-gravity space," as John Yau has put it. The two versions of *Circles Don't Fly They Float* (1990) are good examples of this. A burnt sienna and yellow equine figure floats in the center of each; a sketchy sun like a frosted glass hangs above both. The upright horses are clearly floating, as are the various fishhook, seahorse and other shapes beneath them. *Lion Colored Fish* (1991) is a variation on this pair. In the later painting there are two floating shapes of brighter yellow, and a single animal shape (something between a dog and a buffalo) which is adorned as intricately as a Fabrege egg. *Globe and Brown Light* (1991) is one of the most successful of these anti-gravity works. Shapes that suggest a black light bulb, a blue pipe wrench, other tools (as well as two yellow variations on the globe-and-finger shape) all float freely. The feel is whimsical even while disorienting—housewares designed by Claes Oldenburg thrown into the famous photograph of Salvador Dali with flying cat and spilling water.

Two of the most striking paintings of 1990 can be found side-by-side in *Stand Up to Be Discontinued.* These are *Cinnamon Chops* and *World Crawled Over the Razor.* The first of these is given over to swirls of burnt sienna and umbers, thick enough to look like a topographical map even in reproduction. These are bounded by equally thick areas of white or blocks of black. There is a circulatory-system liveliness and energy about this painting that draws the eye to its swirling heart. *World Crawled Over the Razor,* despite its gruesome title, conveys the feeling of an old-fashioned clown, posed against a bright yellow sun. This could easily be a figure from a Fellini film, a satin-motley trickster reaching down toward us from slightly above, smoke rising from his fist. The blood-red V where a head might be is perhaps meant to be the result of the happening of the title; if so, it fails, and if the painting remains mildly devilish, it certainly is not evocative of pain.

Among the 1991 works are a standout pair of beautifully alive paintings, *Cactus Blanch* and *Wrought Iron Cactus*.[23] These are two versions of the same plant. Wide green leaves, like those of low-growing cacti, rise like plumes above a predominantly yellow and ocher elongated oval—like a golden lily pad; the cacti are surrounded by a hot white, but both send roots downward out of the picture. The second version is more vivid, with black rather than deep green lines separating the leaves, and the leaves themselves are wider. The yellow ground before it is more multi-colored, conveying a healthy teeming effect where the ground in *Cactus Blanch* just looks like broken ground.

Cacti grow in harsh and unforgiving environments, environments which are nonetheless very beautiful and full of specialized life. Van Vliet knows this, having happily lived in the desert much of his life. I vote that these two desert paintings be awarded the title of "self-portraits." This may be romanticizing impulse at work once again, but I am not the only one casting such a vote. Turn the page after looking at the cactus paintings in *Stand Up to Be Discontinued* and you will find a photograph of Van Vliet by Anton Corbijn, the photographer who took the famous *Ice Cream for Crow* photographs and made the *Some Yo-Yo Stuff* film. The photograph appears to have been taken either in the shadow of, or behind the reflection of, a tree of some sort. The spiky irregular shadow that makes Van Vliet visible, as well as the harsh brightness of the sun which shines behind and in some places through this tree, all work together to create a portrait of Van Vliet which is clearly a visual rhyme of these cactus paintings, all three being portraits of spiky beauty, adaption and perseverance under extreme conditions.

The body of Van Vliet's art, too, is just such a portrait. As outlined above, Van Vliet came to the world of art as a kind of refugee. And like many refugees he came nearly penniless, but with his self-pride still intact. He was taken in, but the conditions of his contiuned asylum included having to dismiss parts of his past he valued, and to bear up under continual reminders of those parts he wished to leave behind. He adapted to the pressures of his new environment, the preference for certain styles (of art and attitude),and has become successful and secure.

But there surely must be times when he feels that he has not been accepted on the terms he would have wished. Inside the art world, many even among those who champion his work see him as an eccentric, a primitive not much different from any number of mentally unstable artists carving imaginary beings out of old tree stumps. Many value him as a curiosity, more for his legendary musical past than for his art. These environmental pressures have combined to change Van Vliet's art, perhaps even his most basic feeling for and connection to his world. No longer does happiness shine from the surface of his works, no longer do man and animal, water and light all flow together harmoniously. Instead everything, living or non-living, is on its own, estranged from all others, moving loosely through space. Van Vliet can still produce great beauty when painting, even with this new world view, but the basic feeling, the heart, of his work has changed dramatically.

Van Vliet's 1998 *New Work* exhibit, which was up for just over three weeks in November and December, included oils of various sizes, and ten works on paper which show even more advanced dissociations. The slim catalogue reproduces only six paintings, all with multiple dates. Five of the six *Dreams in the Daytime Colored with Sunshine* (1995 - 96), *Pointed Satchels* (1993 - 94), *The Drazy Hoops* numbers 2 and 3 (both 1997 - 98), and *Curve in the Dirt,* all have much in common with Van Vliet's 1988 - 89 style and 1991's *Lion Colored Fish.* The colors and the arrangement of the forms are very similar. But to this style, Van

Vliet has added watery-looking black lines. Some paintings, *Dreams in the Daylight*, for example, include this minimally. In other paintings, as with the two *Drazy Hoop* works, these lines form heavily gridded sections. These are like wire forms for organic shapes which have yet to grow over them.

Ten Thousand Pistols No Bumblebees, a black and white painting, consists of nothing but these armature-style forms, some of which look like black ice on a white glass pane. In the middle of the painting the black lines form outlines (or, again, armatures) of animal forms much like the dog in *Fire Party for Boomerang Man* (1984). If these works mark the beginning of something new it is not apparent. The effect is rather that of Van Vliet having spliced these watery black lines (even Van Vliet's signatures here are water-wavy black squiggles) onto an older style, to little effect.

The exhibit also included eight pages from intact sketchbooks, all dated within the three months just prior to the exhibit. Upon attending the exhibit, one fan wrote, "They are incredibly simplistic and childlike scribble drawings of pencil, crayon and scratching (as in an empty ballpoint pen).[24]" Such marks are included in such 1989 works as "Dragon Gown" and "Day Barrette," but until this show the sketch books had been known for being filled with Van Vliet's assured, thick-lined, felt pen drawings.

In sum, *New Work* seems a very minor show, one which tells us little of what course Van Vliet may follow in future work. . .

"Thanks For the Hand, But..."

...if there is to be any future work.

Van Vliet last gave interviews by phone in 1993, and by fax in 1994. The fax interview (with Jan typing out Don's answers) was conducted by English journalist Ben Thompson as publicity for the Van Vliet exhibition which opened in Brighton on September 3. In his introductory notes Thompson also noted the change in style:

> When [Van Vliet] had his first British exhibition [fans] gathered in a mixture of pleasure and puzzlement. They will no doubt do the same at this one, perhaps venturing the time-honoured opinion— in view of the increasingly somber tone of Van Vlier's work, the decreasing number of funny animals in it—that they prefer his early stuff.[1]

But the "funny animal" days are likely gone forever, along with the feeling of all living things being interconnected which inspired them.

Also on the list of elements of Van Vliet's arts which seem to be gone forever is his deep and resonant voice. Included with the 1993 catalogue *Stand Up to Be Discontinued* is a short CD of Van Vliet reading some of his poems. On this his voice is thin and wavering, its strength drastically diminished. The CD gives no dates for the readings, but this diminishment is even more apparent in Van Vliet's voice-overs for Anton Corbijn's short film *Some Yo-Yo Stuff,* which was produced in the early 1990s. A number of sources maintain that Van Vliet is now wheelchair-bound. In *Some Yo-Yo Stuff* he is always seen seated, and only from the shoulders up. He is emaciated-looking, and white-haired, his face almost hidden behind swirling clouds of cigar smoke. Watching Van Vliet at this remove calls to mind his words from a 1990 interview:

> It helps when people appreciate what you do, but I'm
> an artist, so thanks for the hand, but don't touch me.[2]

Van Vliet presently lives and paints, if he is still able to do so, in what he has described as a "painted birdcage above a hack-saw ocean with lovely redwood stalks with zillions of raindrops, falling," near Trinidad, California. (He has isolated himself so completely that even this is in doubt. Some say that he has moved to Big Sur, or. . . ?) He no longer makes public appearances, answers no letters, responds to no requests.

In the fax interview Thompson conducted, he asks Van Vliet if he feels cut off from the world. "Cut off just enough to feel well-tailored" he answers. Asked if he has a working routine, Van Vliet answers, "Life."

Notes

Introduction

1. Thompson.
2. Ibid.

Born In the Desert

1. BBC documentary.
2. Wald.
3. Hillman, 134 - 35.
4. The sole source for these accounts is Van Vliet. Long distance attempts—via phone calls, e-mail and fax yielded no information. Others researching in California may have better luck.
5. Reprinted in Walley, [30 - 31].
6. Trakin.
7. Owens.
8. Interview with John French by Justin Sherill, dated November 5, 1998. Posted on *Home Page Replica*.
9. Harkleroad, 27.
10. Quoted in the sleeve notes to *The Legendary A&M Sessions*.
11. French 1999, 25.
12. Ibid., 30.
13. These appear both on the bootleg CD *Captain Beefheart The Early Years 1959 - 69* and the *Grow Fins* set.
14. Dickinson, Jim. From his notes to *Howling' Wolf Memphis Days--The Definitive Edition Vol. 2*. Quoted in Griel Marcus, *Invisible Republic* (NY: Henry Holt & Co., 1998), 226.

Safe As Milk

1. French 1999, 37.
2. Ry Cooder, interviewed in the BBC documentary.
3. DiMartino.
4. "Dali de Clair."
5. French 1999, 41.
6. Ibid., 32.
7. BBC documentary.
8. Eymael.
9. Ferrari, 17 - 18.
10. French 1999, 41 - 42.

11. To this pair could be added another Los Angeles genius who after great triumphs fell prey to the inability to complete further works: Orson Welles.
12. McKnight.

  Strictly Personal

1. These were recorded between October 1967 and May 1968, but not released until 1992, on the *I May Be Hungry But I Sure Ain't Weird* CD.
2. French 1999, 35.
3. "Tim," "The Hollow Cane Clicked Like Ever After," posted on the *Radar Station*
4. Uncredited quote posted in the "Frequently Asked Questions" area of the *Home Page Replica.*
5. "Refusal to Land (Remarks)," posted on *Home Page Replica.*
6. Gore, 40.
7. Duke and DeNunzio.
8. Gore, 42.

  Light the Fire Piano

1. In this same period, Zappa also had Van Vliet record satiric monologues, including "The Grand Wazoo" and "I'm a Bandleader," for his tape archive. The pair also improvised a blues, "Alley Cat," in Zappa's basement studio with John French on drums and Elliot Ingber (later to become "Winged Eel Fingerling" with the Magic Band). These tracks were released more than twenty years later, on Zappa's posthumous *The Lost Episodes.*
2. Many of these recordings were included on the 5 CD set *Grow Fins* released in 1999.
3. French 1999, 59.
4. Zappa comments on this in the BBC documentary, saying this rendered Van Vliet's vocals only vaguely in synch with the music. Zappa sounds appalled at this idea---yet soon after *Trout Mask Replica* was recorded Zappa began making what he termed "xenochronic" recordings: taking the guitar solos from one recording and laying them over a completely different track with a different tempo and/or time signature. One can't help but suspect Van Vliet was an influence on Zappa in this matter.
5. Van Vliet told an interviewer in 1982 that when he was a child his aunt would play "a lot of the current stuff, like Glenn Miller. I thought it was wonderful then and I still like that stuff. . . . My aunt also played a lot of Al Jolson. I heard that stuff in my bassinet as I lay there being rocked back and forth. (McKenna 1982, 16.)

6. Bangs, 46.

7. Winner 1996, 61.

8. Matt Groening, from *Mojo* (December 1993). Posted on the *Radar Station*.

9. Bateson, Mary Catherine. *Our Own Metaphor* (Washington, D.C.: Smithsonian Institution Press, 1991 [reprint of 1972, with new material], 294.

10. Alessandri.

11. Austin, Howard. "A Computational Theory of Physical Skill" (unpublished dissertation, 1976), quoted in Wilson, 105.

12. Wilson, 295.

13. Ingold, Tim. "Tool Use, Sociality and Intelligence," quoted in Wilson, 295 - 96.

14. Fuller, 258.

15. Shore, Michael. "This Is Your Captain Speaking," *The Soho Weekly News* (November 9, 1978), 21.

16. Winner 1996, 59.

17. Harkleroad, 37.

18. These transcriptions, by Mark Steven Brooks, were taken from *Home Page Replica* in July of 1998.

19. McKnight.

Everything's Wrong At the Same Time Its Right

1. Harkleroad writes of Van Vliet seeing a picture of Albert Einstein wearing a fedora and long coat and holding a cigarette, and adopting this exact look soon after (Harkleroad, 81).

2. Winner 1970, 37 - 38, 40.

3. Trakin, 59.

4. Harkleroad, 23.

5. BBC documentary.

6. McKenna 1982, 130.

7. Harkleroad, 38 - 39.

8. Owens.

9. Bangs, 46.

10. Harkleroad, 68 and French 1999, 61.

11. Harkleroad, 85.

12. French 1999, 55.

13. Ibid., 61.

14. Zappa, Frank (with Peter Occhiogrosso). *The Real Frank Zappa Book* (N.Y.: Poseidon Press, 1989).51.

15. Thompson.

16. Alper, 110.

17. Ibid., 115.

18. Ibid.
19. Posted at *members.tripod.com/~RocketteMorton/bands/beef.htmln.*
20. DiMartino.
21. From "The 100 Greatest Albums Ever Made" [#28] *Trout Mask Replica,* in *Mojo* #21 [London, England] (August 1995). Posted on the Mallard Web page: *pagesprodigy.com/FNJD74A/mallard4.htm.*
22. Wilson, 9.
23. Ibid., 4.
24. Ibid., 195 - 96.
25. From "History," 1841.
26. Capra, 7.
27. From Emerson's essay "Nature."
28. Capra, 10. Edited from the original.

Out of the House and On the Road

1. As this book was going to press word began to circulate that Boston was writing a book for the publisher of Harkleroad's book.
2. Barnes, Mike. "The Primer---Captain Beefheart," *The Wire* (April 1998). Posted on the *Radar Station.*
2. An excerpt from this can be seen in the BBC documentary.

Running Hard to Find a Clear Spot

1. Carr.
2. Alessandri.
3. Carr.
4. Harkleroad, 86.
5. Ibid., 91.
6. Cerio & Petros.
7. Harkleroad, 103.
8. Ibid., 108.

Rock and Roll's Evil Doll

1. Brodey.
2. Ames.
3. Harkleroad, 125.
4. Brodey.
5. Jansen, Bert. "Captain Beefheart: Magic for Lonesomes or for the People?" (6/19/74). This interview was originally published in Dutch, and this translation as posted on *Electricity* is at times in awkward English.
6. Harkleroad, 120 - 21.

7. Harkleroad, 126.

Driven Away from His Own Steering Wheel

1. French 1993.
2. Dister, Alain. "Captain Beefheart and the Telepathic Relations," *France Fortdaily [?] Magazine* (May 11, 1972). Posted on the *Electricity* website as a "Gorillacrow translation."
3. Lennon, Nigey. *Being Frank* (L.A.: California Classic Books, 1995), 144 - 45. Lennon's book reproduces two photos of her and Van Vliet, who appears nattily-dressed and at ease. Also reproduced in a whimsical portrait of Lennon drawn and signed "Love" by Van Vliet.
4. Kaiser, 14.
5. The 1972 or earlier compositions are: "Semi-Multicoloured Caucasian," "The Witch Doctor Life," "Ice Cream for Crow," "Best Batch Yet," "Sue Egypt," "A Carrot is As Close As a Rabbit Gets to a Diamond," "Dirty Blue Gene," and "The Past Sure is Tense." The 1976 compositions are "1010th Day of the Human Totem Pole," "'81 Poop Hatch," "Brick Bats," and "Flavor Bud Living." See Kaiser. Also, the poem "Garland I Dig Your Tweed Coat," recorded on *Ice Cream for Crow* dates from 1970.
6. Cerio & Petros.
7. McKenna 1982, 130.
8. Likely Van Vliet intended none of these, but written in arabic numerals 1010 suggests the kind of opposition which inspired "Ice Cream for Crow," and (for all you number fans out there) if it is read as a binary number it would be read as "10," adding another representation of itself.
9. McKenna 1982, 14.

Exuding the Ground He Walks On

1. Perec, Georges. *W or The Memory of Childhood* (trans. David Bellos) (Boston: David R. Godine, 1988), [vii].
2. Carr.
3. In the 1998 exhibit of New Work at Knoedler and Company in New York City, eight pages of intact sketch books were exhibited. These were in a very late, scratchy style bearing no relation to the kind of drawings I refer to here.
4. See Van Vliet's comments in Walley, 147.
5. Eymael.
6. The cover of *Ice Cream for Crow* (1982) reproduces yet another dark painting on a window shade. This is undated, but known to have been done in the *Trout Mask Replica* period. Anton Corbijn's photo of Van Vliet masks part of the painting, and not enough of it is visible to allow for any

idea of its subject matter, if any.

7. Marion Milner [writing as "Joanna Field"]. *On Not Being Able to Paint* (London: Heinemann Educational, 1950). Quoted in Fuller, 132.
8. Ibid., 132 - 33.
9. Berger, John. "The Primitive and the Professional," in *About Looking* (NY: Vintage International, 1980), 75.
10. Quoted in Hillman, *xii.*

"I Fool Myself Gracefully"

1. Schnabel, 27.
2. Jacobs.
3. Schnabel, 206.
4. Lammers, Tjer. "Jeans in the Desert, A Meeting With Captain Beefheart" *Oor* [Dutch music magazine] (April 23, 1983). Posted on *Electricity* as a "Gorillacrow translation."
5. Posted on the *Radar Station* I have not, incidentally, seen these paintings. The *Times* article characterizes them as being much like the covers of the last three Captain Beefheart albums---but these paintings are wildly different! Ms. Boone's comments suggest that they were figurative, which would be consistent with the more widely seen paintings of this same period.
6. Hughes, Robert. *Nothing if Not Critical* (NY: Penguin, 1990), 403.
7. Yau, John. *A.R. Penck* (N.Y.: Harry N. Abrams, 1993), 7.
8. Schnabel, 32.
9. Miller, Arthur A. *Insights of Genius* (N.Y.: Copernicus, 1996), 424.
10. Davenport, Guy. *Objects On a Table* (Washington, D.C.: Counterpoint, 1998), 35.
11. The account here is a conflation of details from several essays in *Parallel Visions: Modern Artists and Outsider Art*, ed. Maurice Tuchman and Carol S. Eliel (Los Angeles/Princeton: Los Angeles Museum of Art/ Princeton University Press, 1992).
12. McKenna 1990.
13. Ibid.
14. DiMartino.
15. Ibid.
16. Ibid.
17. Rogers, John. "Captain Beefheart Gaining International Acclaim---for Painting," Associated Press, June 22, 1995. Posted on the *Radar Station.*
18. Ishmael Reed, *New and Collected Poems* (N.Y.: Atheneum, 1988), 50.
19. *Radar Station.*
20. Comparison of the reproduction of this painting in *Stand Up to Be Discontinued* with that in *Skeleton Breath, Scorpion Blush* will show how

greatly even a change of just a few degrees of saturation can alter the overall effect of a painting. It is the solidity of the colors more than the fact of their greater size which makes the reproductions in the former prefer able to those in the latter. Unless otherwise noted, where reproductions are available in more than one publication, it is on those in *Stand Up...* that my comments are based.

21. An unsigned note in the *New Yorker* at the time of Van Vliet's 1995 solo show at Werner's New York gallery holds that Van Vliet's work has the "raw magic you find only in the work of autodidacts, from the Lascaux cave paintings to the light shows at the Fillmore East."

22. Van Vliet had an exhibit titled "God's Empty Socks and Other Paintings" at Werner New York in the Spring of 1995. The catalogue which was to accompany it was cancelled, according to the gallery by Van Vliet himself. A note in the *New Yorker* reproduced a self-portrait, but this was clearly a drawing, and was unsigned. In the Fall of 1998 Van Vliet had some works on paper in a group exhibit, but these were not seen, and the gallery declined to discuss over the phone the dates of these works.

23. Posted on the *Radar Station.*

"Thanks For the Hand, But . . . "

1. Thompson.
2. McKenna 1990.

Sources

Alper, Gerald. *The Puppeteers Studies of Obsessive Control* (NY: Fromm International, 1994).

Alessandri, Paul. "Captain Crunches Or the Confession of Don Van Vliet" [interview]. *Rock & Folk* [France] #65 (June 1, 1972). Posted as a "Gorillacrow translation" on *Electricity.*

Ames, Roger. "Captain Beefheart," [Original publication unknown] Septem ber, 1974. Posted on the *Radar Station.*

Bangs, Lester. "Captain Beefheart's Iridescent Logic," *Musician Magazine* #29 (January, 1981), 40 - 44, 46. This is surely the best article yet written about the man behind the arts.

BBC documentary. "The Artist Formerly Known as Captain Beefheart" was broadcast on BBC2, August 19, 1997. This included clips from all stages of Van Vliet's music career, and interviews with John French, Ry Cooder, Doug Moon and many more. With this aired "Some Yo-Yo Stuff," a short film by Anton Corbijn produced in 1994.

Bourne, Mike. "Me and Beefheart at Manteno," *Downbeat* v.38, #4 (February 18, 1971), 18-19.

Brodey, Jim. "New Face, New Music." *Rolling Stone* #162 (June 6, 1974). Posted on the *Radar Station*.

Capra, Fritjof. *The Web of Life* (N.Y.: Anchor/Doubelday, 1996).

Carr, Patrick. "Where Are the Animals In This Program? A Study of Captain Beefheart," *Crawdaddy* (March 19, 1972). Posted on the *Radar Station*.

Cerio, Steven and George Petros. "Interview with Gary Lucas," *Seconds Magazine* (April 1996). Also posted on *garylucas.com*.

Corbijn, Anton. *Some Yo-Yo Stuff*. Short documentary film, shown with the BBC documentary above.

Cruickshank, Ben. *Fast and Bulbous The Captain Beefheart Story* (Andover, England: Agenda Books, 1996).

"Dali de Clair" [pseudonym]. "Captain Beefheart or The Crow and the Fox, *Rock & Folk* [France] # 167 (December 1, 1980). Posted on *Electricity* as a Gorillacrow translation.

DiMartino, David. "Yeah I'm Happy. Happy As a Clam," *Mojo Magazine* (December 1993). Posted on the *Radar Station*.

Duke, Alex and Rob DeNunzio. "Our Day with Zoot Horn Rollo" [interview with Bill Harkleroad], *Hi Fi Mundo (http//www.teleport.com/o/o7Ehifim/inter.html)*, 12/29/97.

Electricity [website] *http://people.a2000.nl/tieman*. Maintained by Theo Tieman.

Eymael, Jeff. "I Wanna Howl Like a Werewolf The Kid in the Spotlight," *Aloha* [Netherlands] (May 6, 1972). Posted as a "Gorillacrow translation" on *Electricity*.

Ferrari, Lucia. *Captain Beefheart Pearls Before Swine Ice Cream for Crows* (Rome, Italy: Sonic Books, 1996).

French, John (1993). [Letter to Mojo Magazine], *Mojo* (Dec., 1993). Posted on the *Radar Station*.

-------------(1998). Notes to *O Drumbo Solo* CD.

-------------(1999). Notes to *Grow Fins* CD set.

Fuller, Peter. *Beyond the Crisis in Art* (London: Writers and Readers, 1980).

Gore, Joe. "Zoot Horn Rollo," *Guitar Player* (January 1998), 39-40, 42, 44.

Greer, Jim. "Where's the Beef?" *Spin* v.6, #11 (February 1991), 34-35, 73, 76.

Groening, Matt. [Interview] *Mojo* (Dec., 1993). Posted on the *Radar Station*.

Harkleroad, Bill. *Lunar Notes* (Wembley, England: SAF Publishing, Ltd., 1998).

Hillman, James. *The Soul's Code* (N.Y.: Warner Books, 1996).

Hoffman, Fred. "The Art of Don Van Vliet," *Don Van Vliet* (Santa Monica: Fred Hoffman Gallery, 1990), 3 - 7.

Home Page Replica, [web site] *www.shiningsilence.com*. Maintained by Justin Sherill.

Jacobs, Moze. "Captain Beefheart/Don Van Vliet: Cult Hero," *Vrij Nederland* (?/15/85). Posted as a "Gorillacrow translation" on *Electricity*.

Kaiser, Henry. "Introduction" to Harkleroad (1998), 11 - 16.

Keepnews, Peter. "Captain Beefheart," *Downbeat* v.48, #4 (April 1981), 19-22, 63-64.

Lennon, Nigey. *Being Frank* (L.A.: California Classics Books, 1995).

Loder, Kurt. "Captain Beefheart," in *Bat Chain Puller* (NY: St. Martins Press, 1990).

-----------."*Trout Mask Replica:* Captain Beefheart and the Magic Band," Ibid.

Lucas, Gary. *garylucas.com* [web site].

Marcus, Greil. *Invisible Empire*

McKenna, Kristine. "Captain Beefheart and the Magic Band: Sonic Sculpture in the Mojave," *Musician [issue # unknown]* (1982), 12, 14, 16, 122, 124, 130.

-----------."Where's the Captain?" *Spin* v.3, #8 (January 1988), 16-20.

-----------. "A Crossover of a Different Kind." Originally published in the *Los Angeles Times* (July 29, 1990). Posted on the *Radar Station.*

McKnight, Connor. "Jottings for the Beefheart Archives," *Zig Zag* #29 (5/1/73). Also posted on *Electricity*.

Miller, Jim. "Playing it By Ear with Captain Beefheart," *Vanity Fair* v.46, #2 (April 1983), 101, 161.

Owens, Otis. "An Octafish Speaks," interview posted on *www.beefheart.com* (April 1998).

Radar Station. Actual title is *The Captain Beefheart Radar Station* [website] *www.beefheart.com.* Maintained by Graham Johnston.

Schnabel, Julian. *CVJ: Nicknames of Maitre D's & Other Excerpts from Life* (N.Y.: Random House, 1987).

Shore, Michael. "This is Your Captain Speaking," *The Soho Weekly News* (Nov. 9, 1978), 21, 24.

Springer, Cole. "This is your Captain Speaking..." *Trouser Press* v.6, #2 (February 1979), 24-27.

Stand Up to be Discontinued [No editor credit] (Cantz, 1993)

Tepper, Morris. "Hello/Goodbye: Morris Tepper & Beefheart's Magic Band," *Mojo* #51 (February 1998), 130.

Thompson, Ben. "Reachieving Naivety," *The Independent [England]* (8/21/94). Posted on the *Radar Station* website.

Trakin, Roy. "The Teachings of Captain Beefheart: A Wacky Way of Knowledge," *Creem* (May 1983).

Wald, Eliot. "Conversation with Captain Beefheart," *Oui* (July 1973), 63-64, 104-105.

Walley, David. *No Commercial Potential The Saga of Frank Zappa* (New York: Da Capo, 1996).

Watson, Ben. *Frank Zappa's Negative Dialectics of Poodle Play* (NY: St.

Martins Griffin, 1993).

Werner, Michael (New York City gallery). *Don Van Vliet* Exhibition
catalogue, September 13 to October 26, 1991. [See also Yau, below.]

Wilson, Frank R. *The Hand How its Use Shapes the Brain, Language, and Human Culture* (N.Y.: Parthenon, 1998).

Winner, Langdon. "...The Odyssey of Captain Beefheart," *Rolling Stone* #58
(May 14, 1970),

----------------. "In Search of America Captain Beefheart and the Smithsonian
Institute Blues," *Rolling Stone* #79 (April 1, 1971).

----------------. "Trout Mask Replica," in *Stranded Rock and Roll for a Desert Island*, ed. Greil Marcus (NY: Da Capo Press, 1996), 58-70.

Yau, John. "Introduction," *Don Van Vliet* (NY: Michael Werner, 1991),
unpag.

Selected Discography

(The following is a selection of recordings made by Captain Beefheart and the Magic Band, as well as some of the solo recordings made by the most important of the musicians who have worked with him. This is not a collectors' list, only a selection of pressings, primarily those used for reference in the writing of this book. All are US pressings unless specified.)

Captain Beefheart and the Magic Band

THE LEGENDARY A&M SESSIONS A&M SP-12510 [LP] (1984).

SAFE AS MILK Buddha BDM 1001 / BDS 5001 [mono and stero LPs]
([1967). LP rereleased in 1970 with Langdon Winner quote
on the cover and renumbered BDS 5063. Rereleased in 1999 in the
"Original Master" series with 7 bonus tracks as BMG/Super K/Buddha
7446599605-2 [CD].

CAPTAIN BEEFHEART THE EARLY YEARS 1959 - 1969 Beef Music BF 5969
[bootleg CD].

I MAY BE HUNGRY BUT I SURE AIN'T WEIRD Sequel [UK] NEX CD 215 (1992).

STRICTLY PERSONAL Blue Thumb BTS 1 [LP] (1968).

MIRROR MAN Buddha BDS 5077 [LP] (1971). Rereleased in 1999 in the
"Original Masters" series as THE MIRROR MAN SESSIONS, resequenced and
with 5 bonus tracks as BMG/Super K/Buddha 7446599606-2.

TROUT MASK REPLICA Straight 2MS 2027 [LP] (1969), Reprise JS 2027
[cassette, n.d.], with LP sides resequenced, Reprise 2027-2 [CD] (1989).

LICK MY DECALS OFF, BABY Straight/Reprise RS 6420 [LP] (1970), Bizarre/
Straight/Rhino R4 70364 [cassette] 1989.

SPOTLIGHT KID Reprise MS 2050 [LP] (1972), Reprise 9 26249-2 [CD, with CLEAR SPOT] (1990).

CLEAR SPOT Reprise MS 2115 [LP] (1972), for CD see SPOTLIGHT KID.

UNCONDITIONALLY GUARANTEED Mercury SRM-709 [LP], MCR 4-1-709 [cassette] (1974).

BLUEJEANS AND MOONBEAMS Mercury SRM-1-1018 [LP], MCR 4-1-1018 [cassette] (1974).

LONDON 1974 Movie Play Gold [Portugal] MPG 74025 [CD] (1993).

SHINY BEAST (BAT CHAIN PULLER) Warner Brothers BSK 3256 [LP] (1978).

DOC AT THE RADAR STATION Virgin VA 13148 [LP] (1980), Caroline Blue Plate CAROL 1824-2 [CD] (1986).

ICE CREAM FOR CROW Epic/Virgin ARE 38274 [LP] (1982), Virgin CDV 2237 (n.d.).

GROW FINS Revenant 210 [5-CD set] (1999).

John French

WAITING ON THE FLAME Demon FIENDCD 759 [UK] (1994).

O SOLO DRUMBO Avant AVAN 024 [Japan] (1998).

Gary Lucas

SKELETON AT THE FEAST Enemy EMY 126-2 (1991).

GODS AND MONSTERS Enemy EMY 133-2 (1992).

BAD BOYS OF THE ARCTIC Enemy EMY 146-2 (1994).

EVANGELINE Paradigm PME 0012-2 (1997).

BUSY BEING BORN Tzadik TZ 7121 (1998)

PARADISO Oxygen Music Works OMWCD11 (1998).

Mallard (Bill Harkleroad, Mark Boston, Art Tripp III)

MALLARD Virgin V2045 [LP, UK only] (1975).

IN A DIFFERENT CLIMATE Virgin PZ 34489 [LP] (1978)

MALLARD / IN A DIFFERENT CLIMATE Caroline Blue Plate CAROL 1897, Virgin CDOVD 442 [UK] (1994).

Frank Zappa

THE LOST EPISODES Ryko RCD 40573 (1996).

WEASELS RIPPED MY FLESH RYKO RCD 10163 (1990).

HOT RATS Reprise RS 6356 [LP] 1969; Ryko CDR 10508 (1995).

AN EVENING WITH FRANK ZAPPA AND CAPTAIN BEEFHEART Head [bootleg CD]

BONGO FURY Discreet DS 2234 [LP] (1975); Ryko CDR 10522 (1995).

Paintings Referred to and Sources of Reproductions

Abbreviations used:

FH *Don Van Vliet* The Fred Hoffman Gallery, Santa Monica, in cooperation with MichaelWerner Gallery, New York (July 31 - September 8, 1990).

MW *Don Van Vliet* Michael Werner Gallery, New York (September 13 - October 26, 1991). [See also Yau in sources.]

NW *New Work* Knoedler & Co., in cooperation with Michael Werner Gallery, New York (November 11 - December 5, 1998).

PS *Pearls Before Swine / Ice Cream for Crow.* Ed. Ferrari [see sources].

SB Skeleton Breath, Scorpion Blush (Bern/Berlin: Verlag Gachnang & Springer, 1987).

SU *Stand Up to Be Discontinued* [no editor credit] (Ostfildern: Cantz 1993).

[Note: Untitled and album cover works are source-cited in the text.]

Beezoo, Beezoo (1985) SU 79.
Black Accountant (1989) SU 100.
Black Boar (1989) SU 101.
Black Twig (1991) SU 119.
Boat and Blue Bodagress (1984) SU 59.
Boat and Lock No.2 (1991) MW 12.
Boneless Spirit (1990) SU 113, FH 9.
Bromboline Frenzy (1985) SU 75, SB 32, PS 25.
Cactus Blanch (1991) SU 120, MW 9.
Cage Reservoir (1988) SU 95.
Candle Powered Rodeo Ghosts (1986) SB 76.
Carp Catcher (1986) SB 56.
Castfat Shadows (1987) SU 84, PS 68.
Cat Got His Tail (1985) SU 71.
Cholla (1989) MW 5.
Cinnamon Chops (1990) SU 110, FH 2.
Circles Don't Fly, They Float No.1 (1990) SU 114, MW 7.
Circles Don't Fly, They Float No.2 (1990) SU 115, MW 6.
Copper Diver (1985) SU 77, SB 20.
Crepe and Black Lamps (1985 or '86) SU 82, SB 68, PS 29.
Cross Poked a Shadow of a Crow No.1 (1989) PS 73.
Cross Poked a Shadow of a Crow No. 2 (1989) SU 102.
Curve in the Dirt (1996-97) NW 6.
Dark Light (1988) SU 96.
Day Barrette (1989) SU 103, MW 3, FH 7.
Devil and the Deep Blue Sea (1984) SU 25.

Don't Ruin Step On Thing (1990) FH 4.

Dragon Gown (1989) SU 99.

Drazy Hoops No.2, The (1997-98) NW 4.

Drazy Hoops No.3, The (1997-98) NW 5.

Dreams in the Daytime Colored with Sunshine (1995-96) NW 1 [cover].

Dry Morning Wind That Jingle Like Fish Bones (1987) SU 85.

Dust Devil (1989) SU 105, FH 8.

Dylisheus (1984) SU 68 - 69.

Egyptian Toss Up (1984) SU 16.

Fire Party for Boomerang Man with Wrought Iron Curls (1984) SU 57.

Flashlight In the Daytime (1990) FH 5.

Garden Lion (1986) SB 60.

Ghost Gait, Ghost Gate (1985) SB 28.

Ghost Lemon (1991) MW 11, PS 77.

Ghost Red Wire (1967) SU 51.

Glober and Brown Light (1991) PS 76.

Golden Birdies (1988) SU 90.

Gorillacrow (1990) SU 112, FH 6.

Gray Ape (1988) SU 91, MW 2.

Gray Twist, The (1988) PS 72.

Green Gambler, The (1988) SU 94.

Green Tom (1976) SU 52.

It's Like a White Onion-Fleshed Pumpkin (1985) SU 73, SB 16.

Japan In the Dishpan (1984) SU 55.

Life Walker (1988) SU 92.

Lion Colored Fish (1991) SU 118.

Middle Flower (1990) SU 108.

Night Nitrate (1985) SB 36.

One Bent, One Straight (1989) MW 4.

Parapliers the Willow Dipped (1987) SU 88, PS 65.

Pet Surprises--Pet Surprising Pet (1984) SU 67.

Pointed Satchels (1993-94) NW 2.

Puzzleloaf (1990) MW 8.

Raven Above (1988) SU 97.

Red Cloud Monkey (1985) SB 40.

Riding Some Kind of Unusual Skull Sleigh (1986/87) SU 89.

Rolled Roots Gnarled Like Breakers (1985/86) SB 44.

Rumfhala Horror Puppet (1986) SU 83.

Sea Wig (1986) SB 72.

Striped Light (1985) SU 80 - 81.

Ten Thousand Pistols, No Bumblebees (1995-96) NW 3.

Tiger Boat (1987) SU 87.

Tiger Bow (1988) MW 1.

Tint, Blush, Coo (1987-90) SU 107, FH 1.
Tug (1990) SU 109.
Upsifter (1990) SU 117.
Whalebone Farmhouse (1985) SB 48.
When She Dropped the Flower (1969) SU 49.
White Crepe Boat (1988) PS 69.
With Twinkling Lights and Green Sashes (1986) SB 65.
World Crawled Over the Razor (1990) SU 111.
Wrought Iron Cactus (1991) SU 121, MW 10, PS 80.
Yellow Scarab (1989-90) FH 10.
Yellow Yap (1988-89) SU 98.